BRITISH GOVERNMENT DEPARTMENT

UFO REPORTS DECLASSIFIED MINISTRY OF DEFENCE

FIELD OFFICE AERIAL INVESTIGATION
AND ADMINISTRAIVE FILES

BRITISH GOVERNMENT DEPARTMENT

UFO REPORTS DECLASSIFIED MINISTRY OF DEFENCE

File Number DEFE-24-1926
DEFE-24-1927

1986 SEP 01-1987 AUG 31
1987 AUG 01-1988 FEB 29

DECLASSIFIED

FIELD OFFICE AERIAL INVESTIGATION
AND ADMINISTRAIVE FILES

© UFO Reports Declassified - Ministry Of Defence Vol 1
First Published 2016
Second Publication 2017

The production of this book is to be identified as the Author of this Work
and to be asserted in accordance with the Copyrights, Designs & Patents Act 1988.

British Library Cataloguing in Publication Data:
This book contains Parliamentary information licensed under the Open Parliament
Licence v3.0.

ISBN: 978-1548708702

Typesetting and origination by Philip R Wolfe
Printed and bound in Great Britain.

PREFACE AND ACKNOWLEDGMENTS

This book contains a broad range of genuine UFO-related documents, letters, drawings, photographs and parliamentary questions submitted to the Ministry of Defence (MoD) relating to aerial phenomena. All information within has been collected and documented by the British Government and has been officially declassified after their initial release in May 2008.

All material contained within this book was initially scanned-in by staff at the MoD. After which it was redacted, this was due to portions of the material still containing classified information or personal details; such names and addresses which need to remain anonymous, to protect an individual's rights. Therefore this data was blackout out, as evident on many pages. After this process, the files were then passed to and logged by the National Archives.

Contents within this book where required have been digitally restored, resized and reorganised appropriately by the author for easier reading and reference. We have made every effort to make these documents as readable and clear as possible, and although the majority of the pages are legible any indistinct or illegible text is likely due to the age or the condition of the original documents have been kept in.

We gratefully acknowledge the following for the material and assistance they have provided: The Ministry of Defence, The National Archives.
This book contains Parliamentary information licensed under the Open Parliament Licence v3.0.

VOLUME ONE
NOTABLE FILE HIGHLIGHTS

DEFE 24-1926-1
(Pages 4-168)

Eyewitness observes two very bright objects one foot in size over Bristol Airport. Objects merged then separated and then passed overhead of observer. **Page – 29**

Report made my driver who observed an 'egg shaped' object approximately 10 feet in length with triangular flames emanating from the rear. The object made no noise and 'split' and as it dropped down at Curber Edge in Chesterfield. **Pages – 58**

A technician at Ford reports seeing a transparent upright cylinder with flames moving silently in the skies of Lincoln. **Page – 83-84**

Captain of an aircraft reports unidentified object which passed close by to the port side of aircraft. The object was tracked on radar before being lost. **Page – 160-163**

DEFE 24-1927-1
(Pages 168-366)

Report passed to RAF of a conical shaped object with a 'lacy' tail and orange bar covering 1/8 of the object. Moved unpredictably over skies of Alton as observed by a witness for 35 minutes before it changed shape with a ring of light and disappeared. **Pages 179**

A collection of witness reports involving a sighting of a white ball of light with a long blue emanating tail over West Byfleet. Contains remark about Martian crash-landing. **Pages 209-214**

Witness reports a disk like object with very bright pulsating purple lights and pink overtones before it slowly drops behind houses and out of sight of observer. **Pages 220-221**

Corporal based at RAF Newton in Nottinghamshire observes a large formation of UFO's over RAF base. Two large formations passed by slowly, emitting a sound similar to a jet engine, consisting of approximately 16 lights at the front and 10 at the back containing inner white lights and outer red lights. Contains diagram of the formation. **Pages 222-224**

An incident over Holmfirth in which multiple eye witnesses report observing a bright spherical ball of motionless light in the sky in the early hours of the morning. The ball moved off at tremendous speed leaving an orange fire trail in its wake, witness includes a diagram of the scene and sighting. **Pages 249-256**

RESTRICTED/UNCLASSIFIED

MOD Form 329D
(Revised 3/83)

MINISTRY OF DEFENCE 1993

Date opened

6. SEPT 86

Registered file number

D / Sec (AS) 12/2

Part No. C

1. Attention is drawn to the notes on the inside flap

2. Enter notes of related files on page 2 of this jacket.

DIVISION/ESTABLISHMENT/UNIT/BRANCH

Sec (AS) 2A

SUBJECT UNIDENTIFIED FLYING OBJECTS
U.F.O.s

REPORTS

Referred to	Date	Min/Encl	Referred to	Date	Min/Encl	Referred to	Date	Min/Encl	Referred to	Date	Min/Encl

MOD
DR 1
2 1 DEC 1999
SECOND
REVIEW

2012

CLOSED
NO FURTHER
MINUTES OR
ENCLOSURES
MUST BE PLACED
IN THIS FILE

Section 40

Section 40

File Ref: SEC(AS)12/2
Part: C

RCU000112105 TNT

OR DRO USE ONLY

Review date

d Review date

PA ACTION
(MOD Form 262F must be completed)

SENT OUT DATE
Ext Section 40
From DFNTO(EXP)R2
Bourne Avenue
HAYES MIDDX
UB3 1RF

2 6 SEP 2003

RESTRICTED/UNCLASSIFIED

7

(ii) Key enclosures which support the recommendation are:

_____

_____

_____

_____

(iii) At the end of the specified retention period the file is to be:

Destroyed ☐ ✓

Considered by CS(RM) for ☐
permanent preservation

c.   Of no further administrative value but worthy of consideration by CS(RM) for permanent preservation. ✓

PART 3. BRANCH REVIEWING Section 40	PART 4. DESTRUCTION CERTIFICATE
Signature: _____	It is certified that the specified file has been destroyed.
Name: Section 40	Signature: _____
(Block Capitals)	Name: _____
Grade/Rank: HEO Date: 22|11|99	(Block Capitals)
(Not below HEO/equivalent)	Grade/Rank: _____ Date: _____
Branch Title and Full Address: MINISTRY OF DEFENCE	Witnessed by (TOP SECRET and SECRET only)
(AS) 2 Section 40	Signature: _____
BUILDING	
WHITEHALL	Name: _____
LONDON SW1 2HB	(Block Capitals)
	Grade/Rank: _____ Date: _____
Tel No: Section 40	*(FOR CS(RM) USE ONLY)

Produced by Ministry of Defence, CS (Pr) 2. Tel. Section 40

8

Registered File Disposal Form

MOD Form 262F
(Revised 10/97)

FILE TITLE: (Main Heading - Secondary Heading - Tertiary Heading etc)

UFOs — Reports

Reference:
(Prefix and Number): DISCC(AS) 1212
Part: C

PROTECTIVE MARKING (including caveats & descriptors): UIC

Date of last enclosure: 21.8.87

Date closed: 21.8.87

PART 1. DISPOSAL SCHEDULE RECOMMENDATION
(To be completed when the file is closed)

FOR (HBM) USE ONLY

MOD
DR 1
Date of 1st review: 21 DEC 1999   Date of 2nd review   Forward Destruction Date

Reviewer's Signature: SECOND REVIEW   Reviewer's Signature:

2012

Destroy after _____ years

Forward to CS(RM) after _____ years

No recommendation

PART 2. BRANCH REVIEW
(To be completed not later than 4 years after the date of the last enclosure)
(Delete as appropriate)

a. Of no further administrative value and not worthy of permanent preservation. DESTROY IMMEDIATELY (Remember that TOP SECRET and Codeword material cannot be destroyed locally and must be forwarded to CS(RM))

b. (i) To be retained for _____ years (from date of last enclosure) for the following reason(s):

Section 40

LEGAL		DEFENCE POLICY + OPERATIONS	
CONTRACTUAL		ORIGINAL COMMITTEE PAPERS	
FINANCE/AUDIT		MAJOR EQUIPMENT PROJECT	
DIRECTORATE POLICY		OTHER (Specify)	

PPQ = 100

(Continued overleaf)

9

REPORT OF AN UNIDENTIFIED FLYING OBJECT

A.	Date, Time & Duration of Sighting	21.0130 2 August 1987 10 minutes
B.	Description of Object (No of objects, size, shape, colour, brightness)	Elliptical bright orange. Very thin & bright
C.	Exact Position of Observer Location, indoor/outdoor, stationary/moving	Dereham or bicycle 1 mile south of Wetheringsett, Suffolk.
D.	How Observed (naked eye, binoculars, other optical device, still or movie)	Naked eye
E.	Direction in which object first seen (A landmark may be more useful than a badly estimated bearing)	North East
F.	Angle of Sight (Estimated heights are unreliable)	20° - 30°
G.	Distance (By reference to a known landmark)	1 mile
H.	Movements (Changes in E, F & G may be of more use than estimates of course and speed)	Didn't appear to move but top of object pulsed. Then disappeared.
J.	Met Conditions during Observations (Moving clouds, haze, mist etc)	Stars. Some Cloud. No moon.
K.	Nearby Objects (Telephone lines, high voltage lines, reservoir, lake or dam, swamp or marsh, river, high buildings, tall chimneys, steeples, spires, TV or radio masts, airfields, generating plant, factories, pits or other sites with floodlights or night lighting)	Mendlesham mast. (Radio)

L.	To whom reported (Police, military, press etc)	Sqn Ldr [Section 40] / Ops assistant. Flt/Lt [Section 40] Int /EW Officer RAF Wattisham
M.	Name & Address of Informant	[Section 40] Wattisham, Stowmarket. [Section 40] S'market
N.	Background of Informant that may be volunteered	Had seen down to Leader. Had had a few drinks during the day.
O.	Other Witnesses	None
P.	Date, Time of Receipt	21/1100 B. August 1987
Q.	Any Unusual Meteorological Conditions	None
R.	Remarks	Anxious but not frightened by the object. Requested a reply to the sighting. Flt/Lt [Section 40] mentioned that the moon was due to rise at 0200 in the direction of the sighting. It is possible that it was a part of the moon or a reflection.

[Section 40]

.... Sec (AS)2a

Squadron Leader
Duty Operations Officer
AF Ops

/ Date 21 August 1987 ....

Sec(AS)2 distribution :

Copies to:
Sec(AS)2
AEW/CE
DI 55
File AF Ops/1/11

U N C L A S S I F I E D

QY0238 21/2103 233C3478

FOR C&F

ROUTINE 210958Z AUG 87

FROM   RAF LEUCHARS
TO   MODUK AIR
        HQSTC
        UKRASC

U N C L A S S I F I E D
SIC ZDY
FOR ATTN AFOR(RAF)MOD
A. 16 AUG 87 BETWEEN 2300-2359 LOCAL
B. LOOKED LIKE A STAR
C. STANDING OUTSIDE OF HOUSE
D. NAKED EYE
E. FORFAR AREA TOWARDS DUNDEE THEN LEUCHARS
F. VERY HIGH
G. NOT KNOWN TOO HIGH
H. STOPPED OVER LEUCHARS THEN REVERSED DIRECTION BACK TOWARDS
FORFAR STOPPED AGAIN AND THEN HEADED STRAIGHT UP
J. CLEAR NIGHT LOTS OF STARS SHOWING
K. NOTHING

PAGE 2 RDDXJ 029 UNCLAS
L. CPL ███████ ROYAL AIR FORCE LEUCHARS WG OPS FIFE SCOTLAND
M. ████████████████████ DOUGLAS DUNDEE FIFE SCOTLAND
N. FIRST SIGHTING FOLLOWED FEW MINUTES LATER BY SECOND SIGHTING
WHICH WENT OVER LEUCHARS TURNED LEFT SHOOTING OFF DOWN THE COAST
O. ██████████████████
P. 21 AUG 87 1050 LOCAL
Q. YES IF POSSIBLE
BT

DISTRIBUTION

CAF   1 S&E(AS) ACTION CDJ   1 AF90
STC   1 HQ CC/RAS
CAD   1 DIT/IS
CIW   2 DGI1

12/2
Section
4/8

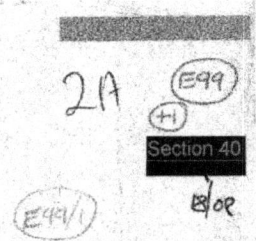

U N C L A S S I F I E D

CYD226 17/1936 229C23Y1

FOR CAS

ROUTINE 171488Z AUG 87

FROM   RAF WEST DRAYTON
TO   MODUK AIR

U N C L A S S I F I E D
SIC Z6F
SUBJECT: AERIAL PHENOMENA A. 161790Z AUG 87, 30 SECS B. ONE, DARK
ROUND OBJECT, NO LIGHTS, NO SOUND C. AT HOME ADDRESS-OUTDOORS-
STATIONARY D. NAKED EYE E. TO THE SOUTH OF PINNER F. 45 DEGREES
WHEN SIGHTED PASSING TO OVERHEAD G. N/K H. STEADY SOUTH-NORTH J.
CLEAR/CAVOK K. RESIDENTIAL AREA L. WATCH MANAGERS DESK LATCC M.
PINNER, MIDDX N. WORKS AT AIS PINNER
O. NIL P. 171230Z AUG 87
BT

DISTRIBUTION   Z6F
F
CAB   1 Sec (AS) ACTION (CXJ   1 AERO)
CYD   1 DD GE/AEW
CAV   1 DI 55
CAV   2 DSTI

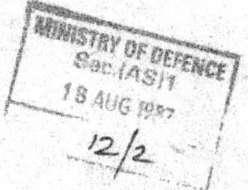

UNCLASSIFIED

CWY059 15/1135 227C0781

FOR CAB

ROUTINE 150715Z AUG 87

FROM   RAF WEST DRAYTON
TO   MODUK AIR

UNCLASSIFIED
SIC Z6F
SUBJECT : AERIAL PHENOMENA
A. 142211 AUG 87, 5 MINS
B. ONE, TRIANGULAR SHAPE, GLOWING
C. MIDDLE ST BLAZE, OUTDOORS, STATIONARY
D. NAKED EYE
E. COMING FROM SEA
F. NOT KNOWN
G. CAME DOWN FROM QUITE HIGH THEN LEVELLED OFF. FLEW OVER HIS HEAD
HEIGHT NOT KNOWN THEN APPEARED TO DISINTEGRATE
H. STEADY
J. CLEAR SKY
K. NONE
L. BT MAWGAN OPERATIONS
M. Section 40   CORNWALL

PAGE 2 RBDAID 001   UNCLAS
N. Section 40 WOULD BE ABLE TO DRAW THE OBJECT
O. NO
P. 142300 AUG 87
BT

MINISTRY OF DEFENCE
Sec.(AS)2
17 AUG 1987
FILE 12/2

DISTRIBUTION   Z6F

CAB   1   Sec (AS) ACTION (CXJ   1   AFDD)
CYD   1   DD GE/AEW
CAV   1   DI 55
CAV   2   DSTI

ANNEX A TO
SOP 502

REPORT OF AN UNIDENTIFIED FLYING OBJECT

A.	Date, Time & Duration of Sighting	102225Z Aug 87
B.	Description of Object (No of objects, size, shape, colour, brightness)	One, Dull orange light brighter than a star
C.	Exact Position of Observer Location, indoor/outdoor, stationary/moving	Outdoor moving slowly East
D.	How Observed (naked eye, binoculars, other optical device, still or movie	Naked eye.
E.	Direction in which object first seen (A landmark may be more useful than a badly estimated bearing)	East
F.	Angle of Sight (Estimated heights are unreliable)	10 above horizon
G.	Distance (By reference to a known landmark	/
H.	Movements (Changes in E, F & Q may be of more use than estimates of course and speed)	Stationary
J.	Met Conditions during Observations (Moving clouds, haze, mist etc)	Clear
K.	Nearby Objects (Telephone lines, high voltage lines, reservoir, lake or dam, swamp or marsh, river, high buildings, tall chimneys, steeples, spires, TV or radio masts, airfields, generating plant, factories, pits or other sites with floodlights or night lighting)	Nil

15

L.	To whom reported (Police, military, press etc)	Nil

M.	Name & Address of Informant	

N.	Background of Informant that may be volunteered	Runs an Employment Agency

O.	Other Witnesses	Nil..

P.	Date, Time of Receipt	

Q.	Any Unusual Meteorological Conditions	

R.	Remarks	He saw a similar object 3 months ago

Sqn Ldr
Duty Ops Officer
AF Ops

Date. 11 Aug 87.

Distribution:

Sec(AS)2
AEW/GE
DI 55
File AF Ops/2/5/1

Spoke Section AS (RAF)

Informed him that we had now received a report on a sighting from Bognor Regis. This was in reply to his earlier 'phone call asking if we had received a report. He asked if we do anything more shall note the sightings. I informed it that we forward them to the RAF department responsible for the air defence of one country.

CWY004 10/0709 222C8375

FOR CAB

ROUTINE 100630Z AUG 87

FROM   RAF WEST DRAYTON
TO   MODUK AIR

UNCLASSIFIED
SIC Z6F
AERIAL PHENOMENA: A. 100300 TO 100310(L) AUG 87. B. ONE LARGE OVAL
SHAPED OBJECT FLAT AT THE EDGES WITH LOTS OF LIGHTS, SOUNDED LIKE
A HELICOPTER STARTING UP. C. INDOORS AT Section 40   BOGNOR
REGIS, SUSSEX. D. NAKED EYE. E. OBJECT HEADING FROM SOUTH TO NORTH
F. STRAIGHT ABOVE. G. BETWEEN 80 TO 100 FEET. H. STEADY. J. CLEAR
SKY, FULL MOON. K. HOUSES. L. POLICE HQ, BOGNOR REGIS, SUSSEX. Section 40
J Section 40   N. NIL. O. HUSBAND
P. 100414(L) AUG 87
BT

DISTRIBUTION   Z6F
F
CAB   1   Sec (AS) ACTION (CXJ   1 AFDO)
CYB   1   DD GE/AEW
CAV   1   DI 55
CAV   2   DSTI

U N C L A S S I F I E D

CY0060 07/0634 219C0472

FOR CAB

ROUTINE 061305Z AUG 87

FROM   RAF WEST DRAYTON
TO   MODUK AIR

U N C L A S S I F I E D
SIC Z6F
AERIAL PHENOMENA
A. 061300 TO 061330(L) AUG 87.OBSERVED FOR APPROX 5MINS BETWEEN TIMES
B. BALL SHAPED SIZE NOT KNOWN
C. Section 40   LUTON, OUT DOORS, STATIONARY
D. TELESCOPE
E. EAST MOVING EASTERLY
F. NOT REPORTED
G. NOT KNOWN
H. STEADY IN AND OUT OF CLOUDS
J. MOVING CLOUDS
K. NOT GIVEN
L. REPORTED INITIALLY TO ATC LUTON
M. Section 40
N. NONE

PAGE 2 RBDAID 060 UNCLAS
O. NONE
P. 061330(L) AUG 87. FURTHER TO ABOVE BALLOON SHAPED OBJECT COLOUR
HALF SILVER HALF BLACK

DISTRIBUTION Z6F

GMB   1 SEC (AS) ACTION C-DSJ   1 MFDC
CYD   1 DD CE/AEW
CAV   1 DI 55
CAV   2 DSTI

MINISTRY OF DEFENCE
Sec.(AS)2
- 7 AUG 1987
FILE 12/2

U N C L A S S I F I E D

CYD004 05/1141 217C1632

FOR CAS

ROUTINE 051045Z AUG 87

FROM   RAF WEST DRAYTON
TO   MODUK AIR

U N C L A S S I F I E D
SIC Z6F
AERIAL PHENOMENA
A. 050655 AUG 87. 10-15 SECS
B. SILVER, NOT VERY LONG; CLOSE TO AN AIRCRAFTS CONTRAILS KEEPING
UP WITH THE AIRCRAFT ABOUT 1 MILE BELOW, 40-50,000 FT
C. A6 ANTRIM-TEMPLE PATRICK RD NEAR BALLY CRAIGY TURNING
D. NAKED EYE
E. SOUTH
F. 30-40 DEGREES
G. N/K
H. STEADY
J. CLEAR
K. N/K
L. ALDERGROVE ATC Section 40
M. Section 40

PAGE 2 RBDA10 002 UNCLAS
O. NONE
P. 050955Z AUG 87 RMK-INFORMANT WOULD LIKE A REPLY
BT

MINISTRY OF DEFENCE
Sec.(AS)2
- 6 AUG 1987

FILE 12/ 2

DISTRIBUTION   Z6F
F
/S   1 Sec (AS) ACTION (CX   1 AFDO
CYB   1 DD GE/AEW
CAV   1 DI 55 — Rang 13/08 to determine outcome. Sec/8 40
CAV   2 DSTI

rang 12/08. 87 58' here
no comments. Section 40

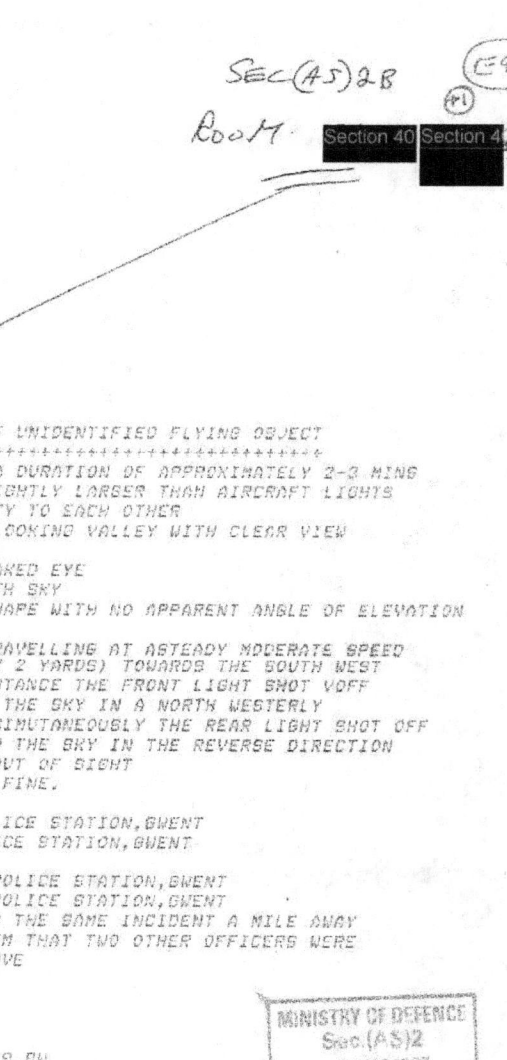
87-08-05 00:44
:
22241 MODDEC B
198228 GWEPOL B

2977 87-08-05 08:51   .

FROM THE CC GWENT POLICE
TO   M.O.D. U.F.O SECTION
FROM RISCA TO HEADQUARTERS
AUTH.OFFICER INSPECTOR SEATON

SIGHTING OF UNIDENTIFIED FLYING OBJECT
+++

A.05/08/87 AT 00:25 HRS. FOR A DURATION OF APPROXIMATELY 2-3 MINS
B.TWO BRIGHT ORANGE LIGHTS SLIGHTLY LARGER THAN AIRCRAFT LIGHTS
  TRAVELLING IN CLOSE PROXIMITY TO EACH OTHER
C.STOOD ON MOUNTAIN ROAD OVERLOOKING VALLEY WITH CLEAR VIEW
  INTO NIGHT SKY
D.OBJECTS OBSERVED WITH THE NAKED EYE
E.OBJECTS OBSERVED TO THE SOUTH SKY
F.BOTH OBJECTS SPHERICAL IN SHAPE WITH NO APPARENT ANGLE OF ELEVATION
G.APPROXIMATELY 3 MILES
H.BOTH LIGHTS WERE OBSERVED TRAVELLING AT ASTEADY MODERATE SPEED
  ONE BEHIND THE OTHER (APPROX 2 YARDS) TOWARDS THE SOUTH WEST
  AFTER TRAVELLING A SHORT DISTANCE THE FRONT LIGHT SHOT VOFF
  AT AFAST SPEED UPWARDS INTO THE SKY IN A NORTH WESTERLY
  DIRECTION AND OUT OF SIGHT.SIMULTANEOUSLY THE REAR LIGHT SHOT OFF
  AT A FAST SPEED UPWARDS INTO THE SKY IN THE REVERSE DIRECTION
  TOWARDS THE SOUTH EAST AND OUT OF SIGHT
J.CLEAR CLOUDLESS SKY.WEATHER FINE.
L.N/A
M.INSPECTOR Section 40 RISCA POLICE STATION,GWENT
  P.C.Section 40   RISCA POLICE STATION,GWENT
N.N/A
O.P.C Section 40   RISCA POLICE STATION,GWENT
  W.P.C. Section 40   RISCA POLICE STATION,GWENT
  BOTH THESE OFFICERS OBSERVED THE SAME INCIDENT A MILE AWAY
  UNAWARE AND UNBEKNOWN TO THEM THAT TWO OTHER OFFICERS WERE
  OBSERVING IT AS OUTLINED ABOVE
P.N/A.
Q.N/A.

MESSAGE ENDS TOE 0348/050887 OP FW
#
22241 MODDEC B
198228 GWEPOL B

SEC (AS) 2 distribution :

   D1 SS
   GS/ AGW

Section 40

20

ANNEX A TO

REPORT OF AN UNIDENTIFIED FLYING OBJECT

A.	Date, Time & Duration of Sighting	4 August 1987 0300 hours approximately 5 mins
B.	Description of Object (No of objects, size, shape, colour, brightness)	3 × size of a star very bright white light. spherical No other colours
C.	Exact Position of Observer Location, indoor/outdoor, stationary/moving	outside in courtyard of old peoples home in courtyard. standing still Croxford House, Westcliff, Southend.
D.	How Observed (naked eye, binoculars, other optical device, still or movie)	Naked eye.
E.	Direction in which object first seen (A landmark may be more useful than a badly estimated bearing)	NN of Southend travelling ESE.
F.	Angle of Sight (Estimated heights are unreliable)	Not known
G.	Distance (By reference to a known landmark)	Not known
H.	Movements (Changes in E, F & G may be of more use than estimates of course and speed)	Moved rapidly initially in a straight line. Then hovered and oscillated. Then moved in a Easterly direction at speed.
J.	Met Conditions during Observations (Moving clouds, haze, mist etc)	Clear skies.
K.	Nearby Objects (Telephone lines, high voltage lines, reservoir, lake or dam, swamp or marsh, river, high buildings, tall chimneys, steeples, spires, TV or radio masts, airfields, generating plant, factories, pits or other sites with floodlights or night lighting)	Buildings

L.	To whom reported (Police, military, press etc)	*Reported to Air Traffic Control, Southend Airport.*
M.	Name & Address of Informant	**Section 40**
N.	Background of Informant that may be volunteered	*Sensible and sober lady*
O.	Other Witnesses	*None*
P.	Date, Time of Receipt	*18 August 1987*
Q.	Any Unusual Meteorological Conditions	*None*
R.	Remarks	

Information received via Third party :

Section 40 *Air Traffic Control, Southend Airport*

Section 40

Section 40

Squadron Leader (*sec(AS)2*)
Duty Operations Officer
AF Ops

Date. *18 August 1987* ...

Copies to:
Sec(AS)2 ✓
AEW/GE
DI 55
File AF Ops/1/11

AIS/FF5

Section 40
8

E93/2

REPORT OF AN UNIDENTIFIED FLYING OBJECT

A. DATE, TIME, DURATION OF SIGHTING 4.8.87 22.30 A 2 HRS.
   (Local times to be used)

B. DESCRIPTION OF OBJECT

   Number   2
   Size   ?
   Shape   TRIANGULAR

   Colours   MULTI
   Brightness VERY BRIGHT.
   Sound   NIL
   Smell   NIL

S/C (AS)2 Distribution:

1. DI 55
2. DE/AEW   Section 40

C. EXACT POSITION OF OBSERVER ST. DAVIDS POST OFFICE EXETER
   Geographical location   OUTDOORS
   Indoors/Outdoors
   Stationary/Moving   STATIONARY

D. HOW OBSERVED

   Naked eye   NAKED EYE INITIALLY THEN BINOCULARS
   Binoculars
   Other optical device
   Still or cine camera   NONE

E. DIRECTION IN WHICH OBJECT WAS FIRST SEEN LOOKING FROM EXETER TOWARDS THE
   (A landmark may be more useful than a badly estimated bearing)   PLOUGH (CONSTELLATION N-E PUB)

F. ANGLE OF SIGHT (Estimated heights are unreliable)   ?

G. DISTANCE (By reference to a known landmark if possible) ?

H. MOVEMENT.
   Steady   STEADY MOVEMENT TOWARDS PLOUGH (CONSTELLATION)
   Changing   THEN RETURNED to OVERHEAD POSITION.
   Erratic

J. MET CONDITIONS DURING OBSERVATION
   Moving clouds
   Haze   CLEAR SKY.
   Mist

K. NEARBY OBJECTS/BUILDINGS ETC   ?

L. TO WHOM REPORTED   OBSERVER LT. COMM. Section 40
   Police   HQ 10 GP ROYAL OBSERVER CORPS,
   Military Organisation POLTIMORE PARK, EXETER.   Tel Section 40
   The Press   OR

M. NAME AND ADDRESS OR INFORMAT Section 40   RD

                                                    EXETER
N. ANY BACKGROUND OF THE INFORMANT THAT MAY BE VOLUNTEERED
                                                    Poltimore

O. OTHER WITNESSES   SEVERAL

P. DATE AND TIME OF RECEIPT OF REPORT   13.00 5.8.87   RAF CHIVENOR

23

From: Reference:

1. Details of Complaint.

    a.   Name: Section 40

    b.   Address: Section 40

2. Sighting:

    a.   Date/Time of Sighting and Duration: 032100 – 2115z AUG 87, so fast only
         sighted for a couple of seconds.
    b.   Position of Observer: Travelling along road between Marston Magna to Mudford

    c.   How Observed: In moving car

    d.   Direction Object first Seen: Parallel with car, heading South.

    e.   Angle of Elevation: 22° from horizontal

    f.   Distance of Object from Observer: Not sure, object was misty.

    g.   Movement of Object: Travelled parallel with car.

    h.   Met Conditions: Dark, slight glow in sky from direction of sun. Clear sky
         with hazy moon.

    i.   Nearby Objects: —

    k.   To Whom Reported: Police and Yeovil air station

    l.   Other Witnesses: Nil

    m.   Comments: The object was the size of a full moon as seen from the Earth.
         It was round and bright.

3. Date and Time Received: 041025z Aug 87

Sec(AS)2 distribution:
DI 55
GE/AEW

        Section 40

Date: 4 Aug 97

MINISTRY OF DEFENCE
Sec.(AS)2
- 6 AUG 1987
FILE 12/2

Signed: Section 40
Name:
Rank: Cpl   Tel No: RM ext Section 40

UNCLASSIFIED

CWD004 04/0740 21AC0500

E93A

FOR CAS

ROUTINE 4   30Z AUG 87

FROM   RAF WEST DRAYTON
TO   MODUK AIR

UNCLASSIFIED

E94

AERIAL PHENOMENA
A. 030330 AUG 87
B. LOOKED LIKE BURNING DEBRIS FALLING FROM SKY, GREEN IN COLOUR,
SPOTTED FOR 30 SECS
C. 20NM SOUTH EAST GATWICK AT FL350 CAPTAIN OF Section 40

D. NAKED EYE
E. 330 DEG FROM POSITION
F. NOT GIVEN
G. MAYBE 100 MILES AWAY
H. STEADY
J. CLEAR
K. NONE
L. LATCC SUPERVISOR

PAGE 2 RBD AIO 001 UNCLAS
M. NOT GIVEN
N. NONE
O. NOT GIVEN
P. RECEIVED 03 AUG 87 2352
BT

DISTRIBUTION Z6P
#
CAD   1 Sec (AS) ACTION (CXJ   1 AFDO)
CYD   4 10 GE/AEW
CAV   1 D1 5
CAV   2 DSTI

25

U N C L A S S I F I E D

CA3017 03/1003 215C0G97

FOR CAB

ROUTINE 030845Z AUG 87

FROM   RAF WEST DRAYTON
TO   MODUK AIR

U N C L A S S I F I E D
SIC ZAF
SUBJECT. AERIAL PHENOMENA
A. 022145(A) AUG 87, 5-10 MINUTES
B. 1 ROUND WITH FLASHING LIGHTS
C. OUTDOORS, MOVING
D. NAKED EYE
E. OBJECT DRWELVZDLC

IFPOBAWNX

CYG

E AB7DCKCEEVWHN/K
H. STEADY TOWARDS SYWELL
J. N/K
K. N/K
L. LONDON ATCC
M. Section 40   NORTHAMPTON
N. N/K
O. N/K
P. 022355(A) AUG 87 TO LATCCIV

PAGE 2 RSDAID 001 UNCLAS
BT

DISTRIBUTION ZAF
F
CAB   1 Sec (AS) ACTION CXJ   1 AFDO
CXD   1 DD GE/AEW
SAV   1 DI 55
SAV   2 DSTI

REPORT OF AN UNIDENTIFIED FLYING OBJECT   (RECEIVED AT RAF COTTESMORE)

A.   DATE, TIME, DURATION OF SIGHTING: 022310 AUG 87
     (Local time to be used)

B.   DESCRIPTION OF OBJECT:

     Number: 1 joined up with another
     Size: large
     Shape: round and long unlike an airmuth (but it was dark) Rather like an airship.
     Colours: not known   creamy yellow
     Brightness: not particularly bright.
     Sound: Very even round, but not jet
     Smell: none

C.   EXACT POSITION OF OBSERVER:

     Geographical Location:
                            Indoors/~~Outdoors~~
                            Stationary/~~Moving~~

D.   HOW OBSERVED:
                            Flashing
     Naked Eye: 1st Red light top + another red. 2nd Green to left of white, not flashing
     Joined up with another white light. Approaching Red and white, retreating R/w and
     flashing red beneath.

E.   DIRECTION IN WHICH OBJECT WAS FIRST SEEN:
                  Great Bowden, Mkt Harborough towards Northampton

F.   ANGLE OF SIGHT:
                  low

G.   DISTANCE: 'close'

H.   MOVEMENT: slow

J.   METEOROLOGICAL CONDITIONS: Clear

K.   NEARBY OBJECTS/BUILDINGS:

L.   TO WHOM REPORTED: Flt Section 40 Ops of RAF Cottesmore

M.   NAME AND ADDRESS OF INFORMANT:

     Section 40

     Great Bowden
     Mkt Harborough   Section 40

27

N. ANY BACKGROUND ON THE INFORMANT THAT MAY BE VOLUNTEERED:

O. OTHER WITNESSES.   *Section 40* daughter.
Publicans dog behaved in a very strange fashion

P. DATE AND TIME OF RECEIPT OF REPORT:

03 0950L Aug 87

Mr Harradine & daughter anxious to assure us they are not cranks and were surprised no one else had seen.

To be sent to: Sec (AS) 2 distribution :
                                   GC/ MEW
Sec (AS) 2   DI 55
Room *Section 40*   *Section 40*
Ministry of Defence   7/3
Main Building
Whitehall
London

Copy to:

COT/116/Ops

2

REPORT OF A SIGHTING OF AN

UNIDENTIFIED FLYING OBJECT
============================

Recieved: 2345hrs. GMT   25th. July '87

A.   252345hrs. GMT

B.   Two objects, very bright, approximately one foot in size
       observed at approximately 50degs. above the horizon. The
       objects merged then separated. One object remained stationary
       the other came towards the observer and passed overhead.

C.   Stanton Drew. Approximately 5nm. ESE of Bristol Airport.

D.   Naked eye.

E.   Not known

F.   50degs. approx.

G.   Not known

H.   Weather report at Bristol Airport, CAVOK.

K.   Nil

L.   Police; then Bristol Airport, Air Traffic Control.

M.

N.   Nil

O.   None

P.   260039hrs GMT.

       NB.   The information was passed by the brother of the observer, who
             was not given information required in p

. . . .
ATC Bristol Airport.

U N C L A S S I F I E D

CY0035 25/1409 20600894

FOR CAB

ROUTINE 251310Z JUL 87

FROM   RAF WEST DRAYTON
TO   MODUK AIR

U N C L A S S I F I E D
SIC Z6F
SUBJECT: AERIAL PHENOMENA
A. 251115(L) JULY 87, 30 SECONDS TO 1 MINUTE
B. 3 ORBS (SPHERICAL) APPROX 4 FEET IN DIAMETER
C. OUTDOORS AND INDOORS, SEEN FROM Section 40   LONDON N3
D. NAKED EYE
E. OBJECTS OBSERVED OVERHEAD FINCHLEY GOLF COURSE
F. 3 TIMES THE HEIGHT OF TREES AT GOLF COURSE
G. N/K
H. STEADY SLOW CONTROLLED MOVEMENT
J. SKY MAINLY CLEAR APART FROM SLIGHT CLOUD
K. N/K
L. GOLDERS GREEN POLICE STATION
M. Section 40
N. N/K

PAGE 2 RBDAID 001 UNCLAS
O. N/K
P. 251300Z JUL 87 TO AIS(M)
BT

DISTRIBUTION   Z6F
F
CAB   1 Sec (AS) ACTION (CXJ   1 AFDO)
CAM   1 ACS(P)
CYD   1 DD GE/AEW
CAV   1 DI 55
CAV   2 DSTI

Section 40

U N C L A S S I F I E D

CAB#08 24/1949 265C4548

FOR CAB

ROUTINE 241900Z JUL 87

FROM   RAF WEST DRAYTON
TO   MODUK AIR

U N C L A S S I F I E D
SIC Z6F
SUBJECT: AERIAL PHENOMENA
A. 241900(L) JUL 87, 5 MINUTES
B. BALL SHAPED OBJECT FLAT UNDERSIDE SHINEY ON TOP
C. OUTDOORS, OUTSKIRTS OF KIDDERMINSTER
D. NAKED EYE
E. FROM SOUTHWEST TO NORTHEAST
F. N/K
G. ONE QUARTER TO ONE HALF MILE APPROXIMATELY
H. MOVED STEADILY TOWARDS OBSERVER, THEN STOPPED. HUNG IN THE AIR
BEFORE IT SHOT UPWARDS AT SPEED
J. SCATTERED CLOUD, DULL DAY, WIND SPEED 10 MILES PER HOUR
K. TELEPHONE LINES
L. KIDDERMINSTER POLICE
M. Section 40   KIDDERMINSTER, TELEPHONE

MINISTRY OF DEFENCE
Sec.(AS)2
27 JUL 1987
FILE 12/2

PAGE 2 RDGID 007 UNCLAS
Section 40
N. NIL
O. TWO FRIENDS WITNESSED
P. 241905(L) JUL TO POLICE
BT

DISTRIBUTION Z6F
F
CAB   1 Sec (AS) ACTION (CXJ   1 AFDO)
CAM   1 ACS(P)
CYD   1 SO GE/AEW
CAV   1 DI 55
JAV   2 DSTI

UNIDENTIFIED FLYING OBJECT PROFORMA

From: FCF
HQ P.SS(UK)
RUDLOE MANOR
HAWTHORN.

Reference:

21/07

1. Details of Complaint.

   a. Name: Section 40

   b. Address: Section 40

      To

2. Sighting:

   a. Date/Time of Sighting and Duration: 14 1800-1815 & FOR 5 MINUTES

   b. Position of Observer: IN AN AREA CALLED THE STRAY IN HARROGATE

   c. How Observed: WHILST WALKING.

   d. Direction Object first Seen: ——

   e. Angle of Elevation: HIGH IN SKY ABOVE HIM.

   f. Distance of Object from Observer: OBJECT WAS AT CLOUD LEVEL.

   g. Movement of Object: VERY FAST. FASTER THAN AN AIRCRAFT.

   h. Met Conditions: A FEW LIGHT CLOUDS

   j. Nearby Objects: NIL

   k. To Whom Reported: Cpl Section 40

   l. Other Witnesses: NIL

   m. Comments: HE SAW A BRIGHT LIGHT FLASHING IN THE SKY. HE SAID A LOT OF UFO's ARE SEEN IN YORKSHIRE

3. Date and Time Received: 151320 & JULY 87

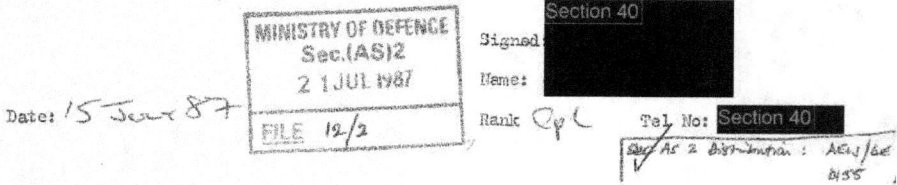

MINISTRY OF DEFENCE
Sec.(AS)2
2 1 JUL 1987
FILE 12/2

Signed: Section 40

Name: Section 40

Date: 15 JULY 87

Rank Cpl   Tel No: Section 40

Sec AS 2 Distribution : AEW/AE
0/55

32

REPORT OF AN UNIDENTIFIED FLYING OBJECT

A.	Date, Time & Duration of Sighting	14 July 1987 1900 hours. 5 - 7 minutes
B.	Description of Object (No of objects, size, shape, colour, brightness)	Very bright white object. Spherical with small tail. Larger than an aeroplane.
C.	Exact Position of Observer location, indoor/outdoor, stationary/moving	Standing still in outside garden. (The steay)
D.	How Observed (naked eye, binoculars, other optical device, still or movie)	Naked eye
E.	Direction in which object first seen (A landmark may be more useful than a badly estimated bearing)	East
F.	Angle of Sight (Estimated heights are unreliable)	45°
G.	Distance (By reference to a known landmark)	Not Known
H.	Movements (Changes in E, F & G may be of more use than estimates of course and speed)	Travelling towards west. Direct movement. Moved until vanished over horizon.
J.	Met Conditions during Observations (Moving clouds, haze, mist etc)	Bright evening. Good visibility. High Clouds.
K.	Nearby Objects (Telephone lines, high voltage lines, reservoir, lake or dam, swamp or marsh, river, high buildings, tall chimneys, steeples, spires, TV or radio masts, airfields, generating plant, factories, pits or other sites with floodlights or night lighting)	None

L.	To whom reported (Police, military, press etc)	Not previously reported.
M.	Name & Address of Informant	Harrogate. Yorkshire
N.	Background of Informant that may be volunteered	---
O.	Other Witnesses	None known.
P.	Date, Time of Receipt	1245 15 July 1987
Q.	Any Unusual Meteorological Conditions	None
R.	Remarks	Seemed a sober gentleman.

. . . .

Squadron Leader
Duty Operations Officer
AF Ops

Date..15 July 1987.....

Sec(AS) 2

Copies to:
Sec(AS)2
AEW/GE
DI 55
File AF Cps/1/11

Sec (AS) 2 distribution :
AEW/GE
DI/55
File 12/2

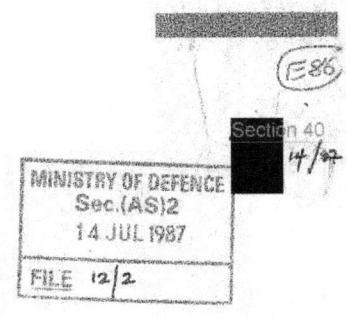

U N C L A S S I F I E D

CWY019 14/0603 19SC0401

FOR CAB

ROUTINE 140600Z JUL 87

FROM   RAF WEST DRAYTON
TO   MODUK AIR

U N C L A S S I F I E D
SIC Z6F
SUBJECT: AERIAL PHENOMENA
A. 13222SL JUL 87 B. ONE, =346)-403, SQUARE SHAPED OBJECT. BLACK
SHADOW WITH BRIGHT WHITE LIGHT IN EACH CORNER C. W12 LONDON,)
B. 3)-5
(-)49,3, STATIONARY D. NAKED EYE E. IN SOUTH F. UNKNOWN BUT
GIVEN AS SAME HEIGHT AS AN A/C SEEN A FEW MINUTES LATER G. 2-)% ,0)3
-2-6 Z. MOVING SOUTH TO NORTH J. CLEAR SKIES K. NONE CLEAR VIEW
L. BY TELEPHONE TO AIS(M? CATEGRIC?M. Section 40
Section 40   N. NONE O. Section 40   NEXT DOOR
NEIGHBOUR R. ?SE325 LOCAL JUL 87

DISTRIBUTION   Z6F
F
CAB   1 Sec (AS) ACTION (CXJ   1 AFDO)
CAM   1 ACS(P)
CYD   1 DD CE/AEW
CAV   1 DI 55
CAV   2 DBTI

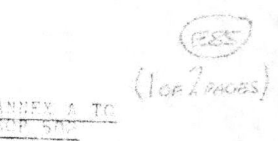

REPORT OF AN UNIDENTIFIED FLYING OBJECT

A.	Date, Time & Duration of Sighting	Saturday 11 July 1987 10.50 pm 30 seconds
B.	Description of Object (No of objects, size, shape, colour, brightness)	Large thick hoop. Even spaced white lights with orange-grey tinge.
C.	Exact Position of Observer Location, indoor/outdoor, stationary/moving	Outside in the garden. Gidea Park, Romford, Essex
D.	How Observed (naked eye, binoculars, other optical device, still or movie)	Eye
E.	Direction in which object first seen (A landmark may be more useful than a badly estimated bearing)	West → East direction.
F.	Angle of Sight (Estimated heights are unreliable)	directly overhead
G.	Distance (By reference to a known landmark)	Not known
H.	Movements (Changes in E, F & G may be of more use than estimates of course and speed)	Direct motion. Slow speed. Unnoticed.
J.	Met Conditions during Observations (Moving clouds, haze, mist etc)	Blue black night sky. Clear. Starlight.
K.	Nearby Objects (Telephone lines, high voltage lines, reservoir, lake or dam, swamp or marsh, river, high buildings, tall chimneys, steeples, spires, TV or radio masts, airfields, generating plant, factories, pits or other sites with floodlights or night lighting)	Buildings.

L.	To whom reported (Police, military, press etc)	Sec As (2). Brother of informant.
M.	Name & Address of Informant	
N.	Background of Informant that may be volunteered	Housewife
O.	Other Witnesses	3 others.
P.	Date, Time of Receipt	1300 hours 13 July 1987.
Q.	Any Unusual Meteorological Conditions	None
R.	Remarks	

Sec (AS) 2 distribution :
AEW/GE
DI 55

File 12/2

4/07

. . . .

Squadron Leader
Duty Operations Officer
AF Ops

Date. . . . .

Copies to:
Sec(AS)2
AEW/GE
DI 55
File AF Ops/1/11

MoD Sec AS 2
with Compliments

pt off
oc Supply / PSO

With the Compliments of

THE HOME OF CLOSE CONTROL

Royal Air Force   Sherburn
Staxton Wold   GPTN
Scarborough   Ext
North Yorks   AOTN
YO12 4TJ   Ext

STAX/453/5/Ops

REPORT OF AN UNIDENTIFIED FLYING OBJECT

A.　Date, time and duration of sighting.　(Local times to be quoted).

　　1 July 87　　　2215 - 2240

B.　Description of object.　(Number of objects, size, shape, colours, brightness, sound, smell, etc).

　　One, spherical, bright gold, and 'whirring' noise, size not known.

　　('Whirring' noise was stressed during report).

C.　Exact position observer.　(Geographical location.　Indoors or outdoors. Stationary or moving.

　　In the direction looking from Malton, moving from side to side then disappeared. (Hovered for a time).

D.　How observed.　(Naked eye, binoculars, other optical device, still or movie camera.

　　Naked eye.

E.　Direction in which object was first seen.　(A landmark may be more useful than a badly estimated bearing).

　　From East of Malton, moving West, then hovering.

F.　Angle of sight.　(Estimated heights are unreliable).

　　Near horizon.

G.　Distance.　(By reference to a known landmark wherever possible).

　　Fairly close, but hard to judge.

H.　Movements.　(Changes in E, F, and G may be of more use than estimates of course and speed).

　　As C.

J.　Meteorological conditions during observations.　(Moving clouds, haze, mist etc).

　　Broken, still cloud.

K.　Nearby objects　(Telephone lines; high voltage lines; reservoir, lake Swamp or marsh; river, high buildings, tall chimneys, steeples, spires, TV or radio masts; airfields, generating plant; factories, pits or other sites with flood-lights or other night lighting).

　　Thought to be over open country.

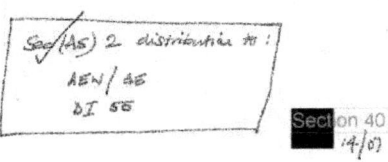

Sec(AS) 2 distribution to :
AEW/ AE
DI 55

MINISTRY OF DEFENCE
Sec (AS)2
13 JUL 1987

FILE 12/2

L. To whom reported. (Police, military organisations, the press etc).
RAF Staxton Wold no one else.

M. Name and address of informant.

N. Any background on the informant that may be volunteered.

O. Other witnesses.

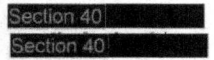

P. Date and time of receipt of report.

1 July   2240 A.

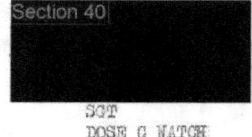

SGT
DOSE C WATCH

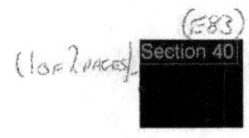

ANNEX A TO
SOP 502

REPORT OF AN UNIDENTIFIED FLYING OBJECT

A.	Date, Time & Duration of Sighting	300100Z Jun 87 15 - 20 Minutes
B.	Description of Object (No of objects, size, shape, colour, brightness)	1 Large White Light and 5 smaller lights which were also white
C.	Exact Position of Observer Location, indoor/outdoor, stationary/moving	Outdoor/Stationary
D.	How Observed (naked eye, binoculars, other optical device, still or movie	Naked eye.
E.	Direction in which object first seen (A landmark may be more useful than a badly estimated bearing)	Large White light was travelling West to East. Other 5 lights in various directions
F.	Angle of Sight (Estimated heights are unreliable)	From West to above.
G.	Distance (By reference to a known landmark	Over Newcastle
H.	Movements (Changes in E, F & G may be of more use than estimates of course and speed)	Varied
J.	Met Conditions during Observations (Moving clouds, haze, mist etc)	Clear visibility
K.	Nearby Objects (Telephone lines, high voltage lines, reservoir, lake or dam, swamp or marsh, river, high buildings, tall chimneys, steeples, spires, TV or radio masts, airfields, generating plant, factories, pits or other sites with floodlights or night lighting)	To high to estimate

L.	To whom reported (Police, military, press etc)		Duty Staff RAF Boulmer

M.	Name & Address of Informant		Section 40
			NEWCASTLE UPON TYNE
			Tel: Section 40

N.	Background of Informant that may be volunteered		Night Security Guard Ex member of Armed Forces

O.	Other Witnesses		Nil..

P.	Date, Time of Receipt		300120Z Jun 87

Q.	Any Unusual Meteorological Conditions		No.

R.   Remarks

Section 40

Sqn Ldr
Duty Ops Officer
AF Ops

Date. 30 Jun 87...

Distribution:

Sec(AS)2
AEW/GE
DI 55
File AF Ops/2/5/1

U N C L A S S I F I E D

CAB002 25/615B 145C0041

FOR CAB

ROUTINE/ROUTINE 242330Z MAY 87

FROM   RAF NEATISHEAD
TO   MODUK AIR
INFO   UKRADC
        HQ 11 GP

U N C L A S S I F I E D
SIC I3F/Z6F
(CORRECTED COPY)
MSGID/UNIDENTIFIED FLYING OBJECT REPORT
A 242335A, FOR 30 SECS
B ONE INTENSE SCARLET LIGHT, APPROX STREET LIGHT SIZE, CIRCULAR
IN SHAPE, NO SOUND OR SMELL DETECTED
C FIVE MILES SOUTH OF BUNGAY ON HALESWORTH RD, OBSERVER IN
STATIONARY CAR
D NAKED EYE
E ABOVE CAR
F OBSERVED BELOW CLOUD LEVEL, MET REPORTS CLOUD AT 100-200FT

G OBSERVER UNSURE
H FIRST STATIONARY, THEN MOVING SLOWLY SOUTH EAST, THEN DISAPPEARED
J COLTISHALL MET REPORT SOLID CLOUD BASE 190-200FT, WIND SOUTH
WESTERLY 10KTS, NO MIST/HAZE
K NIL NEAREST LIGHT SOURCE 3-4 MILES AWAY
L DUTY CONTROLLER RAF NEATISHEAD
M [Section 40]   BECCLES, NORFOLK
N NONE VOLUNTEERED
O THERE WAS ANOTHER WITNESS IN CAR, OBSERVER REFUSED TO GIVE NAME.
P 25 1150L
BT

DISTRIBUTION I3F
F
CXJ   1 AFDO-ACTION (CXJ   1 AFDO)

DISTRIBUTION Z6F
F
CAB   1 Sec (AS) ACTION (CXJ   1 AFDO)
CAM   1 ACS(P)
CYD   1 DD QE/AEW
CAV   1 DI 55
CAV   2 DSTI

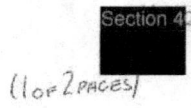

(1 of 2 PAGES)

REPORT OF AN UNIDENTIFIED FLYING OBJECT

A.	Date, Time & Duration of Sighting	182245A May 87 5 – 10 seconds
B.	Description of Object (No of objects, size, shape, colour, brightness)	2 oval objects side by side, approx 10 ft wide with blue and green lights — no sound
C.	Exact Position of Observer Location, indoor/outdoor, stationary/moving	Driving vehicle towards object
D.	How Observed (naked eye, binoculars, other optical device, still or movie	Naked eye.
E.	Direction in which object first seen (A landmark may be more useful than a badly estimated bearing)	SE to NW SOUTH FAMBRIDGE (5862 1949)
F.	Angle of Sight (Estimated heights are unreliable)	approx 45%
G.	Distance (By reference to a known landmark	25 to 30 yards from observer
H.	Movements (Changes in E, F & G may be of more use than estimates of course and speed)	NIL
J.	Met Conditions during Observations (Moving clouds, haze, mist etc)	Clear visibility & high clouds
K.	Nearby Objects (Telephone lines, high voltage lines, reservoir, lake or dam, swamp or marsh, river, high buildings, tall chimneys, steeples, spires, TV or radio masts, airfields, generating plant, factories, pits or other sites with floodlights or night lighting)	Sodium Street lights Near river and mooring area

L.	To whom reported (Police, military, press etc)	Police

M.	Name & Address of Informant	Section 40

N.	Background of Informant that may be volunteered	Stores Manager at Southend airport

O.	Other Witnesses	Nil..

P.	Date, Time of Receipt	190630Z May 87

Q.	Any Unusual Meteorological Conditions	No.

R.	Remarks _____	Southend ATC contacted by Police and stated that an aircraft departed in the direction of the sighting at 182249A May 87

Section 40

Sqn Ldr
Duty Ops Officer
AF Ops

Date. 19 May 87...

Distribution:

Sec(AS)2
AEW/GE
DI 55
File AF Ops/2/5/1

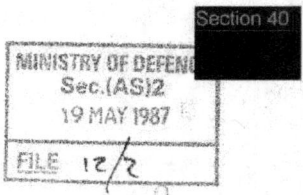

U N C L A S S I F I E D

CAB137 18/2036 138C4106

FOR CAB

ROUTINE 182013Z MAY 87

FROM   RAF WEST DRAYTON
TO   MODUK AIR

U N C L A S S I F I E D
SIC Z4F
SUBJECT: AERIAL PHENOMENA
A. 181935Z MAY 87. 2 MINS B. ONE, CIGAR SHAPED WITH SMALLER METAL
ATTACHMENTS, SILVER C. SALFORD, OUTDOORS, STATIONARY D. NAKED
EYE E. EAST F. 90 DEGREES G. 2 TO 3 MILES H. STEADY J. CAVOK K. NONE
L. MANCHESTER SUB-CENTRE M. Section 40
N. NONE O. WIFE P. 181940Z MAY 87
BT

DISTRIBUTION   Z4F
F
CAB   1 Sec (AS) ACTION (CXJ   1 AFDO)
CAM   1 ACS(P)
CYD   1 DD GE/AEW
CAV   1 DI 55
CAV   2 DSTI

46

Section 40  E79

Date, Time Duration of Sighting.

15/5/87   0100.

Description of Object

2 INTERMITTENT FLASHING LIGHTS.

Exact Position of Observer.

Section 40   JOHNSHILL   LOCHWINNOCH.

How Observed.

NAKED EYE.

Direction in which Object was first seen.

EASTERLY.

Angular Elevation of Object

90° ABOVE HORIZON.

Distance of Object from Observer.

A LONG WAY OFF.

Movements of Object.

Meteorological Conditions During Observations.
Moving Clouds, Haze, mist etc.   CLEAR.

Nearby Objects.

NONE.

To Whom Reported.   Section 40

D WATCH
ATLANTIC HOUSE.

Name & Address of Informant.

Section 40

Any Background Information on the Informant that
may be Volunteered.   NONE.

Other Witnesses.

WIFE.

MINISTRY. OF DEFENCE
Sec.(AS)2
19 MAY 1987

Date & Time of Receipt of Report.

0215   15/5/87

FILE   12/2

U N C L A S S I F I E D

GRW151 11/2948 131C4405

FOR CAB

ROUTINE 139839Z MAY 87

FROM   RAF BINBROOK
TO   MODUK AIR

U N C L A S S I F I E
BIC LAZ/Z6F
BIC Z6F INS BY DCC.
A 082230Z MAY 87
B 1 TENNIS BALL SIZE, BRIGHT WHITE IN COLOUR WITH RED TAIL BEHIND
C AT HIS HOME IN GRIMSBY FROM FRONT WINDOW
D NAKED EYE
E TRAVELLED EAST TO WEST LOW ELEVATION
F ESTIMATED 20 DEGREES
G ESTIMATED 6.5 MILES
H AS IN E ABOVE
J NIGHT, CLEAR SKY, NO STREET LIGHTS
K NIL
L GRIMSBY POLICE
M Section 40   GRIMSBY, SOUTH
HUMBERSIDE
N DOES NOT BELIEVE IN UFOS

O NIL
P 8 MAY 87 2146 ALFA (GRIMSBY POLICE)
BT

DISTRIBUTION LAZ
F
NO SDL

DISTRIBUTION / Z6F
F
CAB   1 Sec (AS) ACTION (CXJ   1 AFOC)
CAM   1 ACS(F)
CYD   1 DG GE/AEW
CAV   1 DI 55
CAV   2 DSTI

49

Section 40

U N C L A S S I F I E D

CWP074 80/?587 128C2603

FOR CAS

ROUTINE 0812452 MAY 87

FROM   RAF WEST DRAYTO
TO   MODUK AIR

MINISTRY OF DEFENCE
Sec IAS)2

12/2

U N C L A S S I F I E
SIC Z6F
SUBJECT AERIAL PHENOMENA. A. 081125Z MAY 87 DURATION 10 MINS. B. ONE
SIZE AND SHAPE NOT GIVEN, WHITE VERY BRIGHT NO SOUND OR SMELL. C.
BRACKNELL, OUTDOORS, STATIONARY. D. NAKED EYE. E. 10 NORTH. F.
30 TO 45 DEG THEN DIPPED LOWER BEFORE DISAPPEARING. G. NO IDEA OF
DISTANCE. H. STEADY TO NORTH. J. CAVOK. K. ON INDUSTRIAL ESTATE
PYLONS 400 YDS AWAY. L. LATIC SUPERVISOR. M. Section 40
Section 40   . N. NON. O. MIL
F. 081210Z MAY 87
BT

DISTRIBUTION   Z6F
F
CAB   1   Sec (AS). ACTION (CXJ   1 AFDO)
CAR   1   ACS(P)
CYD   1   DD GE/AEW
CAV   1   DI SS
CAV   2   DSTI

U N C L A S S I F I E D

CAS089 30/0431 120C0570

FOR CAS

ROUTINE 300531Z APR 87

FROM   RAF WEST DRAYTON
TO   HQUK AIR

U N C L A S S I F I E D
519 XAF
SUBJECT: AERIAL PHENOMENA
A. 292200(L) APR 87, 2 MINS
B. ONE, HOT AIR BALLOON SHAPED, YELLOW AND RED GLOW
C. WINCHMORE HILL, NORTH LONDON, OUTDOORS, STATIONARY
D. NAKED EYE
E. SOUTH EAST
F. 60 DEGREES
G. 500FT
H. STEADY
J. CAVOK
K. TWO GARDEN TREES
L. ENFIELD POLICE
M. Section 40
N. NIL

PAGE 2 RDDAID 001 UNCLAS
O. BOYFRIEND
P. 292243(L) APR 87
87

DISTRIBUTION X6F

CAS   1 SAS (AS) ACTION (CXJ   ,1 AFBS)
CAN   1 RU9(F)
CYD   1 DD CE/AEW
CAV   1 DI 55
CAV   2 DST1

U N C L A S S I F I E D

CWD050 24/1194 114C0615

FOR CAS

ROUTINE 240640Z APR 87

FROM   RAF WEST DRAYTO.
TO   MODUK AIR

U N C L A S S I F I E D
610 Z&F
SUBJECT: AERIAL PHENOMENA A. 220039Z APR AND 232139Z APR 87
10-15 MINS B. ONE, INDISTINCT GLOBE POSSIBLY TWO, IN VARYING
DEGREES OF BRIGHTNESS C. HUNGERFORD BRIDGE, RIVER THAMES
LONDON D. NAKED EYE E. OVER WATERLOO BRIDGE F. OVER THE SHELL
MEX BUILDING AND DESCEND TO 100-150FT (APPROX 10 STOREYS) G. AS
E H. STEADY DESCENT J. A LITTLE HAZY K. SHELL MEX BUILDING
M. Section 40
*TE. TEL Section 40   N. Section 40 IS VERY KEEN TO HEAR ANY FURTHER
INFORMATION ON THIS SIGHTING O. Section 40 WIFE AND 4 OTHER PASSERS
BY P. 232206Z APR 87
BT

DISTRIBUTION Z&F
F
COB   1 Sec (AS). ACTION (CXJ   1 AFBO)
CAM   1 ACS(P)
CYB   1 DD GE/AEW
CAV   1 DI 55
CAV   2 DSTI

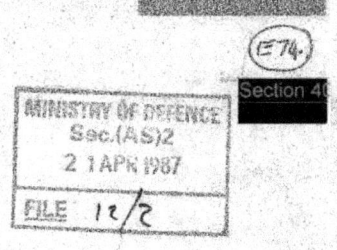
UNCLASSIFIED FILE 12/2

CWD045 21/1633 111C1511

FOR CAS

ROUTINE 211140Z APR 87

FROM : RAF WEST DRAYTON
TO : MODUK AIR

UNCLASSIFIE
SIC ZSF
SUBJECT: AERIAL PHENOMENA
A. 210423Z APR 87
B. SMALL, VERY BRIGHT WHITE LIGHT
C. OBSERVER ON BOARD BOAT TRAVELLING DOWN RIVER
D. NAKED EYE
E. MOVING WEST TO EAST OVER DEVONPORT NUCLEAR SUBMARINE COMPLEX
F. OVERHEAD
G. N/K
H. VERY FAST, DIRECT LINE, NO VARIATION
J. CAVOK
K. DEVONPORT DOCKYARD COMPLEX
L. N/A
M. NO. Section 40 POLICE CONSTABLE Section 40 MOD POLICE, DEVONPORT
N. PC Section 40 THOUGHT THE LIGHT MIGHT BE A SATELLITE AS THE INTENSITY

PAGE 2 RADAID 045 UNCLAS
OF THE LIGHT DID NO
O. NONE
P. 210446Z APR 87
BT

DISTRIBUTION ZSF
F
CAS   1 Sec (AS) ACTION (CKJ, 1 AFDD)
CAN   1 ACS(P)
CTO   2 BD GE/AEW
CAV   1 B1 SS
CAV   2 DSTI

MINISTRY OF DEFENCE
Sec.(AS)2
- 7 APR 1987

UNCLASSIFIED

FILE

CAB141 QA/P162 89AC4747

FOR CAB

ROUTINE 062015Z APR 87

FROM   RAF WEST DRAYTON
TO   MODUK AIR

UNCLASSIFIED
SIC Z6F
SUBJECT AERIAL PHENOMENA
A. 0622004(L) APRIL
B. ONE LARGISH INVERTED FUNNEL SHAPED OBJECT, SHINING, WITH BRIGHTER
LIGHT AT BASE ACCOMPANIED BY SPARKS
C. DRIVING IN CAR NORTH ALONG A396 EXETER TO TIVERTON ROAD
D. NAKED EYE
E. RIGHT HANDSIDE OF ROAD APPROX POSITION GRID 889302
F. LOW ANGLE
G. HARD TO TELL
H. DESCENDING
J. SLIGHT HAZE
K. NIL
L. EXETER POLICE
M.

PAGE 2 RBBAID 010 UNCLAS
N. SOBER SENSIBLE LADY
O. NIL
P. 0617452 APRIL. (AION ASSUMED REPORTED OBJECT WAS A HOT AIR BALLON
VIEWED AT DUSK)
BT

DISTRIBUTION Z6F
F
CAB   1 SEC (AS) ACTION (CX)   1 AFDO)
CAR   6 ACR(F)
CYB   1 DD GE/AEW
CAV   1 DI 55
CAU   2 DSTI

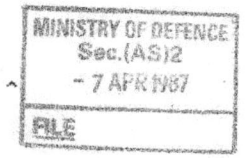
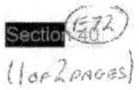
MINISTRY OF DEFENCE
Sec.(AS)2
- 7 APR 1987
FILE

REPORT OF AN UNIDENTIFIED FLYING OBJECT

A.	Date, Time & Duration of Sighting	6 Apr 87 0925-0930Z
B.	Description of Object (No of objects, size, shape, colour, brightness)	Bright, like flood light large, white far away.
C.	Exact Position of Observer Location, indoor/outdoor, stationary/moving	Outside
D.	How Observed (naked eye, binoculars, other optical device, still or movie	Naked eye.
E.	Direction in which object first seen (A landmark may be more useful than a badly estimated bearing)	South
F.	Angle of Sight (Estimated heights are unreliable)	High
G.	Distance (By reference to a known landmark	1 - 2 miles.
H.	Movements (Changes in E, F & G may be of more use than estimates of course and speed)	Moved towards, Overhead. Circled then went. No Noise.
J.	Met Conditions during Observations (Moving clouds, haze, mist etc)	Clear sky.
K.	Nearby Objects (Telephone lines, high voltage lines, reservoir, lake or dam, swamp or marsh, river, high buildings, tall chimneys, steeples, spires, TV or radio masts, airfields, generating plant, factories, pits or other sites with floodlights or night lighting)	Nil

1

L.   To whom reported (Police,
     military, press etc)

M.   Name & Address of Informant

N.   Background of Informant that
     may be volunteered   Painter & Decorator

O.   Other Witnesses

                                           Nil..

P.   Date, Time of Receipt

                                           060950Z Apr 87

Q.   Any Unusual Meteorological
     Conditions   No.

R.   Remarks
     ------

       7 Apr 87
Date.............   Sqn Ldr
                                          Duty Ops Officer
Distribution: AF Ops

Sec(AS)2
AEW/GE
DI 55
File AF Ops/2/5/1

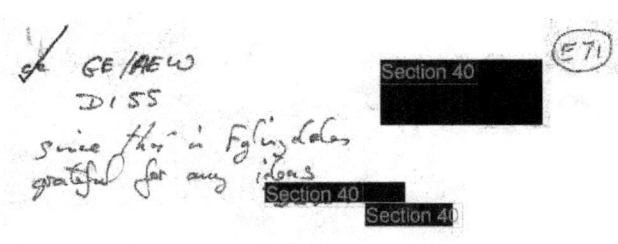

U N C L A S S I F I E D

CYL004 26/0132 085G0286

FOR CYL

ROUTINE/ROUTINE 260947Z MAR 87

FROM   RAF FYLINGDALES
TO   MODUK AIR
INFO   UKRAOC
        HQ 11 GP

U N C L A S S I F I E D
SIC EUJ
SUBJECT: REPORT OF AN UNIDENTIFIED FLYING OBJECT
A. 252114Z MAR 87. 3 SECONDS
B. FLAMING GREEN LIGHT WITH YELLOW GOLD PIECES DROPPING OFF
C. WEST OF LOCKWOOD BECK RESERVOIR NEAR BECK BROW ON A173
D. NAKED EYE
E. OBSERVER LOOKING SW WITH OBJECT TRAVELLING TO SE
F. ABOUT 30 DEGREES
G. ESTIMATED IN EXCESS OF 10 MILES TOWARDS HELMSLEY
H. HORIZONTAL, MOVING DOWNWARDS AT END OF SIGHTING
J. CLEAR SKIES WITH SOME PATCHES OF MEDIUM CLOUD
K. LOCKWOOD BECK RESERVOIR
L. SQN LDR Section 40 900

PAGE 2 R8DOXH 003 UNCLAS
M. Section 40   MIDDLESBOROUGH
N. RAF FYLINGDALES PBX OPERATOR AND EX-SERVICEMAN
O. NO OTHER WITNESSES
P. 252255Z MAR 87

DISTRIBUTION EUJ
F
CYL   1 CPR ACTION /(OAK   1 DUTY PRESS OFFR)

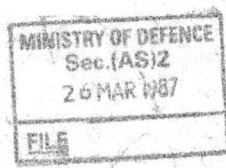

MINISTRY OF DEFENCE
Sec.(AS)2
2 6 MAR 1987

FILE

DISS
GE/AEW

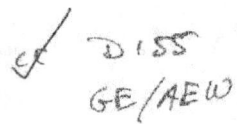

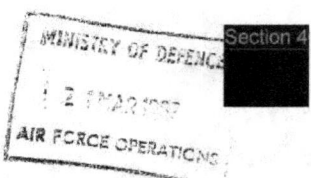

MINISTRY OF DEFENCE
1 2 MAR 1987
AIR FORCE OPERATIONS

U N C L A S S I F I E D

CWV029 21/1118 080C1062

FOR CWV

PRIORITY 211000Z MAR 87

FROM   HQP AND SSUK
TO   AFOR

U N C L A S S I F I E D
SIC I3F/I8J
FOR DUTY OPS OFF. UFO SIGHTING. AT 210300Z MAR 87 SGT Section 40
Section 40   CIVILIAN POLICE HQ, DERBYSHIRE Section 40
REPORTED THE FOLLOWING. SIGHTED AT 210005Z MAR 87 AT CURBER IN
DERBYSHIRE. OS MAP SHT 27 MAP REF 260747 TRAVELLING S TO N. SEEN
BY Section 40   CHESTERFIELD, DERBYSHIRE Section 40
Section 40 VIEWED FROM A MOVING VEHICLE WITH 1 X PAX AS WITNESS.
DESCRIPTION: EGG SHAPED, APPROX 10 FEET IN LENGTH, FLAMES FROM
THE REAR IN A TRIANGULAR PATTERN, TRAVELLED SE TO NW OVER CURBER
EDGE AND WAS DESCENDING APPEARING TO COME DOWN ON CURBER EDGE.
ANGLE OF SIGHT 30 DEGREES DISTANCE FROM VIEWER APPROX 150 YDS.
OBJECT APPEARD TO SPLIT AS IT DROPPED. NO NOTICABLE NOISE, NO
LIGHTS. UNABLE TO ESTIMATE SPEED. WEATHER FINE AND CLEAR WITH LIGHT
CLOUD. CIVILIAN POLICE PATROL TO THE AREA - NEGATIVE RESULTS.
CIVILIAN POLICE CHECKED WITH MANCHESTER AND E MIDLAND AIRPORTS -

PAGE 2 RBDAPJ 001 UNCLAS
NEGATIVE RESULTS
BT

MINISTRY OF DEFENCE
Sec.(AS)2
23 MAR 1987
FILE

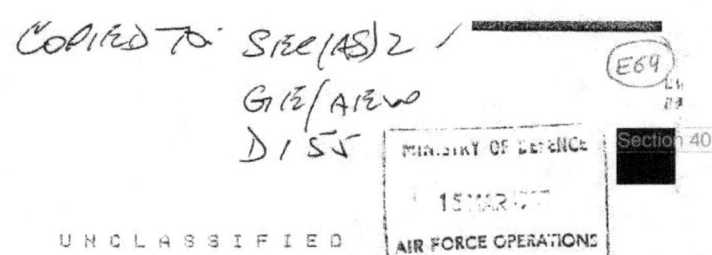

MINISTRY OF DEFENCE

15 MAR 87

AIR FORCE OPERATIONS

Section 40

U N C L A S S I F I E D

CXJ011 15/0211 074C0367

FOR CXJ

PRIORITY 150100Z MAR 87

FROM   UKRADC
TO   MODUK AIR

U N C L A S S I F I E D
SIC ISF/IBJ
 SUBJECT UNIDENTIFIED FLYING OBJECT. MODUK FOR AFD. HQSTC FOR WG CDR
GE
 A 150010Z MAR 87 FIVE MINUTES
 B THREE. MOVING. HELICOPTER SIZE. VARIOUS BRIGHT ORANGE LIGHTS
 C ON ROAD FROM COOKHAM TO MAIDENHEAD
D NAKED EYE
 E FROM MAIDENHEAD TO SLOUGH
 F 3000 TO 5000 FEET
G DIRECTLY ABOVE
 H MOVING EAST
J FULL MOON. CLEAR SKY. NO WIND
 K NO SIGNIFICANT OBJECTS
L CIVILIAN POLICE
M Section 40

PAGE 2 R800YI 004 UNCLAS
N NIL
O NONE
 P 150040Z MAR 87
 BT

DISTRIBUTION ISF
F
 CXJ   1 AFDO ACTION < CXJ   1 AFDO >

DISTRIBUTION IBJ
F
 CYO   1 DD EW&R ACTION < CXJ   1 AFDO >

MINISTRY OF DEFENCE
Sec.(AS)2
16 MAR 1987

FILE

59

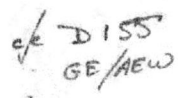

UNIDENTIFIED FLYING OBJECT PROFORMA

From: PCF   Reference: PSS/214/3/AIR
      HQ P&SS (UK)
      RAF RUDLOE MANOR
      HAWTHORN, WILTS, SN13 OPQ

1.   Details of Complaint.

     a.   Name: PC Section 40

     b.   Address: WAREHAM POLICE STATION   TEL; Section 40

2.   Sighting:

     a.   Date/Time of Sighting and Duration:THUR 12 MAR 2105 - 2120 (3 PASSES OVER AREA)

     b.   Position of Observer: CHIDEOCK MANOR, LOOKING NORTH WITH PC Section 40

     c.   How Observed: BINOCULARS - NAKED EYE

     d.   Direction Object first Seen:TRAVELLING WEST TO EAST, 12 - 16% ABOVE HORIZON

     e.   Angle of Elevation:

     f.   Distance of Object from Observer:IN EXCESS OF 3 MILES

     g.   Movement of Object:STRAIGHT LINE, UNIFORM SPEED

     h.   Met Conditions:CLEAR, INTERMITTANT CLOUD, DRY, STARLIT

     i.   Nearby Objects:COPSE OBLITERATES WEST HORIZON, OBSERVER IN VALLEY

     k.   To Whom Reported:SGT Section 40 DUTY SGT

     l.   Other Witnesses:PC Section 40

     m.   Comments:2 LINES OF LIGHTS 4 ON TOP 4 BELOW, YELLOWISH WHITE IN COLOUR
               BETWEEN LIGHTS 1 OR 2 OTHER LIGHTS COLOUR NOT DISCRIBABLE
               OBJECT TRAVELLING 2 x OWN LENGTH EVERY SECOND

3.   Date and Time Received:
     031410Z APR 87

     ┌─────────────────────┐
     │ MINISTRY OF DEFENCE │   Section 40
     │   Sec.(AS)2   │   Signe
     │   - 8 APR 1987   │   Name:
     ├─────────────────────┤
Date: 6 APR 87   FILE   Rank WO   Tel No: RM EXT Section 40

                                                              PTO

PC Section 40 IS ONE OF THE STAFF AT HRH's RESIDENCE AT CHIDEOCK, HE IS INTERESTED IN
ASTRONOMY,   HAS LIVED NEAR RAF UNITS AND IS ABLE TO RECOGNISE AIRCRAFT.   _,
HE OBSERVED THE OBJECT FROM 2 OR 3 DIFFERENT POSITIONS , THE SHAPE HE SAW LOOKED LIKE AN F 111,
WINGS SWEPT BACK BUT NO DISCHIBABLE ENGINE NOISES, HE VIEWED THE OBJECT THROUGH 7x50
BINOCULARS.

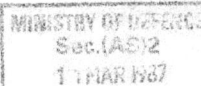
U N C L A S S I F I E D

CWD063 11/0734 07OC1832

FOR CAB

ROUTINE 110707Z MAR 87

FROM   RAF WEST DRAYTON
TO   MODUK AIR

U N C L A S S I F I E D
SIC Z6F
SUBJECT AERIAL PHENOMENA
A. 110055 FIVE TO TEN MINUTES
B. ONE OBJECT ROCK LIKE IN SHAPE CONSISTING MAINLY OF LIGHTS WITH
A RIM ABOVE IT
C. ON THE B4524 (BRIDGEND TO OGMORE BY SEA RD.) WHILST RIDING HIS
BIKE
D. NAKED EYE
E. WEST TOWARDS RIVER
F. 15 FEET ABOVE THE RIVER
G. ACROSS THE ESTUARY
H. NOT KNOWN
J. FINE
K. N/A
L. HQ SOUTH WALES POLICE (SGT Section 40

PAGE 2 RBDAID 001 UNCLAS
M. Section 40
N. 17 YRS OLD
O. NONE
P. 110327Z MAR
BT

DISTRIBUTION   Z6F
A
CAB   1 Sec (AS) ACTION (CXJ   1 AFDO)
CAM   1 ACS(P)
CYD   1 DD GE/AEW
CAV   1 DI 55
CAV   2 DSTI

MINISTRY OF DEFENCE
Sec.(AS)2
- 9 MAR 1987
FILE

Section

U N C L A S S I F I E D

OAB236 04/2251 04B06V47

FOR CAV

ROUTINE 042000Z MAR 87

FROM   RAF WEST DRAYTON
TO   MODUK AIR

U N C L A S S I F I E D
STC IAF
SUBJECT AERIAL PHENOMENA
A. 061840Z MAR 87 TWO MINUTES
B. ONE PALE BRIGHT GREEN OBJECT, GLOWING ON AND OFF. NIL SOUND
OR SMELL
C. Section 40 SOUTH GOSFORTH, IN HIS HOUSE LOOKING OUT OF
WINDOW
D. NAKED EYE
E. NOT KNOWN
F. NOT KNOWN
G. NOT KNOWN
H. STEADY MOVEMENT THEN JUST DISAPPEARED
J. CLEAR SKY
K. NIL
L. INITIALLY TO NORTHUMBERLAND POLICE THEN NEWCASTLE AIRPORT

PAGE 2 RODAZG 047 UNCLAS
M. Section 40
N. NIL
O. NIL
P. 061938Z MAR 87
BT

DISTRIBUTION ZAF
#
AWS   1 Sec (AS) ACTION (CAJ   1 AF(DC))
CAN   1 ASB(P)
CYS   1 DD SE/AEW
CAV   1 DI-55
CAV   2 DST)

WITH THE COMPLIMENTS OF

SATCO

Newcastle Airport,
Woolsington,
Newcastle upon Tyne,
NE13 8BZ

Telephone:
Tyneside Section 40
Ext. Section 40

64

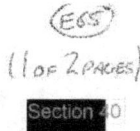

NEWCASTLE AIRPORT

Report on Unidentified Flying Object

A. Date, Time (local) Duration of Sighting.

B. Description of Object.
    Number, size, shape, colour, brightness, sound, smell etc.

C. Exact Position of Observer.
    Geographical Location, indoors/outdoors, moving/stationary

D. How Observed.
    Naked eye, binoculars etc, still/movie camera

E. Direction in which Object First Seen.
    Landmark may be more use.

F. Angular Elevation of Object.
    Estimated heights are unreliable.

G. Distance of Object from Observer.
    By reference to a known landmark wherever possible.

H. Movements of Object.

    Change in E, F and G may be of more use than estimates of course and speed.

J. Meteorological Conditions During Observations.
    Moving clouds, haze, mist etc.

K. Nearby Objects.
    Telephone or high-voltage lines; reservoir, lake or dam; swamp or marsh; river;
    high buildings, tall chimneys, steeples, spires, TV or radio masts; airfields;
    generating plant; factories; pits or other sites with floodlights or other
    lighting.

L. To Whom Reported.
    Police, military organisations, the press, etc.

M. Name and Address of Informant.

N. Any Background Information on the Informant that may be Volunteered.

O. Other Witnesses.

P. Date and Time of Receipt of Report.

The details are to be telephoned immediately to AIS (Military) LATCC W/D Section Ext.

The completed report is to be sent by the originating air traffic service unit to the
Ministry of Defence (AFOR)   R.A.F.
                               Main Building
                               Whitehall SW1

SEE (AS)2
Kean Section 40

NEWCASTLE AIRPORT

Report on Unidentified Flying Object

A. .... 6th March 1840   5mins. ....

B. .... Pale Green Sphere ....

C. .... Longbenton - Outdoors ....

D. .... Naked Eye ....

E. .... Not Reported ....

F. .... 55° ....

G. .... 1/4 Mile ....

H. .... Not Reported ....

J. .... 1850 Metar   16015   2500m   68 RASN   7 STOO5. *RAIN + SNOW*

K. .... NONE ....

L. .... POLICE ....

M. ....   South Gosforth, Newcastle upon Tyne. ....

N. .... --- ....

O. .... ---- ....

P. .... 6/3/87   1858. ....

With The Compliments

of

O i/c AF Ops

Room Section 40
Ministry of Defence
Main Building
Whitehall
London
SW1A 2HB

Section 40

E64
Section 40

Date, Time Duration of Sighting.

6TH MARCH   1840   FEW MINS

Description of Object

PALE BRIGHT GREEN GLOWING

Exact Position of Observer.

OUTSIDE HIS HOUSE.

How Observed.

—

Direction in which Object was first seen.

UNKNOWN

Angular Elevation of Object

—

Distance of Object from Observer.

UNKNOWN

Movements of Object.

SLOW MOVING THEN LARGE FLASH AND DISAPPEARED.

Meteorological Conditions During Observations.
Moving Clouds, Haze, mist etc.

CLEAR SKY -

Nearby Objects.

HOUSING ESTATE

To Whom Reported.

NORTHUMBERLAND POLICE

Name & Address of Informant.

Section 40   S. GOSFORTH NEWCASTLE

Any Background Information on the Informant that
may be Volunteered.

—

Other Witnesses.

NONE

Date & Time of Receipt of Report.

1915. 6TH MARCH 87

MINISTRY OF DEFENCE
Sec. (A.G)2
·16 MAR 1987
FILE ...

UNCLASSIFIED   OIC AFOR

CYD 160 27/2324 0580 6175

FOR CYD

ROUTINE 271935Z FEB 87

MINISTRY OF ...

- 2 MAR 1987

AIR FORCE OPERATIONS

FROM CBFASI
TO   MODUK AIR

UNCLASSIFIED
SIC KHA/IUQ
FOR MODUK AIR OPERATIONS. SUBJECT: UFO OBSERVATION. TIME OF
OBSERVATION 271935Z FEB 87. LARGE BRIGHT GREEN OBJECT TRAILING
TAIL OF ORANGE SPARKS 200 TO 300FT LONG WHICH SEPARATED AFTER
10 TO 15 SECONDS. POSITION 2150S 2326W. SEEN WITH NAKED EYE.
LEFT AIRCRAFT ON HEADING OF 090 DEGREES FLIGHT LEVEL 280 DESCEN-
DING AT AN ANGLE 10 DEGREES DOWN FROM HORIZON. DISTANCE 2 TO 5NM
LEFT OF AIRCRAFT TRACK OF 060 DEGREES MOVING IN A STRAIGHT LINE.
MET CONDITIONS WERE ON TOP BKN CU, VISIBILITY UNLIMITED, WINDS
LIGHT AND VARIABLE, TEMPERATURE MINUS 23-
BT

DISTRIBUTION   KHA
F
CYD   1 DD AIR (Support) ACTION (CXJ   1 AFDO)

DISTRIBUTION   IUQ
F
CXP   1 Mov Ops(RAF) ACTION (CXJ   1 AFDO)
CAB   1 D Mov(RAF)
CWN   4 Q (Mov) 2/ DOMS

COPIED TO: SRC (AS)2
           AEW/GR
           D/55

MINISTRY OF DEFENCE
Sec.(AS)2
- 3 MAR 1987

FILE

69

DOCLFS. — please hand to this,

Humberside Police

HUMBERSIDE POLICE
H.Q.
2 4 FEB 1987
ADMIN.
OPERATIONS SUPPORT DIVISION

With Compliments

HQ OPERATIONS

MESSAGE FROM GOOLE SUB

SIGHTING OF UFO
****

ABOUT 0140HRS ON TUESDAY 24TH FEBRUARY 1987. Section 40
Section 40 WAS DRIVING HIS TAXI ALONG THE A18 EAST
BOUND TOWARDS SCUNTHORPE. WITH AT THE TIME WAS A 16 YEAR OLD NEIGHBOUR
Section 40 AND THREE FRIENDS FROM SCUNTHORPE. ASV THE VEHICLE
APPROACHED PILFREY BRIDGE. Section 40 BECAME AWARE OF A STATIONARY
OBJECT IN THE SKY TO HIS RIGHT. THE OBJECT RESEMBLED AN AIR BALLOON IN
THE SHAPE OF A SAUSAGE. AND HAD THREE SEPARATE FLASHING RED LIGHTS IN
A HORIZONTAL LINE. THERE WAS A CONSTANT GREEN LIGHT TO THE LEFT OF THE
RED LIGHTS AND WHAT APPEARED TO BE A CLUSTER OF BRIGHT WHITE LIGHTS
ON THE UNDERSIDE OF THE OBJECT BENEATH THE RED LIGHTS.
Section 40 CONTINUED TO SCUNTHORPE WERE HE LEFT HIS THREE FRIENDS AND
RETURNED TO CROWLE VIA THE SAME ROUTE. WITH ▇▇▇▇ AS HIS ONLY
PASSENGER.
AS HE APPROACHED THE SAME LOCATION. PILFREY BRIDGE. HE SAW THE OBJECT
IN THE SAME POSITION. Section 40 CONTINUED FOR ABOUT ONE MILE AND
PULLED INTO THE LAYBY JUST BEFORE CROWLE CROSSROADS. WHERE THE TWO OF
THEM GOT OUT OF THE CAR TO VIEW. THE OBJECT. AT THIS TIME THE OBJECT
WAS JUST ABOVE TREE LEVEL AND SLOWLY RISING. AND THE ONLY NOISE THAT
COULD BE HEARD WAS A LOW HUMMING SOUND.
THE TWO OF THEM GOT BACK INTO THE VEHICLE AND AS THEY PULLED OFF THE
OBJECT QUICKLY FLEW PAST THEM TOWARDS CROWLE BRICKYARD. A DISTANCE OF
ABOUT A MILE AND HALF WHICH WAS COVERED IN A COUPLE OF SECONDS.
FROM THAT POSITION Section 40 COULD SEE THEAT THE OBJECT WAS ROUGHLY
THE SAME SIZE AS A SINGLE DECKER BUS. AND SAW IT CIRCLE ROUND TOWARDS
STUBLEYS FARM ON THE SOUTH SIDE OF THE A18 AND INTO THE WOODS.
Section 40 WENT HOME AND THEN RETURNED TO THE CANAL BRIDGE ON THE A161
NEAR TO CROWLE CROSSROADS. WITH HIS BINOCULARS. FROM THERE HE SAW THE
OBJECT TRAVEL TOWARDS SANDTOFT AND DISSAPEAR FROM VIEW.
Section 40 STATES THAT HE SAW THE OBJECT ABOUT ONE MONTH AGO NEAR THE
A18 AT TUDMARSH CORNER. ABOUT 1930HRS. WHEN THE OBJECT APPEARED TO
FOLLOW HIM FOR A SHORT DISTANCE BEFORE DISAPPEARING.

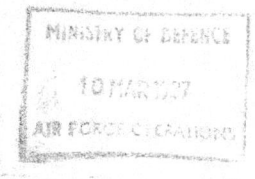

Authorised by PS Section 40   Sent by PC Section 40

*With the
Chief Constable's
Compliments*

Constabulary Headquarters,
Butterley Hall,
RIPLEY, Derby.
DE5 3RS

ALFRETON DHQ
HEADQUARTERS
TO THE CHIEF CONSTABLE, DERBYSHIRE
FROM THE DIVISIONAL COMMANDER, ALFRETON,
SERIAL NO. A 10
LOG NO. 18/2105/FEB/87

UNIDENTIFIED FLYING OBJECT
==================================

A. DATE/TIME/DURATION -BETWEEN 1806+1807HRS 180287-LESS THAN 1 M NUT
   OF SIGHTING
B. DESCRIPTION OF   -ORANGE GLOW TURNING TO WHITE LEAVING VAPOUR
   OBJECT(S)   TRAIL WHICH DISPE SED IMMEDIATELY, SHAPE
                         UNKNOWN
C. EXACT POSITION   -WITNESS AT SOMERCOTES FACING ALFRETON
   OBSERVED   OBJECT IN E/N.E DIRECTION
D. HOW OBSERVED   -NORMAL VISION
E. DIRECTION IN WHICH   -N.E OVERHEAD,.THEN TRAVELLED E/N.E TOWARDS
   OBJECT FIRST SEEN   HOPE VALLEY DIRECTION
F. ANGLE OF SIGHT   -70% FROM HORIZONTAL THEN 30% WHEN TRAVELLING
G. DISTANCE   -2 MILES
H. MOVEMENTS   -DESCENDED,THEN CROSSED,CURVED AWAY,ASCENDING
                         AT GREAT SPEED
J. METEOROLOGICAL   -CLEAR,CLOUD BANK TO SOUTH,MOVING WESTWA DS
   CONDITIONS AT TIME
K. NEARBY OBJECTS   -NIL
L. OFFICER DEALING   -P.C Section 40   HEANOR

   THE WITNESS Section 40   SECURITY OFFICE ,OF
Section 40   HEANOR, IS AN AMATEUR ASTRONOMER WHO HAS MADE ONE
PREVIOUS REPORT OF A SIGHTING OF A U.F.O.

AUTHORISED BY SERGEANT Section 40

AS PER TEL. CONVERSATION BETWEEN

SGT. Section 40   and your Section 40

of 19.02.87

REPORT OF AN UNIDENTIFIED FLYING OBJECT

A. Date, time and duration of sighting.   18 Feb 87 1806-1807 hours
                                                     1 minute duration

B. Description of object.   Orange glow turning to white leaving
                                                     vapour trail.

C. Exact position observer.   Somercotes, Derbyshire, facing
                                                     Alfreton E/NE

D. How observed.   Naked eye

E. Direction in which object was first seen.   NE overhead

F. Angle of sight.   70° from horizontal, 30° when
                                                     travelling

G. Distance.   Hope valley, 2 miles

H. Movements.   Descended and crossed, moved away at
                                                     speed

J. Meteorological conditions during observations.   Clear weather

K. Nearby objects.   Not known

L. To whom reported.   HQ Derbyshire Police, Ripley

M. Name and address of informant.   Section 40

N. Any background on the informant that may be volunteered.   N/K

O. Other witnesses.   N/K

P. Date and time of receipt of report.   1330 19.2.87

    A-1

MINISTRY OF DEFENCE
Sec.(AS)2
26 FEB 1987
FILE

74

Section 40
(E59)

From: Reference:

1. Details of Complaint.

    a. Name:

    b. Address: HENOR,
        DERBYSHIRE

2. Sighting:

    a. Date/Time of Sighting and Duration: 1815067 feb 87   1 min

    b. Position of Observer: SOMERCOATES,
        DERBYSHIRE

    c. How Observed: NORMAL VISION

    d. Direction Object first Seen: EAST - NORTHEAST.

    e. Angle of Elevation: 70% when horizontal & 30% when
        travelling

    f. Distance of Object from Observer: 2 miles.

    g. Movement of Object: descended, stopped then
        ascended very quickly.

    h. Met Conditions: Clear, cloud bank south, moving
        westwards.

    j. Nearby Objects: —

    k. To Whom Reported: Derbyshire police

    l. Other Witnesses: —

    m. Comments: Previous sightings. There was an orange
        glow turning to white leaving a vapour trail
3. Date and Time Received: that vanished immediately.
        @ 1910302 feb 87

Signed: Section 40

Name:

Date: 19 feb 87   Rank: AA   Tel No: Section 40

U N C L A S S I F I E D

DTG189 16/2399 847C4453

FOR CAS

ROUTINE/ROUTINE 161725Z FEB 87

FROM   RAF WATTISHAM
TO   MODUK AIR
INFO   UKRADC
        HQ 11 GP

U N C L A S S I F I E D
BTG 25P
SUBJECT UNIDENTIFIED FLYING OBJECT SIGHTING REF. 110/345/8/OPS DATED
23 MAR 74
A 1515372 FEB 87
B RED GREEN AND WHITE FLASHING LIGHTS
C INDOORS
D NAKED EYE
E SSE, FROM CLACTON TOWARDS WATTISHAM
F/G VERY HIGH IN THE SKY
H MOVING VERY SLOWLY
J CLEAR SKY
K MIL
L SGT Section 40   DUTY OPS CLERK RAF WATTISHAM

PAGE 2 RAFDUKG 452 UNCLAS
M Section 40   GREAT ASHFIELD, ELMSWELL.
N NONE
O FIRST REPORTED TO Section 40   BY FRIENDS IN BURY ST EDMUNDS
P 1515302 IN BURY
Q YES
AMPN. LOCAL CONTROLLER SAW OBJECT AS A VERY BRIGHT LIGHT OF CHANGING
COLOUR ON BEARING OF 160. HE OBSERVED LIGHT FROM 1855 UNTIL 1902 AND
IT APPEARED TO BE HOVERING. AN AC TRANSITING FROM CLACTON TO WTM
PASSED BENEATH OBJECT AND VERIFIED OBJECT VERY HIGH. LIGHT ALSO SEEN
BY CC PLT ____ DRIVING ALONG A45
BT   Section 40

DISTRIBUTION Z6
F
CAS   1 Sec (AS) ACTION (CXJ   1 AFOO)
CAM   1 ACS(F)
CYD   1 DS QE/ACM
CAU   1 DI 55
CAU   2 DGTI

UNCLASSIFIED

CAB054 11/0346 042C0444

FOR CAB

ROUTINE/ROUTINE 1013397 FEB 87

FROM   RAF VALLEY   CORRECTED VERSION?
TO   MODUK AIR
INFO   HQRAFSC

UNCLASSIFIED
SIC ZAF
REPORT OF UNIDENTIFIED FLYING OBJECT. MOD FOR DFC, HQRAFSC FOR
ESYD
A. 25 JAN 87 1630Z TO 1650Z
B. ROUND SINGLE WHITE LIGHT
C. RMT.
D. NAKED EYE
E. TO THE WEST TOWARDS LLANDUDNO
F. LOW IN SKY AT ROOFTOP LEVEL OF ADJACENT 2 STOREY HOUSE
G. APPROX 1 TO 2 MILES
H. STATIC
J. DRY, GOOD VISIBILITY, NO CLOUD
K. ELECTRICITY PYLON
L. ATC RAF VALLEY
M.   KINMEL BAY, RHY   TEL RHYL
N. DRIVING INSTRUCTOR WITH BSM SCHOOL OF MOTORING
O. INSTRUCTING PUPIL AT TIME
P. 9 FEB 87 2200Z
BT

DISTRIBUTION ZAF

CAB   1   Sec (AS) ACTION (DXJ   1 AFDC
SAH   1   ACS(P)
CYS   1   SO SE/SEN
TAU   1   DI 55
IAU   2   DDII

UNIDENTIFIED FLYING OBJECT PROFORMA

From: F.C.F. RAF Rudloe Manor   Reference:

1.   Details of Complaint.

    a.   Name: Section 40

    b.   Address: Section 40   Pany Cae-Mawr Gwent

2.   Sighting:

    a.   Date/Time of Sighting and Duration: 09.02.87 0630(L) 2 minutes approx.

    b.   Position of Observer: Upstairs bedroom of home

    c.   How Observed: Naked Eye

    d.   Direction Object first Seen: North East

    e.   Angle of Elevation: _____

    f.   Distance of Object from Observer: 500 to 600 feet

    g.   Movement of Object: Nil

    h.   Met Conditions: Dawn Breaking, conditions clear, no cloud, little wind

    j.   Nearby Objects: Nil

    k.   To Whom Reported: Sqn Ldr Section 40 RAF ~~Castleon~~ CAERLWEAST, Gwent

    l.   Other Witnesses: See over

    m.   Comments:

3.   Date and Time Received: 1515L 09.02.87.

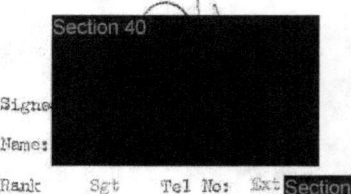

Signe~~d~~

Name:

Date: Rank   Sgt   Tel No: Ext Section 40 appeared to be a sensible lady, who maintained throughout that the object she saw was not a figment of the imagination. She was awoken by a very bright light shinning into her bedroom. On looking out she saw an object approx 7-8' across, round and on the ground. There was no noise coming from it and it was stationary. She watched the object for a couple of minutes and during this time there was no movement. Later that morning her son visited the area and found 3 circles in the grass. Inside these circles the grass appeared brighter than the surrounding area. The circles were indented about 1-1½ inches. The area was also visited by Sqn Ldr The discription of the area is produced below.

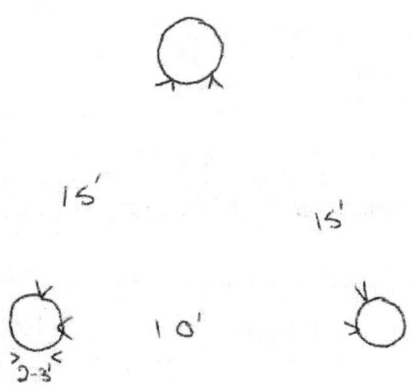

79

Copy to
DI 55
Sec (AS) ✓
AEW/GE
D/AF Ops 2/5/1

U N C L A S S I F I E D

CXJ042 05/1132 05602109

FOR CXJ

PRIORITY/ROUTINE 051100Z FEB 87

FROM   UKRAOC
TO   MODUK AIR
INFO   RAF WADDINGTON

U N C L A S S I F I E D
SIC I3F/IBJ
MODUK AIR FOR AFDO. WADDINGTON FOR OPS. SUBJECT REPORT OF AN
UNIDENTIFIED FLYING OBJECT
A. 0100Z TO 0115Z FEB 87 DURATION 30 SECS
B. UPRIGHT CYLINDER. TRANSPARENT WITH FLAMES WITHIN. MOVING AWAY
SILENT
C. OUTDOORS. GARRATS BRIDGE. LINCOLN. ROYAL NAVY CLUB
D. NAKED EYE. PHOTO TAKEN
E. WEST. MOVING NORTH. TOWARDS CATHEDRAL
F. DIFFICULT TO TELL. QUITE LOW AT FIRST
G. DIFFICULT TO TELL
H. GRADUAL MOVEMENT
J. CLEAR OPEN SKY
K. TERRACED HOUSES

PAGE 2 RBDOYI 064 UNCLAS
L. RAF WADDINGTON OPERATIONS
M. Section 40
N. TECHNICIAN AT FORD GARAGE
O. Section 40
P 011710 FEB 87
NOTE RAF WADDINGTON OPS TO NOTE ADDRESS FOR UFO REPORTS PLUS HQSTC
FOR UKRAOC AND HQ CDR GE
BT

DISTRIBUTION   I3F
F
  CXJ   1   AFDO   ACTION (CXJ   1   AFDO)

DISTRIBUTION   IBJ
F
  CYD   1   DD ENAR ACTION (CXJ   1   AFDO)

        END   U N C L A S S I F I E D

U N C L A S S I F I E D

CWD011 05/0152 036C0456

FOR CAB

ROUTINE 042250Z FEB 87

FROM　　RAF WEST DRAYTON
TO　　　MODUK AIR

U N C L A S S I F I E D
SIC Z6F
SUBJECT: AERIAL PHENOMENA
A. 032255Z TO 2303Z FEB 87
B. ONE LARGE SPHERICAL OBJECT, SILVER GREY COLOUR WITH FOUR RED
LIGHTS AT REAR. ROTATING BRIGHT WHITE LIGHTS AROUND CENTRE. VERY
QUIET MUFFLED NOISE (WHIRLING SOUND)
C. LANCASTER VALE ESTATE, OUTDOORS INITIALLY STATIONARY THEN SLOW
MOVING
D. NAKED EYE. INFORMANT APPROACHED OBJECT, WHILE IT WAS STATIC,
WALKING FAST WITH DOG. HE GOT TO APPROX 150FT WHEN OBJECT MOVED OFF,
TILTED, VEERING TO RIGHT IN WSW DIRECTION FOLLOWING RAILWAY LINE
E. LANCASTER VALE ESTATE TOWARDS SKERTON
F. FIVE DEG
G. 150 TO 200 YDS
H. STEADY

PAGE 2 RBDAID 010　UNCLAS
J. BLANKET OF MIST WHICH DIDNT START UNTIL A FEW FEET OFF GROUND.
OBJECT VERY CLEAR
K. HOUSING ESTATE RAILWAY LINE
L. AIS(M) BY TELEPHONE
M. ████████████████████████████████VALE ESTATE, LANCASTER,
LANCASHIRE
N. NIL
O. INDEPENDENT SIGHTING BY FRIEND AND WIFE IN CAR OVER CARLISLE
BRIDGE. OBJECT WAS BULKY, FAT, GLOWING AND VEERED OF AT AN ANGLE.
WITNESS ADDRESS ████████████████████████████████████
LA1 2BZ
P. 042200Z FEB 87
BT

DISTRIBUTION　Z6F
F
CAB　　1　Sec (AS) ACTION (CX.)　　1　AF90)
CAM　　1　ACS(P)

U N C L A S S I F I E D

WD113 04/1910 035C496J

OR CAB

ROUTINE/ROUTINE 041555Z FEB 87

ROM   RAF VALLEY
O   MODUK AIR
NFO   HQRAFSC

U N C L A S S I F I E D
ITC Z6F
MODUK AIR FOR DS8, HQRAFSC FOR CSYC. SUBJECT REPORT OF UNIDENTIFIE
FLYING OBJECT
A. 31 JAN 87 0130HR FOR 30MIN
B. ONE OBJECT FLASHING LIKE STAR: RED, GREEN, WHITE AND BLUE LIGHT
C. OUTDOORS
D. NAKED EYE.
E. OVERHEAD

DISTRIBUTION   Z6F
F
CAB   1 Sec (AS) ACTION (CXJ   1 AFDO)
CYD   1 DD GE/AEW
CAV   1 DI 55

ADE 2 RDDSVS 016 UNCLAS
. Section 40   BRYNGWRYN (TEL Section 40)
. MIL
. SGN
. 31 JAN 87 0210HRS

DISTRIBUTION   Z4
F
CAB   1 Sec (AS) ACTION (1 AFDO)
CAM   1 ACS(P)
CYD   1 DD GE/AEW
CAV   1 DI SB
CAV   2 DSTI

82

REPORT OF AN UNIDENTIFIED FLYING OBJECT

A. <u>Date, Time and Duration of Sightings</u>. (Local Times to be Quoted)

~~31st Feb~~ 1st Feb. 0100 - 0115.

DURATION 30 SECS.

B. <u>Description of Object</u>. (Number of objects, size, shape, colours, brightness, sound, smell etc).

UPRIGHT CYLINDER TRANSPARANT WITH FLAMES WITHIN MOVING AWAY. SILENT.

C. <u>Exact Position Observer</u>. (Geographical location. Indoors or outdoors. Stationary or moving).

OUTDOORS GLARRATS BRIDGE, LINCOLN. ROYAL NAVY CLUB.

D. <u>How Observed</u>. (Naked eye, binoculars, other optical device, still or movie camera).

NAKED EYE PHOTO's TAKEN.

E. <u>Direction in which Object was First Seen</u>. (A landmark may be more useful than a badly estimated bearing).

WEST MOVING NORTH. TOWARDS CATHEDRAL.

F. <u>Angle of Sight</u>. (Estimated heights are unreliable).

DIFFICULT TO TELL. QUITE LOW AT FIRST.

G. <u>Distance</u>. (By reference to a known landmark wherever possible).

DIFFICULT TO TELL

H. <u>Movements</u>. (Changes in E, F and G may be of more use than estimates of course and speed).

GRADUAL MOVEMENT.

I. <u>Meteorological Conditions during Observations</u>. (Moving clouds, haze, mist etc).

CLEAR OPEN SKY

J.   Nearby Objects. (Telephone lines; high voltage lines; reservoir, lake swamp or marsh; river; high buildings, tall chimneys, steeples, spires, TV or radio masts; airfields, generating plant; factories, pits or other sites with flood-lights or other night lighting).

TERRACED HOUSES.

K.   To Whom Reported. (Police, military organisation, the press etc).

RAF WADDINGTON. OPERATIONS.

L.   Name and Address of Informant.

M.   Any Background on the Informant that may be Volunteered.

TECHNICIAN AT FORD GARAGE.

N,   Other Witnesses.

O.   Date and Time of Receipt of Report

1ST FEB. 1710 HRS.

84

REPORT OF AN UNIDENTIFIED FLYING OBJECT

A.	Date, Time & Duration of Sighting	30 Jan 87, 2006Z Several minutes (20 mins)
B.	Description of Object (No of objects, size, shape, colour, brightness)	Size of star. Stationary white flashing light. Red flashing light on circular rim. Bright.
C.	Exact Position of Observer Location, indoor/outdoor, stationary/moving	Indoor, stationary.
D.	How Observed (naked eye, binoculars, other optical device, still or movie	Naked eye.
E.	Direction in which object first seen (A landmark may be more useful than a badly estimated bearing)	Northwards towards Brookward County First School, Neath Hill, Milton Keynes.
F.	Angle of Sight (Estimated heights are unreliable)	Directly above house.
G.	Distance (By reference to a known landmark	None.
H.	Movements (Changes in E, F & G may be of more use than estimates of course and speed)	Stationary.
J.	Met Conditions during Observations (Moving clouds, haze, mist etc)	Clear sky.
K.	Nearby Objects (Telephone lines, high voltage lines, reservoir, lake or dam, swamp or marsh, river, high buildings, tall chimneys, steeples, spires, TV or radio masts, airfields, generating plant, factories, pits or other sites with	None.

L.	To whom reported (Police, military, press etc)	Thames Valley Police, Divisional HQ, 302 Witan Gate East, Central Milton Keynes, Buck.
M.	Name & Address of Informant	████████
N.	Background of Informant that may be volunteered	Not known.
O.	Other Witnesses	Nil..
P.	Date, Time of Receipt	30 Jan 87. 2026.
Q.	Any Unusual Meteorological Conditions	No.
R.	Remarks -------	Informant interested in UFOs. Seemed clear-headed coherent.

████████

Sqn Ldr
Duty Ops Officer
AF Ops

30 Jan 87
Date............

Distribution:

Sec(AS)2
AEW/GE
DI 55
File AF Ops/2/5/1

U N C L A S S I F I E D

CWD113 04/1910 03SC4963

FOR CAS

ROUTINE/ROUTINE 041555Z FEB 87

FROM   RAF VALLEY
TO   MODUK AIR
INFO   HQRAFSC

U N C L A S S I F I E D
SIC ZAF
MODUK AIR FOR DSS. HQRAFSC FOR CBYO. SUBJECT REPORT OF UNIDENTIFIED
FLYING OBJECT
A. 31 JAN 87 0130HR FOR 30MIN
B. ONE OBJECT FLASHING LIKE STAR: RED, GREEN, WHITE AND BLUE LIGHTS
C. OUTDOORS
D. NAKED EYE, NEAR RAF VALLEY
E. OVERHEAD
F. N/A
G. N/A
H. N/A
J. CLEAR SKY
K. NONE
L. ATC RAF VALLEY

PAGE 2 RODBVS 016 UNCLAS
M. Section 40   BRYNGWRYN (TEL Section 40
N. NIL
O. SGN
P. 31 JAN 87 0210HRS 1
87

DISTRIBUTION IGF
W
CAB   1 Sec (AS) ACTION (CXJ   1 AFDO)
CAM   1 ACB(F)
CYD   1 DD CE/AEW
CAV   1 DI 55
CAV   2 DSTI

87

MINISTRY OF DEFENCE
27 JAN
AIR FORCE (ESO)

COPY TO
Sec(AS)2
AEW/SE
DI 55
D/AF Ops 2/5/1

KT0435 27/1416 0270510

ROUTINE 0542X07 JAN 97

FROM: MOSTC
TO: MODUK AIR

R E S T R I C T E D
SIC IZF/IBJ
MODUK AIR FOR AFO
SUBJECT: UFO
A. APPROX FOUR WEEKS AGO BETWEEN 0515Z AND 0600Z ON TWO SUCCESSIVE
DAYS.
B. LIKE A LARGE BRIGHT WHITE CHANDELIER OCCASIONALLY SMALLER
OBJECTS LEFT THE REAR OF MAIN OBJEC.
C. TOP FLOOR OF BLOCK OF FLATS.
D. THROUGH RACING GLASSES, ALTHOUGH INITIALLY OBSERVED WITH
NAKED EYE BY WIFE
E. TO LEFT OF FRONT FACE OF FLATS.
F. HALFWAY UP SKY APPROX 4 DEGREES
G. NIL
H. INITIALLY STATIONARY THEN UPWARDS AT HIGH SPEED
J. SKY CLEAR.

PAGE 2 RBGGYI 116 R E S T R I C T E D
K. NIL
L. WEST MIDLANDS POLICE CONTROL ROOM, BOURNVILLE LANE STN
BIRMINGHAM. [Section 40] REPORTED AM 27 JAN 97.
M. [Section 40] WEDNESBURY
MIDLANDS
N. 7 YEARS NAVAL EXPERIENCE GUES
O. WIFE
P 2710007 JAN 97
BT

DISTRIBUTION IXF
F
CXJ 1 AFDO ACTION (CXJ 1 AFOO)

DISTRIBUTION IBJ
F
CYD 1 DD EMAR ACTION (CXJ 1 AFOO)

88

U N C L A S S I F I E D

CWD033 88/0010 007C5136

FOR CAS

ROUTINE 071115Z JAN 87

FROM   RAF BINBROOK
TO   MODUK AIR

U N C L A S S I F I E D
SIC L6Z/Z6F
(SIC Z6F INSERTED BY DCC)
A 0612302 JAN
B BRIGHT RED/CIRCULAR OBJECT FOLLOWED BY THICK TRAIL OF BLACK SMOKE
C LOOKING NORTH FROM KITCHEN WINDOW WHILE OBJECT WAS MOVING IN A
WESTERLY DIRECTION
D NAKED EYE
E NOT REPORTED
F JUST ABOVE BUILDING HEIGHTS
G N/K
H STRAIGHT LINE LOSING HEIGHT
J FINE SLEAT FALLING BUT VISIBILITY GOOD
K NONE REPORTED
L BRANSHOLME POLICE STATION HULL
M Section 40   BRANSHOLME, HULL TEL Section 40
ection 40
N AND O NONE
P 0613172 JAN
BT

DISTRIBUTION   L6Z
F
NO SDL

DISTRIBUTION   Z6F
F
CAB   1   Sec (AS) ACTION (CXJ   (1 AFDG)
CAM   1   AC9(P)
CYB   1   DD SE/AEW
CAV   1   DI 55
CAV   2   DSTI

U N C L A S S I F I E D

CAB033 07/0730 007C0453

FOR CAB

ROUTINE 070700Z JAN 87

FROM   RAF WEST DRAYT
TO   MODUK AIR

U N C L A S S I F I E D
SIC Z6F
SUBJECT: AERIAL PHENOMENA
A. 070130Z JAN 87, 5 MINUTES
B. ONE BOWL SHAPED OBJECT GLOWING DULL ORANGE
C. OUTDOORS, OPENSHAW, MANCHESTER
D. NAKED EYE
E. OVER MANCHESTER
F. FORTY FIVE DEGREES
G. NOT KNOWN
H. CHANGING
J. SKY CLEAR
K. IN CITY
L. POLICE
N. NIL

PAGE 2 RBDAID 001 UNCLAS
O. NO
P. 070240Z JAN 87
87

DISTRIBUTION   Z6F
F
CAB   1   Sec (AS)   ACTION (CXJ   1   AFDO)
CAN   1   ACAS(P)
CVB   1   DS GE/AEW
CAV   1   DI 55
CAV   2   DSTI

To: MOD Sec (AS) 2b
Room
Main Building
Whitehall
London

From:HQ P&SS (UK)
FCF
RAF Rudloe Manor
Hawthorn
Wilts SN13 0P:

FLYING COMPLAINT   **06 JAN 87**

1.   The attached complaint was recieved at this Headquarters as per date stamp from a "first time" complainant.

2.   The complaint location is/is not listed as an avoidance area and is situated as follows:

   a.   OS Sheet Number .... *110* ....

   b.   Grid Reference .... *S.E. 8902* ...

   c.   LFA .... *8* ....

3.   This Headquarters will take no further action unless directed by you.

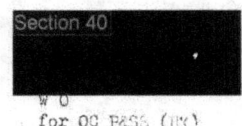

W O
for OC P&SS (UK)

UFO   FLYING COMPLAINT FORM

From: RAF Finningley   Reference: FIN/2325/3/P1
To: HQ P&SS (UK) Flying Complaints Flight

1.   Details of Complainant.

    a.   Name   Section 40

    b.   Address

                     WOMBWELL BARNSLEY

    c.   Nearest Large Town

    d.   Tel No   BARNSLEY   Section 40

2.   Details of Incident.

    a.   Date   05TH JAN 87

    b.   Time (Local or GMT)   2359 LOCAL

    c.   No of Ac Involved

    d.   Direction   HOVERING

    e.   Height   ?

3.   Details of Aircraft (Tick as appropriate)

    Jet Ac   Propellor Ac   Military Ac   Civil Ac   Fighter
    Bomber   Helicopter   Light Ac   Other ✓   Camouflaged
    Silver   Red and White   Other Colours/Special Markings (specify

4.   Location of Complaint.

    a.   Address as 1b

OR b.

5.   Claims.   Is there any injury to persons and/or livestock or damage to
property which will result in a claim? If so, is complainant owner of the
property? (Details)

6.   Full Details of Complaint.   RED FLASHING LIGHT. OBJECT
WAS DEFUSED BUT SAUSER SHAPED SURROUNDED BY
WHITE GLOW. SEEMED TO BE HOVERING OVER WOMBWELL
NO HEIGHT COULD BE GUESSED AT BUT FAIRLY HIGH

7.   Date and Time Report received   06TH JAN 87   1330L

                            Signed   Section 40

                            Name   SGT.

U N C L A S S I F I E D

CAB027 02/1250 ваддана

FOR CAB

ROUTINE 0210002 JAN 87

FROM   RAF WEST DRAYTON
TO   MODUK AIR

U N C L A S S I F I E D
UIC 26F
SUBJECT: AERIAL PHENOMENA. A. 31 DEC 1986 BETWEEN 1900 AND 1930 HRS
LOCAL B. ONE CIRCULAR VERY BRIGHT WHITE LIGHT SURROUNDED BY A
RECTANGULAR HALO OF PULSATING LIGHTS C. INDOORS D. BINOCULARS
E. SOUTH OF THAXTED F. 15 TO 20 DEGS G. IN OUTER SPACE H. STEADY
J. NOT GIVEN K. NONE L. FIRST TO STANSTEAD ATC THEN POLICE M. Section 40
       THAXTED, ESSEX N. SOME O. WIFE AND SON.
Section 40
SON AT UNIVERSITY IS A KEEN AMATEUR ASTRONOMER P. 620925L
17.

DISTRIBUTION Z6F
F:
CAB   1 Sec (AS) ACTION (EX)   1 SF8O)
CAM   1 AES(A)
CYB   1 AD GE/AEW
CAV   1 D1 SS
CAW   2 DSII

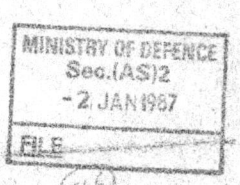

U N C L A S S I F I E D

CAB019 02/1138 002C0451

FOR CAB

ROUTINE 020915Z JAN 87

FROM   RAF WEST DRAYTON
TO   MODUK AIR

U N C L A S S I F I E
SIC Z6F
SUBJECT: AERIAL PHENOMENA. A. 0430 HRS ON 2 JAN FOR 60 MINS.
RED AND YELLOW GLOWING LIGHTS WITH TWO CENTRES. C. HOME ADDRESS.
D. NAKED EYE AND BINOCULARS. E. 30 MILES SOUTH OF WOKING. F. 25 TO
30 DEGREES ABOVE THE HORIZON. G. SEE E. J. CAVOK. K. NOT KNOWN.
L. LATEC MIL. M. Section 40   KENISHFORD,
MAYFORD WOKING Section 40   N. NONE. O. NONE. P. 0207452 JAN 87
87

DISTRIBUTION   Z6F
F
CAB   1 Sec (AS) ACTION (CXJ   1   AFDG)
CAB   1 ACS(P)
CYD   1 DD GE/AEW
CAV   1 DI 55
CAV   2 DSTI

94

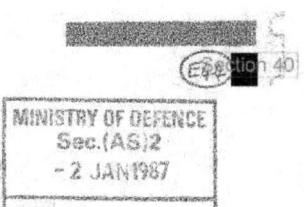

MINISTRY OF DEFENCE
Sec.(AS)2
- 2 JAN 1987

FILE

UNCLASSIFIED

CAB003 02/0838 002C0217.

FOR CAB

ROUTINE 020810Z JAN 87

FROM   RAF WEST DRAYTON
TO   MODUK AIR

UNCLASSIFIED
SIC Z6F
SUBJECT: AERIAL PHENOMENA
A. 0729 HRS ON 23 DEC 86 FOR 15 SECONDS B. 3 LARGE PLUS VARIOUS SMALL
ROUND BRILLIANT WHITE OBJECTS C. JUNCTION OF BURNEY ROAD AND
SEVERLEY WAY, NEW MALDEN D. NAKED EYE E. NIL F. DIRECTLY OVERHEAD
G. NOT KNOWN H. STEADY, SOUTH TO NORTH J. THIN PATCHY CLOUD COVER
K. BUILT UP AREA L. TO LATCC MIL M. Section 40
Section 40   N. NONE O. NONE P. 231825Z DEC 86
2T

DISTRIBUTION   Z6F
F
CAB   1   Sec (AS) ACTION (CXJ   1   AFDC)
CAM   1   ACS(P)
CYD   1   DD GE/AEW
CAV   1   DI 55
CAV   2   DSTI

95

U N C L A S S I F I E D

CAB050 23/1309 257C145R

FOR CAB

ROUTINE 231045Z DEC 86

FROM   RAF WEST DRAYTON
TO   MODUK AIR

U N C L A S S I F I E D
SIC Z6F
REFERENCE MY Z6F 231015Z DEC 86. PHENOMENA ALSO SIGHTED OVERHEAD
HUYTON LIVERPOOL AT 239725Z DEC 86 BY MR YOUNG Section 40
LIVERPOOL 8. REPORTED TO LIVERPOOL AIRPORT
ST

DISTRIBUTION   Z6F
F
CAB   1 Sec (AS) ACTION (CXJ   1 AFDO)
CAM   1 ACS(P)
CYD   1 GD GE/AEW
CAV   1 DI 55
CAV   2 DST1

U N C L A S S I F I E D

CWD040 9X/1234 357C1325

FOR CAB

ROUTINE 231015Z DEC 86

FROM   RAF WEST DRAYTON
TO   MODUK AIR

U N C L A S S I F I E D
SIC ZGF
AERIAL PHENOMENA:
A. 230730 DEC 86 - 2 MINUTES
B. SIX GOLDEN SPHERES WITH VAPOUR TRAIL
C. OUTDOORS, STATIONARY, KINGSLEY, CHESHIRE
D. NAKED EYE
E. OVERHEAD LIVERPOOL SPEAKE AIRFIELD MOVING TOWARDS MANCHESTER
F. N/K
G. N/K
H. WEST TO EAST MOVING VERY FAST
J. CLEAR SKY
K. NONE
L. LIVERPOOL AIRPORT, CIVIL SUPERVISOR LATCC
M.

PAGE 2 RBDAID 005 UNCLAS
N. EX-NAVY, KEEN ASTROLOGER
O. NIL
P. 230940Z DEC 86
BT

DISTRIBUTION   ZGF
F
CAB   1 Sec (AS) ACTION (CXJ   1 AFDO)
CAM   1 ACS(P)
CYD   1 DD GE/AEW
CAV   1 DI 55
CAV   2 DSTI

U N C L A S S I F I E D

CWD012 23/0950 357C0715

FOR CAB

ROUTINE 230820Z DEC 86

FROM   RAF WEST DRAYTON
TO   MODUK AIR

U N C L A S S I F I E D
SIC Z6F
AERIAL PHENOMENA:
A. 230720 DEC 86
B. LARGE, BURNING-UP AS IT REENTERED EARTHS ATMOSPHERE, PROBABLY
A SATELITE
C. OUTDOORS INFRONT OF ATLANTIC HOUSE, THE SCOTTISH AIR TRAFFIC
CONTROL CENTRE
D. NAKED EYE
E. HEADING 130 DEG
F. MOVING FROM 010 DEG TO 090 DEG ABOVE THE HORIZON
G. REFER TO ITEM O
H. STEADY HEADING OF 130 DEG MOVING VERY FAST
J. CLEAR AND FROSTY
K. NONE
L. N/A

PAGE 2 RBD01D/002 UNCLAS
M. Section 40   PRESTWICK, Section 40
N. WATCH MANAGER SCATCC
O. THE PILOTS OF Section 40 ABERDEEN TO HEATHROW AT TALLA REPORTING
POINT FL370 AND Section 40 TORONTO TO HEATHROW 30 MILES NW BELFAST
REPORTING POINT FL370. BOTH PILOTS REPORTED THAT THE SIGHTING WAS
ABOVE THEM
P. 230735Z DEC 86
BT

DISTRIBUTION   Z6F
F
CAB   1   Sec (AS) ACTION (CRJ   1   AFDO)
CAM   1   ACB(P)
CYD   1   D9 GE/AEW
CAV   1   D1 55
CAV   2   DSTI

With Compliments

Watch Manager.

Sc & OATCC
National Air Traffic Services
Atlantic House, Sherwood Road, Prestwick, Ayrshire KA9 2NR
Telephone Section 40 Ext

A joint Civil Aviation Authority — Ministry of Defence Service

MINISTRY OF DEFENCE
Sec.(AS)2
– 5 JAN 1987
FILE

Section 40

Date, Time Duration of Sighting.

23ʳᵈ DEC. 1986   0728½

Description of Object

LARGE OBJECT RE-ENTERING EARTHS ATMOSPHERE & BURNING UP

Exact Position of Observer.

OUTSIDE FRONT DOOR OF ScOATCC ATLANTIC HOUSE

How Observed.

BY NAKED EYE

Direction in which Object was first seen.

HEADING APPROXIMATELY 130°

Angular Elevation of Object

VIRTUALLY 90° to 10° ABOVE THE HORIZON

Distance of Object from Observer.

SEE SECTION O

Movements of Object.

HEADING APPROXIMATELY 130° VERY FAST

Meteorological Conditions During Observations.
Moving Clouds, Haze, mist etc.

CLEAR & FROSTY

Nearby Objects.

NONE

To Whom Reported.

WATCH MANAGER ScATCC.

Name & Address of Informant.   PRESTWICK AYRSHIRE   Section 40
Section 40

Any Background Information on the Informant that
may be Volunteered.

AIR TRAFFIC CONTROL OFFICER AT ScATCC

Other Witnesses. PILOTS OF Section 40 —CELL POSITION OVER TWA VOR FL370 &
OF Section 40 —CELL POSITION 30NM NORTHWEST BSL VOR FL370. BOTH PILOTS
REPORTED OBJECT WELL ABOVE THEM

Date & Time of Receipt of Report.

23ʳᵈ DEC 1986   0735½

U N C L A S S I F I E D

CND@@5 23/9939 357C0473

FOR CAS

ROUTINE 230515Z DEC 86

FROM   RAF WEST DRAYTON
TO   MODUK AIR

U N C L A S S I F I E D
BIC Z6F
UFO REPORT:

A. 2196@@ DEC 86
B. SINGLE OBJECT WITH BRIGHT ORANGE VAPOUR TRAIL TINGED GREEN AT
TIMES

C. TRAVELLING EAST ON A27 CHICHESTER BY PASS IN CAR WITH PASSENGER
D. NAKED EYE
E. TO SOUTH SOME DISTANCE AWAY

F. NOT STATED
G. NOT STATED

H. FALLING

J. COLD DRY DARK
K. OPEN FIELDS AND GRAVEL PITS
L. CHICHESTER POLICE STATION
M. Section 40

PAGE @ RRDAYS 001 UNCLAS
Section 40
N. NONE
O. PASSENGER IN CAR AND RE
P. 230800Z DEC 86
RT

DISTRIBUTION Z6F
F
CAV   1 Sec (AS) ACTION (CXJ   (1 AFDO)
CAV   1 ACDS(P)
CYD   1 DD GE/RAW
CAV   1 DI 53
CAV   2 DGTI

COPY TO: SEC(RS)2
DI 55
GE/AEW .

CKJ115 22/2354 35603959 ******

FOR CKJ

PRIORITY/ROUTINE 222330Z DEC 96

FROM   UKRADC
TO   MODUK AIR
INFO   HQSTC

U N C L A S S I F I E D
SIC I3F/IBJ
MODUK AIR FOR AFO0. HQSTC FOR NG CDR GE
A. 222140 DEC 96. DURATION 5 TO 6 MINS
B. ONE SHIMMERING OBJECT WITH TWO ROTATING LIGHTS. NO COLOUR
SIZE ETC
C. MOVING THEN STATIONARY CAR AT HAGLEY NEAR STOURBRIDGE. WEST
MIDLANDS
D. NAKED EYE
E TO H. OBJECT MOVED FROM LEFT TO RIGHT FROM OVER STOURBRIDGE
GOLF CLUB TOWARD CLENTHILLS TO THE SW OF BIRMINGHAM. OBJECT WENT
NEARLY O/H AND HT ESTIMATED (?) AT APPROX 1000FT. SPEED VERY
SLOW. EMITTED WHAT LOOKED LIKE A SHOOTING STAR ONCE
J. VIS PERFECT
K. NIL

PAGE 2 RBDOYI 249 UNCLAS
L. UKRADC
M. Section 40
Section 40
N0. Section 40
H. WORKS IN A BANK
O. NO
P. 222215Z DEC 96
BT

DISTRIBUTION   I3F
F
  CKJ   1 AFOO ACTION (CKJ   1 AFOO)

DISTRIBUTION   IBJ
F
  CYD   1 OD EWGR ACTION (CKJ   1 AFOO)

EMG   U N C L A S S I F I E D

UNCLASSIFIED

CAB034 20/0921 354C0812

FOR CAB

ROUTINE 200825Z DEC 86

FROM   AIS LONDON
TO   MODUK AIR

U N C L A S S I F I E D
SIC Z6F
FROM AIS(M) WEST DRAYTON
AERIAL PHENOMENA
A. 2007+0 DEC 86, 3 MINUTES
B. SINGLE, BRIGHT. WHITE LIGHT
C. HAMMERSMITH, WEST LONDON, OUTDOORS, IN CAR
D. NAKED EYE
E. SOUTHWARDS OVER HAMMERSMITH BRIDGE
F. VERY HIGH
G. N/K
H. ANTI-CLOCKWISE CIRCLING
J. CLEAR SKY
K. BUILT-UP AREA
L. N/A
M. Section 40

PAGE 2 RBDAID 001 UNCLAS
N. N/K
O. NIL
P. 200730 DEC
BT

DISTRIBUTION   Z6F
F
CAB   1 Sec (AS) ACTION (CXJ   - 1 AFDC
CAM   1 ACS(P)
CYD   1 DD GE/AEW
CAV   1 DI 55
CAV   2 DSTI

103

UNCLASSIFIED

CAS193 19/8341 353C5051

FOR CAS

ROUTINE 192140Z DEC 84

FROM   RAF WEST DRAYTON
TO   MODUK AIR

UNCLASSIFIED
SIC ZAF
SUBJECT: AERIAL PHENOMENA
A. 192044 DEC, STILL VISIBLE AT TIME OF REPORT 20
B. TWO OBJECTS, VERY BRIGHT, RED AND WHITE LIGHTS. SOUND OR
SMELL, LOOKED TO BE ABOUT HALF AN INCH TO THE MAX
MUST HAVE BEEN QUITE LARGE CLOSE UP, VERY HIGH
C. IN CAR INITIALLY THEN OUTDOORS
D. NAKED EYE AND BINOCULARS, ALSO TOOK STILL PHOT
E. NORTHEAST OF BIRMINGHAM
F. APPROXIMATELY 30 DEGREES FROM HORIZONTAL
G. DIFFICULT TO JUDGE BUT A FAIR DISTANCE AWAY
H. STEADY
J. SOME MOVING CLOUDS
K. TOO DARK TO SEE BUILDINGS CLEARLY
L. BIRMINGHAM AIRPORT WHO PASSED HIM TO AIS(M)

PAGE 2 RSDA10 010 UNCLAS
M. Section 40   ERDINGTON, BIRMINGHAM Section 40
TELEPHONE Section 40
N. Section 40 SOUNDED SOBER, SENSIBLE AND CONCERNED
O. EVENTUALLY WHOLE FAMILY WITNESSED THEM
P. 192055 DEC 84, FOLLOW UP CALL AT 2130 OBJECTS HAD VANISHED
BT

DISTRIBUTION   ZAF
P
CAS   1   Sec (AS) ACTION (CXJ   1 APDO)
CAM   1   ACM(F)
CYD   1   DD SE/AEM
CAV   1   DI 55
CAV   2   DSTI

104

U N C L A S S I F I E D

CXJ083 19/1807 353C3722

FOR CXJ

PRIORITY/ROUTINE 191646Z DEC 86

FROM   UKRAOC
TO   MODUK AIR
INFO   HQSTC

U N C L A S S I F I E D
SIC I3F/IBJ
MODUK AIR FOR (AFDO) HQSTC FOR WNG CDRE GE
A. 182140Z DEC 86 FOR 4 MINUTES
B. TWO LIGHTS. SUBTENDED THE SIZE OF A 2P PIECE AT ARMS LENGTH
CIRCULAR. ORANGE. VERY BRIGHT. CAST A SHADOW
C. LIKAY HILLS, COTTERIDGE, KINGS NORTON. OUTDOOR. STATIONARY
D. NAKED EYE
E. FROM AREA OF BIRMINGHAM AIRPORT. (IE EAST)
F. 45 DEGREES
G 1 MILE, THEN OVERHEAD, THEN STOPPED
H. CAME TO OVERHEAD. HOVERED FOR 16 SECS AT ABOUT 100 FEET. DEPARTED
VERTICALLY
J. HAZE
K. BIRMINGHAM AIRPORT 6 MILES

PAGE 2 RBDOYI 255 UNCLAS
L. TO BIRMINGHAM AIRPORT, WHO SET HIM ON TO Section 40   (TEL
Section 40   , KINGS STANDING, Section 40
M. Section 40   KINGS NORTON
N. TAKING DOG FOR A WALK. A COMPUTER SYSTEMS ANALYST
O. Section 40   GREAT BAR, BIRMINGHAM Section 40
P. 191600Z DEC 86
BT

DISTRIBUTION   I3F
F
  CXJ   1 AFDO ACTION (CXJ   1 AFDO)

DISTRIBUTION   IBJ
F
  CYD   1 DD EW&R ACTION (CXJ   1 AFDO)

END   U N C L A S S I F I E D

UNCLASSIFIED

CXJ064 19/1704 353C3278

FOR CXJ

PRIORITY 191530Z DEC 86

FROM   UKRAOC
TO   MODUK AIR

UNCLASSIFIED
SIC I3F/IBJ
MODUK AIR FOR AFDO.
SUBJECT UNIDENTIFIED FLYING OBJECTS
    182140Z DEC 86 THREE TO FOUR MINUTES
d. LARGE A/C TYPE WITH LONG WINGSPAN, ONE OBJECT DARK TWO SQUARE
LIGHTS
C. MOVING IN CAR ALONG BRISTOL RD IN NORTHFIELD, WORCS
D. NAKED EYE
E. APPROACHED RIGHT TO LEFT TURNED SOUTH IN SAME DIRECTION AS CAR
F. LOW SEVERAL HUNDRED FEET
G. NO REPORT
H. SLOW SEEMED TO PACE CAR (40 MPH) THEN ACCELERATED AWAY
J. CLEAR SHARP NIGHT LOTS OF STARS
K. NONE KNOWN
L. NO REPORT

PAGE 2 RBODYI 177 UNCLAS

PAG 2 RBDOYI 177 UNCLAS
M. Section 40   BLACKWELL, WORCS
N. WORKS FOR POLICE AS A CLERK TRAVELLING HOME FROM DUTY
O. NONE
P. 191455Z DEC 86
BT

DISTRIBUTION   I3F
F
  CXJ   1 AFDO ACTION (CXJ   1 AFDO)

DISTRIBUTION   IBJ
F
  CYD   1 DD EW&R ACTION (CXJ   1 AFDO)

END   UNCLASSIFIED

106

U N C L A S S I F I E D

CMD140 16/2842 35904829

FOR CAS

ROUTINE 151500Z DEC 86

FROM   RAF BINBROOK
TO   MODUK AIR

U N C L A S S I F I E D
SIC L6Z/Z6F
   (SIC Z6F ADDED BY DCC TO EFFECT DISTRIBUTION)

A 092100Z DEC
B FLASH OF GREEN LIGHT WITH RED SPOT INSIDE
C NOT REPORTED
D NAKED EYE
E NOT REPORTED, OBJECT TRAVELLED ACROSS THE SKY
F NOT KNOWN APPEARED TO BE HIGH
G NOT REPORTED
H SEEN AT FIRST FOR ABOUT 3 SECONDS TRAVELLING IN A STRAIGHT LINE
DISAPPEARED FOR 30 SCONDS TO ONE MINUTE AND THEN RE-APPEARED
DIRECTION EMABY TO LOUTH
J AFTER DARK NOT KNOWN
K NOT REPORTED
L STATION DUTY OFFICER RAF BINBROOK
M Section 40   LOUTH LINCOLN
N NOT KNOWN
O Section 40
P 092130Z DEC
BT

DISTRIBUTION   L6Z

NO SIU

DISTRIBUTION   L6Z
F
CAB   1   Sec (AS)   ACTION   (CXJ   1   AFDQ
CAM   1   ACS(P)
CYD   1   DD GE/AEW
CAV   1   DI 55
CAV   2   DSTI

REPORT OF AN UNIDENTIFIED FLYING OBJECT

A. DATE, TIME, DURATION OF SIGHTING: 5 Dec 86   2115 hrs   Duration not given.
   (Local time to be used)

B. DESCRIPTION OF OBJECT:

   Number: One
   Size: Football size
   Shape: Circular
   Colours: Red centre with blue surrounds
   Brightness: -
   Sound: -
   Smell: -

C. EXACT POSITION OF OBSERVER:

   Geographical Location: Stenborough Mill, Leics
                           ~~Indoors~~/Outdoors
                           ~~Stationary~~/Moving

D. HOW OBSERVED:

   Naked Eye: Yes

E. DIRECTION IN WHICH OBJECT WAS FIRST SEEN: East to West

F. ANGLE OF SIGHT: Looking North from house.

G. DISTANCE: Not given

H. MOVEMENT: Very fast, like shooting star.

J. METEOROLOGICAL CONDITIONS: Clear but no stars visible.

K. NEARBY OBJECTS/BUILDINGS: No details given

L. TO WHOM REPORTED: Leicester Police who reported sighting to SDO.

M. NAME AND ADDRESS OF INFORMANT: Section 40

1

108

N. ANY BACKGROUND ON THE INFORMANT THAT MAY BE VOLUNTEERED:

Ex- Royal Navy.

O. OTHER WITNESSES.   None given.

P. DATE AND TIME OF RECEIPT OF REPORT:

Received by SDO at 2158 hrs on 5 Dec 86, at RAF Cottesmore.

To be sent to:

Sec (AS) 2
Room Section 40
Ministry of Defence
Main Building
Whitehall
London

Copy to:

COT/116/Ops

Section 40

Royal Air Force Newton
Nottingham NG13 8HL

Telephone 0949 20771 Ext 212

MOD
(Attn Sec (AS)2)
Rm Section 40
Main Building

Please reply to
Officer Commanding
Your reference

Our reference
NEW/2/3/Air
Date
28 November 1986

REPORT OF UNIDENTIFIED FLYING OBJECT

1. Details of Person reporting incident:

    a. Name: Section 40

    b. Address: Section 40
        Sutton-in-Ashfield

    c. Nearest Town: Mansfield

    d. Telephone Number: Mansfield Section 40

2. Details of Incident:

    a. Date 17 Oct 86

    b. Time: Approx 2230

    c. Were a/c Involved: Yes one jet, type unknown

    d. Height N/K

3. Full details of incident: Section 40 saw what appeared to be a jet aircraft and following in its wake was a bright mushroom shaped object. The jet flew on but the object hovered over Pixton Village about 8 miles from Mansfield. The object was glowing and eventually flashed away into the distance at great speed.

Section 40

Flt Lt
for OC

MINISTRY OF DEFENCE
Sec.(AS)2
-3 DEC 1986

FILE 12/7

UNCLASSIFIED
RESTRICTED

UNCLASSIFIED

CWD016 27/0952 331C1114 CORRECTED VERSION

FOR CAB

ROUTINE 2707002 NOV 86

FROM   RAF WEST DRAYTON
TO   MODUK AIR

UNCLASSIFIED
SIC Z6F
SUBJECT: AERIAL PHENOMENA
A. 262228Z, NOT KNOWN
B. ONE, NOT KNOWN, BALL, WHITE, VERY BRIGHT, NONE   NONE
C. AS PER HOME ADDRESS, OUTDOORS, STATIONARY
D. NAKED EYE, BINOCULARS
E. NNW OF READING
F. 7000FT DOWN TO SURFACE
G. 8 TO 9 MILES
G. STEADY
J. MOVING CLOUDS
K. NONE
L. LONDON HEATHROW ATC
M. Section 40   GORING ROAD, WOODCOATE, NR
READING, BERKS, TEL Section 40

PAGE 2 RDDAID 001 UNCLAS
N. AMATEUR ASTRONOMER
O. NONE
P. 2623302 NOV 86
BT

DISTRIBUTION Z6F
P.
CAB   1 Sec (AB) ACTION (CXJR   1 AFDO)
CAM   1 ACS(F)
CYB   1 DD GE/AEW
CAV   1 DZ 55
CAV   2 D8TI

FROM: .....RAF WITTERING........................ Reference:

TO: HQ P&SS (UK) Flying Complaints Flight

1. Details of complainant   UFO REPORT

    a. Name   [Section 40]

    b. Address   [Section 40]

    c. Nearest large town   PETERBOROUGH

    d. Telephone No   [Section 40]

2. Details of Incident

    a. Date   24 NOV 86

    b. Time (Local or GMT)   2320Z + 2340Z

    c. No of Ac involved   N/A

    d. Height   'REASONABLY LOW'

    e. Direction   HEADING NORTH-EAST

3. Details of aircraft (Tick as appropriate)

Jet ac	Propellor ac	Military ac	Civil ac	Fighter
Bomber	Helicopter	Light ac	Other Markings	Camouflaged
Silver	Red and White	Other colours/ Special markings (specify)		

4. Location of Complaint

    a. Address as 1b above

or

    b.

5. Claims (do not prompt complainant. Is there any injury to persons and/or lievestock or damage to property which will result in a claim? If so is complainant owner of the property? (Details)

1

6. **Full details of complaint** said that he saw two bright white lights in the sky as he was driving along the A605 by the Peterborough Show Ground on Monday night. As he was watching he noticed a third light appear and then all three lights, their intensity varying, moved over the Show Ground heading towards Peterborough. The lights seemed to move as one body but could not discern any shape or structure between them. At 2340 he saw the lights again between Wassington and Fotheringay and watched them for some minutes before they departed to the north-west. was certain that the lights were not from a conventional aircraft, and could only describe it as similar in size to an airship.

7. **Date and time report received**   250930Z Nov 86

Signed:

Name:

Date: 27 Nov 86

Rank: Sgt   Tel No:

2

2 1 NOV 1986

Section 40

ANNEX A TO
SOP 502

+1 E3⊕

(1 of 2 PAGES)

FILE

REPORT OF AN UNIDENTIFIED FLYING OBJECT

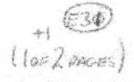

A.	Date, Time & Duration of Sighting	18 Nov 86, 0300Z for about 5 minutes
B.	Description of Object (No of objects, size, snape, colour, brightness)	1 object, Ball of bright light
C.	Exact Position of Observer Location, indoor/outdoor, stationary/moving	Observer in a car which was moving
D.	How Observed (naked eye, binoculars, other optical device, still or movie)	Naked eye.
E.	Direction in which object first seen (A landmark may be more useful than a badly estimated bearing)	In the south, shot off at amazing speed toward N. Reappeared in S aft. 2 mins. moved, shot off at amazing speed to N.
F.	Angle of Sight (Estimated heights are unreliable)	None give.
G.	Distance (By reference to a known landmark)	None given.
H.	Movements (Changes in E, F & G may be of more use than estimates of course and speed)	See para E
J.	Met Conditions during Observations (Moving clouds, haze, mist etc)	Clear night.
K.	Nearby Objects (Telephone lines, high voltage lines, reservoir, lake or dam, swamp or marsh, river, high buildings, tall chimneys, steeples, spires, TV or radio masts, airfields, generating plant, factories, pits or other sites with floodlights or night lighting)	On main road between Inverness and Stoak End

L.	To whom reported (Police, military, press etc)	Sgt [Section 40] Operations Lossiemouth.
M.	Name & Address of Informant	[Section 40] Ballachulish, [Section 40]
N.	Background of Informant that may be volunteered	None given.
O.	Other Witnesses	None given
P.	Date, Time of Receipt	20 Nov 1350Z - Delay because she didn't think that she would be believed
Q.	Any Unusual Meteorological Conditions	No
R.	Remarks	Witness sound calm and sensible.

[Section 40]

Squadron Leader
Duty Operations Officer
AF Ops

Date. 20 Nov 86 .....

Copies to:
Sec(AS)2
AEW/GE
DI 55
File AF Ops/2/5/1

U N C L A S S I F I E D

CH84R2 18/0086 321C4326

FOR CAS

ROUTINE 172004Z NOV 86

FROM   RAF WEST DRAYTON
TO   MODUK AIR

U N C L A S S I F I E D
SIC ZAF
SUBJECT/AERIAL PHENOMENA:
A. 171840Z NOV 86, 2 MINS
B. ONE, BIG, CRUCIFIX, WHITE, VERY BRIGHT, NIL, NIL
C. CHORLEY OLD ROAD, HORWICH, OUTDOORS, STATIONARY
D. NAKED EYE
E. NOT KNOWN
F. NOT KNOWN
G. NOT KNOWN
H. CHANGING
J. MOVING CCW90
K. OPPOSITE WINTER HILL TV MAST
L. MANCHESTER POLICE AND MANCHESTER ATC
M. Section 40 ████████████████████████, HORWICH, NR BOLTON, LANCS
N. NONE

PAGE 2 RBDA22 013 UNCLAS
O. NONE
P. 172004Z NOV 86
BT

DISTRIBUTION ZAF

CAS   1 S&G (AS) ACTION (CX)   1 AFDO 1
DAS   1 AC86 P
CVD   1 DB DS/AD4
CAV   1 DT S5
CAV   2 DGTI

Copy to
Sec (AS)
AEW/GE
DI 55

To be forwarded as UFO Report

U N C L A S S I F I E D

Section 40

Section 40

CXJ032 16/2243 32000880

FOR CXJ

PRIORITY/ROUTINE 162137Z NOV 86

FROM   UKRADC
TO   MODUK AIR
INFO   HQSTC

U N C L A S S I F I E D
SIC I3F/IBJ
MODUK AIR FOR AFDO
HQSTC FOR WNG CDRE GE
A. 161930Z NOV 86 FOR 45 MINUTES
B. TWO LARGE STAR SIZE. TWO. PULSING. WHITE. LIKE VERY BRIGHT
STAR
C. Section 40 WEDNESFIELD. INDOORS. STATIONARY. THEN
OUTDOORS. ONE ABOVE OTHER
D. NAKED EYE
E. NORTH EAST
F. 45 DEGREES - 45 DEGREES
G. NIL
H. UPPER MOVED RIGHT. MOVED DUE EAST. LOWER MOVED LEFT MOVED DUE
NORTH

PAGE 2 RBDDYI 024 UNCLAS
J. CLEAR
K. NOTHING
L. PC. Section 40 WEDNESFIELD POLICE STATION, ALFRED SQUARE
ROAD
M. Section 40 WEDNESFIELD. AGED 32
PLUS 6 YOUNGSTERS SAW 4 LIGHTS IN A CROSS FORMATION
N. WITNESS SEEMED SENSIBLE AND SOBER
O. ALSO SOBER
P. 162020Z NOV 86
BT

DISTRIBUTION   I3F
F
CXJ   1 AFOS ACTION (CXJ   1 AFDC)

DISTRIBUTION   IBJ
F
CYO   1 DO EWAR ACTION (CXJ   (AFDO)

END   U N C L A S S I F I E D

with the compliments of

MINISTRY OF DEFENCE

AIR FORCE OPS RM

MOD FORM 195

118

Date, Time and **12TH NOVEMBER, 1986   0105Z**
Duration of Sighting ① 5 SECONDS   ② 7 SECONDS

Description of Object ① Group of 3 small 'triangular' lights. Dull orange
in colour
② Group of 5 small dull orange lights, triangular shaped.

Exact Position of outside kitchen door of home in SPRINGBURN, Glasgow
Observer

How Observed naked eye.

Direction in Which ① to North, near "The Plough"
Object was First Seen ② Overhead.

Angular Elevation of ① approx 65°
Object ② approx 90°

Distance Of Object unknown ("very high")
from Observer

Movements of Object all headed north and rapidly changed formation,
moving very quickly.

Meteorological Conditions Clear, starlit, small amount of distant
During Observations cloud.

Nearby Objects Trees, 40 feet high, 150 feet distant.

To Whom Reported ATC Supervisor, ▓Section 40▓ CAA/NATS,
Glasgow Airport.

Name and Address of ▓Section 40▓ SPRINGBURN, GLASGOW.
Informant
Tel: ▓Section 40▓

Any background Informaton Had drunk only cocoa. Both "stunned" by what
that may be Volunteered they had seen. Had to tell someone. Police
referred them to ATC. No sound. Not like aircraft.

Other witnesses Husband: MR A. CONVERY, said "not Aurora Borealis,
meteors military aircraft or like civil aircraft they have seen."

Date and Title of Receipt ▓ ▓ N1V. 1986.
of Report ▓Section 40▓ ATC Supervisor.

To: The Ministry of Defence (AFOR)   Phone: AIS Military
Royal Air Force ▓ LATCC 7 NOV 1986
Main Building
Whitehall   AIR FORCE OPERATIONS
LONDON SW 1
PTO

The observers seemed genuine to me. They seem to have seen something which they consider very unusual.

Scottish military had no record of any military aircraft activity.

ATC Supervisor.

REPORT OF AN UNIDENTIFIED FLYING OBJECT

A.	Date, Time & Duration of Sighting	061930A Nov 86 20 secs
B.	Description of Object (No of objects, size, shape, colour, brightness)	Delta shape object. One.
C.	Exact Position of Observer Location, indoor/outdoor, stationary/moving	Northampton In the back garden hanging out washing.
D.	How Observed (naked eye, binoculars, other optical device, still or movie	Eye.
E.	Direction in which object first seen (A landmark may be more useful than a badly estimated bearing)	Norhtwest, high in the sky.
F.	Angle of Sight (Estimated heights are unreliable)	Over the house.
G.	Distance (By reference to a known landmark	Not Known
H.	Movements (Changes in E, F & G may be of more use than estimates of course and speed)	None.
J.	Met Conditions during Observations (Moving clouds, haze, mist etc)	Clear sky, but getting dark.
K.	Nearby Objects (Telephone lines, high voltage lines, reservoir, lake or dam, swamp or marsh, river, high buildings, tall chimneys, steeples, spires, TV or radio masts, airfields, generating plant, factories, pits or other sites with floodlights or night lighting)	None.

121

L.	To whom reported (Police, military, press etc)	Wooton Park Police & MOD Air Force Operations
M.	Name & Address of Informant	Section 40 Parkland, Northampton. Tel: Section 40
N.	Background of Informant that may be volunteered	None given.
O.	Other Witnesses	None.
P.	Date, Time of Receipt	071935A Nov 86.
Q.	Any Unusual Meteorological Conditions	Nil
R.	Remarks	None

Section 40

Sqn Ldr
Duty Ops Officer
AF Ops

7 Nov 86
Date.............

Distribution:

Sec(AS)2
AEW/GE
DI 55
File AF Ops/2/5/1

U N C L A S S I F I E D

CA9079 06/9955 31OC1183

FOR CAB

ROUTINE 060835Z NOV 86

FROM   RAF WEST DRAYTON
TO   MODUK AIR

U N C L A S S I F I E D
SIC Z6F
SUBJECT: AERIAL PHENOMENA
A. 060600(L) NOV 86
B. A GROUP OF NINE FLASHING WHITE AND RED LIGHTS
C. HAZLEMERE, SURREY, INDOORS, STATIONARY
D. NAKED EYE
E. SOUTH
F. NOT KNOWN
G. NOT KNOWN
H. STEADY
J. SKY CLEAR
K. URBAN AREA
L. POLICE, GODALMING, SURREY
M. Section 40
N. NIL

PAGE 2 RBDAID 001 UNCLAS
O. WIFE AND HIS TWO CHILDREN
P. 060720(L) NOV 86
BT

DISTRIBUTION   Z6F
P
CAB 1 Sec (AS) ACTION (CXJ   1 AFDG)
CAM 1 ACS(P)
CYD 1 DD GE/AEW
SAV 1 DI 55
CAV 2 DSTI

123

Section 40

F.a 1113.
(E26/2)

A   Date, time and duration of sighting (Local times to be quoted)

6 Nov 86   0600   for   4 - 5   mins

B   Description of object (Number of objects, size, shape, colours, brightness, sound, smell, etc).

Two sets of green, red and white steady lights with 2 flashing red lights to side of the L a straight line

C   Exact position observer (Geographical location. Indoors or outdoors. Stationary or moving).

WORTHING STATION.

D   How observed (Naked eye, binoculars, other optical device, still or movie camera).

Naked Eye.

E   Direction in which object was first seen (A landmark may be more useful than a badly estimated bearing).

SE to overhead — NW.

F   Angle of sight (Estimated heights are unreliable).

60 - 70° from horizontal.

G   Distance (By reference to a known landmark wherever possible).

H   Movements (Changes in E, F and G may be of more use than estimates of course and speed).

Kept station throughout sighting

J   Meteorological conditions during observations (Moving clouds, haze, mist etc).

Still dark. Good vis

K   Nearby objects (Telephone lines; high voltage lines; reservoir, lake or dam; swamp or marsh; river; high buildings, tall chimneys, steeples, spires, TV or radio masts; airfields; generating plant; factories, pits or other sites with flood-lights or other night lighting).

L   To whom reported (Police, military organisations, the press etc).

M   Name and address of informant   Section 40

N   Any background on the informant that may be volunteered

O   Other witnesses

P   Date and time of receipt of report   11071625

Q   Is a reply requested?   WOULD BE INTERESTED IF ANYTHING FOUND.

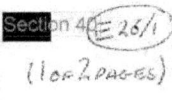
ANNEX A TO
SOP 502

REPORT OF AN UNIDENTIFIED FLYING OBJECT

A.	Date, Time & Duration of Sighting	272340Z Oct 86 15 secs
B.	Description of Object (No of objects, size, shape, colour, brightness)	3 x white/mauve lights in line, west to east. then triangle and vanished.
C.	Exact Position of Observer Location, indoor/outdoor, stationary/moving	In car driving down Peacock Gardens, Selsdon.
D.	How Observed (naked eye, binoculars, other optical device, still or movie	Eye.
E.	Direction in which object first seen (A landmark may be more useful than a badly estimated bearing)	South, over NT bird sanctuary.
F.	Angle of Sight (Estimated heights are unreliable)	30 degrees up.
G.	Distance (By reference to a known landmark	Distant.
H.	Movements (Changes in E, F & G may be of more use than estimates of course and speed)	As B above.
J.	Met Conditions during Observations (Moving clouds, haze, mist etc)	Clear, visibility, but cloudy. Lights below cloud.
K.	Nearby Objects (Telephone lines, high voltage lines, reservoir, lake or dam, swamp or marsh, river, high buildings, tall chimneys, steeples, spires, TV or radio masts, airfields, generating plant, factories, pits or other sites with floodlights or night lighting)	Above NT bird sanctuary.

L.	To whom reported (Police, military, press etc)	AF Ops.

M.   Name & Address of Informant   Section 40

N.   Background of Informant that may be volunteered   Section 40 is a police officer

O.   Other Witnesses   None

P.   Date, Time of Receipt   272355Z Oct 86

Q.   Any Unusual Meteorological Conditions   Nil

R.   Remarks   None

Section 40

Squadron Leader
Duty Operations Officer
AF Ops

28 Oct 86
Date............

Distribution:

Sec(AS)2
AEW/GE
DI 55
File AF Ops/2/5/1

MINISTRY OF DEFENCE Section 40
Sec.(AS)2
22 OCT 1986
FILE

ANNEX A TO
SOP 502

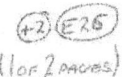
(lof 2 pages)

REPORT OF AN UNIDENTIFIED FLYING OBJECT

A.	Date, Time & Duration of Sighting	21 Oct 86 2146A 5-10 Mins.
B.	Description of Object (No of objects, size, shape, colour, brightness)	Very bright orange light 1 object Round
C.	Exact Position of Observer Location, Indoor/outdoor, stationary/moving	Bottom of garden Indoors through window. Stationary
D.	How Observed (naked eye, binoculars, other optical device, still or movie)	Naked Eye
E.	Direction in which object first seen (A landmark may be more useful than a badly estimated bearing)	West side of Aberdeen
F.	Angle of Sight (Estimated heights are unreliable)	Up in the sky? No other more precise details
G.	Distance (By reference to a known landmark)	Near Tree Tops Hotel, Aberdeen. No distance available
H.	Movements (Changes in E, F & G may be of more use than estimates of course and speed)	Slowly towards the sea eastwards.
J.	Met Conditions during Observations (Moving clouds, haze, mist etc)	Clear Sky
K.	Nearby Objects (Telephone lines, high voltage lines, reservoir, lake or dam, swamp or marsh, river, high buildings, tall chimneys, steeples, spires, TV or radio masts, airfields, generating plant, factories, pits or other sites with floodlights or night lighting)	About 6 miles from Dyce airport

L.	To whom reported (Police, military, press etc)	Constable Section 40 Aberdeen Police
M.	Name & Address of Informant	Section 40
N.	Background of Informant that may be volunteered	None given
O.	Other Witnesses	Husband of Section 40
P.	Date, Time of Receipt	Received in MOD AF Ops at 2270A 21 Oct 86.
Q.	Any Unusual Meteorological Conditions	None
R.	Remarks	None given

Section 40

. . .

Squadron Leader
Duty Operations Officer
AF Ops

Date. 21 Oct 86 ....

Copies to:
Sec(AS)2
AEW/GE
DI 55
File AF Ops/2/5/1

U N C L A S S I F I E D

copy to: SAC (AS)2
ARW/GR
D155
FILE

CXJ099 21/1652 2940C3438

FOR CXJ

ROUTINE 211029Z OCT 86

FROM   UKRAOC
TO   MODUK AIR

U N C L A S S I F I E D
SIC I3F
MOD FOR AFOR SUSPECT UFO REPORT
A. 191045Z OCT 86 FOR APPROX 5-6 MINUTES
B ONE OBJECT, CIGAR SHAPED, VERY BRIGHTLY ILLUMINATED
C INSIDE AT FIRST, THEN OUTSIDE, OBSERVER STATIONARY
D. NAKED EYE AND BINOCULARS
E. TRAVELLING IN AN EASTERLY DIRECTION
F. APPROX 45 (FORTY FIVE) DEGREES
G. NOT KNOWN (OVER SEA)
H. VERY FAST EAST
I. SKY CLEAR
J. VIEWED OVER SEA
K. NO OTHER AGENCIES CONTACTED
L. Section 40   SKEGNESS. TELEPHONE NUMBER,
SKEGNESS Section 40

PAGE 2 RBODYI 093 UNCLAS
0. 191105Z OCT 86. SAC Section 40 OPERATIONS ROOM, RAF WADDINGTON
BT

DISTRIBUTION   I3F
F
CXJ   1 AFDO ACTION (CXJ   1 AFDO)

END   U N C L A S S I F I E D

Section 40

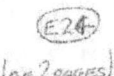

ANNEX A TO
SOP 502

(1 of 2 pages)

REPORT OF AN UNIDENTIFIED FLYING OBJECT

A.	Date, Time & Duration of Sighting	20 Oct 86 1955A 5 mins
B.	Description of Object (No of objects, size, shape, colour, brightness)	White/Gray light 1 Object Roundish Very bright
C.	Exact Position of Observer Location, indoor/outdoor, stationary/moving	Outdoor walking
D.	How Observed (naked eye, binoculars, other optical device, still or movie)	Naked Eye
E.	Direction in which object first seen (A landmark may be more useful than a badly estimated bearing)	Nelson St. East side of Aberdeen, near Mounthooly Rouhd-about
F.	Angle of Sight (Estimated heights are unreliable)	High in the sky.
G.	Distance (By reference to a known landmark)	None given
H.	Movements (Changes in E, F & G may be of more use than estimates of course and speed)	None given
J.	Met Conditions during Observations (Moving clouds, haze, mist etc)	Clear sky
K.	Nearby Objects (Telephone lines, high voltage lines, reservoir, lake or dam, swamp or marsh, river, high buildings, tall chimneys, steeples, spires, TV or radio masts, airfields, generating plant, factories, pits or other sites with floodlights or night lighting)	4 miles from Dyce airport

L.	To whom reported (Police, military, press etc)	W/Constable Section 40 Aberdeen Police
M.	Name & Address of Informant	Section 40
N.	Background of Informant that may be volunteered	None given
O.	Other Witnesses	None
P.	Date, Time of Receipt	Reported to AF Ops at 212230A Oct 86
Q.	Any Unusual Meteorological Conditions	None
R.	Remarks	None given

Section 40

Squadron Leader
Duty Operations Officer
AF Ops

Date... 21 Oct 86 ......

Copies to:
Sec(AS)2
AEW/GE
DI 55
File AF Ops/2/5/1

131

MINISTRY OF DEFENCE
Sec.(AS)2
27 OCT 1986
FILE

. Date, Time Duration of Sighting.

20/10/86 — 0007 —   15 MINS

. Description of Object   ALTERNATING GREEN & WHITE LIGHT.

. Exact Position of Observer.   GLASGOW. (POLLOCK) SW

. How Observed.   NAKED EYE

. Direction in which Object was first seen.   EAST OF OBSERVER

. Angular Elevation of Object   ·   50°. (ESTIMATED)

F. Distance of Object from Observer.   NOT KNOWN

I. Movements of Object.   STRAIGHT LINE THEN STATIONARY.
SOUTH EAST TO NORTH WEST.

J. Meteorological Conditions During Observations.
Moving Clouds, Haze, mist etc.   CLEAR SKY THEN LIGHT CLOUD.

K. Nearby Objects.   NONE

L. To Whom Reported.   SCATCC ATC WATCH MANAGER

M. Name & Address of Informant.   Section 40   POLLOCK
GLASCOW

N. Any Background Information on the Informant that   BASIC INTEREST. IN
may be Volunteered.   ASTRONOMY

O. Other Witnesses.   Section 40   (OBSERVERS MOTHER

MINISTRY OF DEFENCE
24 OCT 1986
AIR FORCE OPERATIONS

P. Date & Time of Receipt of Report.
20/10/86 — 0007.

MINISTRY OF DEFENCE
Sec.(AS)2
20 OCT 1986
FILE

U N C L A S S I F I E D

CAB033 19/2265 292C099B

(E24)

FOR CAB

ROUTINE 192010Z OCT 86

(E23/1)

FROM   RAF WEST DRAYTON
TO   MODUK AIR

U N C L A S S I F I E D
SIC Z6F
SUBJECT AERIAL PHENOMENA
A. 191945L OCT 86, 1 MINUTE
B. LARGE, BRIGHT BLUE STAR-SHAPE
C. SCARCROFT, NEAR LEEDS, OUTDOORS, STATIONARY
D. NAKED EYE
E. NIL
F. NIL
G. NIL
H. FROM HORIZON TO VERY HIGH, SPEEDED-UP WITH HEIGHT
J. CLOUD
K. NIL
L. MANCHESTER ATC SUPERVISOR
M. Section 40   SCARCROFT, NEAR LEEDS, WEST YORKSHIRE
N. NIL

PAGE 2 RDDAID 001 UNCLAS
O. NIL
P. 191945Z OCT 86
BT

DISTRIBUTION Z6F
F
CAB   1 Sec (AS) ACTION (CXJ   1 AFDO)
CAM   1 ACB(P)
CYD   1 DD GE/AEW
CAV   1 DI 55
CAV   2 DSTI

133

REPORT OF AN UNIDENTIFIED FLYING OBJECT

(1 of 2 pages)

A. Date, Time and Duration of Sightings. (Local Times to be Quoted)

19ᵗʰ OCTOBER 1986   1145L   5-6 MINUTES.

B. Description of Object. (Number of objects, size, shape, colours, brightness, sound, smell etc).

CIGAR SHAPED VERY BRIGHTLY ILLUMINATED

C. Exact Position Observer. (Geographical location. Indoors or outdoors. Stationary or moving).

INSIDE AT FIRST, THEN OUTSIDE, OBSERVER STATIONARY !

D. How Observed. (Naked eye, binoculars, other optical device, still or movie camera).

NAKED EYE AND BINOCULARS.

E. Direction in which Object was First Seen. (A landmark may be more useful than a badly estimated bearing).

TRAVELLING IN AN EASTERLY DIRECTION

F. Angle of Sight. (Estimated heights are unreliable).

APPROX 45°

G. Distance. (By reference to a known landmark whereever possible).

NOT KNOWN (OVER SEA).

H. Movements. (Changes in E, F and G may be of more use than estimates of course and speed).

FLEW FAST EAST

I. Meteorological Conditions during Observations. (Moving clouds, haze, mist etc).

SKY CLEAR.

134

J. Nearby Objects. (Telephone lines; high voltage lines; reservoir, lake swamp or marsh; river; high buildings, tall chimneys, steeples, spires, TV or radio masts; airfields; generating plant; factories, pits or other sites with flood-lights or other night lighting).

VISUAL OVER SEA.

K. To Whom Reported. (Police, military organisation, the press etc).

NO OTHER AGENCIES CONTACTED

L. Name and Address of Informant.

SAG-X33   RL' - SAIG-X6-55

M. Any Background on the Informant that may be Volunteered.

N, Other Witnesses.

O. Date and Time of Receipt of Report

19th OCTOBER 1986

1205 h .

OPERATIONS ROOM

RAF WADDINGTON

6PN

(E22/1)

→ Sec (AS)2a please
(RM Section 40) Section

UNCLASSIFIED

CAB845 17/0717 290C0766

FOR CAB

ROUTINE 162200Z OCT 86

FROM   RAF WEST DRAYTON
TO   MODUK AIR

Section 40

Section 40   Pre- deal.

UNCLASSIFIED
SIC ZGF/Z99
(Z99 - DCC USE ONLY, NOT TO BE USED IN REPLY)
SUBJECT: AERIAL PHENOMENA
A. 162240(L) OCT 86 40 MINUTES
B. 2 LARGE VERY BRIGHT ROUND OBJECTS RED IN COLOUR
C. ST IVES, CAMBRIDGESHIRE. OUTDOORS IN GARDEN, STATIONARY.
D. NAKED EYE
E. NIL
F. NIL
G. VERY HIGH
H. SPREAD
J. CLEAR SKY
K. NIL
L. RAF WYTON, Section 40
N. NIL
O. Section 40   HUSBAND, MOTHER AND HER FRIEND Section 40
P. 162143Z OCT 86
BT

DISTRIBUTION   ZGF
F
WO 8DI

DISTRIBUTION   Z99
Z
CAB 1 89(AIR) ACTION (CXJ 1 JDC/AFDD)

cf AEW/GE3
DI 55

UNIDENTIFIED FLYING OBJECT PROFORMA

From: HQ PESS(UK) FCF   Reference: FILE

1. Details of Complaint.

   a. Name: ███Section 40███

   b. Address: ███Section 40███
       NR SHERBOURNE   DORSET

2. Sighting:

   a. Date/Time of Sighting and Duration: 161510Z OCT 86

   b. Position of Observer: IN REAR GARDEN OF ABOVE ADDRESS

   c. How Observed: EYESIGHT ONLY

   d. Direction Object first Seen: MOVING NORTH

   e. Angle of Elevation: ALMOST DIRECTLY ABOVE

   f. Distance of Object from Observer: HIGH ALTITUDE COULD NOT ESTIMATE

   g. Movement of Object: MOVED TO REAR OF AIRLINER HOVERED CLOSE THEN MOVED AWAY AT HIGH SPEED

   h. Met Conditions: CLEAR BLUE SKY

   j. Nearby Objects: AIRLINER

   k. To Whom Reported: FIRSTLY TO RM BARRACKS LYMPSTONE

   l. Other Witnesses: MOTHER

   m. Comments: NONE

3. Date and Time Received: 1655L 16 OCT 86

                         Signed ███Section 40███

                         Name:

Date: 16 OCT 86   Rank CPL   Tel No: ██Section 40██

137

U N C L A S S I F I E D

CAB051 16/0759 28OCT1986

FOR CAB

ROUTINE/ROUTINE 152224Z OCT 86

FROM   COMMCEN LINDHOLME
TO   MODUK AIR
INFO   HQRAFSC

U N C L A S S I F I E D
SIC Z6F
RECVD OVER TELEX FROM GWENT CONSTABULARY Section 40
TLX REF 0385
ATTN MODUK AIR FOR S4K (AIR)
     HQRAFSC FOR CP SY O
UNIDENTIFIEDFLYING OBJECTS
A.15.10.86 20.00HRS FOR 10-15 MINS.
B.ONE ROUND OBJECT, SMALL IN SIZE WITH RED, WHITE AND GREEN
  FLASHING LIGHTS.
C.ON GROUND LEVEL.
D.THROUGH BINOCULARS.
E.STATIONARY OVER TWMBARLEM.
F.TO RIGHT OF TWMBARLEM ABOUT 3 MILES UP INTO SKY.
G.2 MILES AWAY.

PAGE 2 RSDPCU 037 UNCLAS
H.STATIONARY.
J.FINE CLEAR NIGHT.
K.NIL.
L.CWMBRAN POLICE STATION.
M.Section 40
N.LOCAL FARMER
BT

DISTRIBUTION   Z6F
F
CAB   1 Sec (AS) ACTION (CXJ   1 AFDD)
CAM   1 ACS(P)
CYD   1 DD GE/AEW
CAV   1 DI 55
CAV   2 DSTI

REPORT OF AN UNIDENTIFIED FLYING OBJECT

A.	Date, Time & Duration of Sighting	12 Oct 86. 1330 hrs. 5 minutes.
B.	Description of Object (No of objects, size, shape, colour, brightness)	1 object. Bright yellow ball of light.
C.	Exact Position of Observer Location, indoor/outdoor, stationary/moving	Outdoors in stationary vehicle.
D.	How Observed (naked eye, binoculars, other optical device, still or movie	Naked eye.
E.	Direction in which object first seen (A landmark may be more useful than a badly estimated bearing)	West of Milton Keynes.
F.	Angle of Sight (Estimated heights are unreliable)	On horizon.
G.	Distance (By reference to a known landmark	Not known.
H.	Movements (Changes in E, F & G may be of more use than estimates of course and speed)	Stationary but object disappeared and reappeared.
J.	Met Conditions during Observations (Moving clouds, haze, mist etc)	Dull but clear.
K.	Nearby Objects (Telephone lines, high voltage lines, reservoir, lake or dam, swamp or marsh, river, high buildings, tall chimneys, steeples, spires, TV or radio masts, airfields, generating plant, factories, pits or other sites with floodlights or night lighting)	Open country but object seen through trees.

L.	To whom reported (Police, military, press etc)	Thames Valley Police Central Room Section 40 Tel Section 40
M.	Name & Address of Informant	Section 40 Road, Milton Keynes, Bucks.
N.	Background of Informant that may be volunteered	Not given.
O.	Other Witnesses	Mother (same address)
P.	Date, Time of Receipt	121630 Oct 86
Q.	Any Unusual Meteorological Conditions	None
R.	Remarks	None

Section 40

12 Oct 86

Date. . . . .

Squadron Leader
Duty Operations Officer
AF Ops

Distribution:

Sec(AS)2
AEW/GE
DI 55
File AF Ops/2/5/1

140

U N C L A S S I F I E D

CWD673.11/1329 2840i163

FOR CAS

ROUTINE 111200Z OCT 86

FROM   RAF WEST DRAYTON
TO   MODUK AIR

U N C L A S S I F I E D
SIC Z6F
SUBJECT: AERIAL PHENOMENA
A. 111105Z MOMENTARILY
B. 10 BRIGHT GLASS BALLS
C. IN FLIGHT
D. NAKED EYE, FROM FLIGHT DEC
E. ABOVE AIRCRAFT
F. 10,000FT ABOVE
G. NIL
H. IN A SOUTH EASTERLY DIRECTION
J. CAVOK
K. NIL
L. CONTROLLER OF BRISTOL SECTOR LATCC
M. PILOT OF AER LINGUS Section 40   PARIS TO DUBLIN FLT NO SEE M
N. CABIN CREW

PAGE 2 RBDAID 001 UNCLAS
P. PILOT WILL FILE REPORT ON LANDING/AT DUBLIN
BT

DISTRIBUTION   Z6F
F.
CAB   1 Sec (AS) ACTION (CXJ   1 AFDO)
CAM   1 ACS(P)
CYR   1 DD GE/AEW
CAV   1 DI 55
CAV   2 DSTI

U N C L A S S I F I E D

CWD028 11/0116 283C5083

FOR CAB

ROUTINE 161436Z OCT 86

FROM   RAF BINBROOK
TO   MODUK AIR

U N C L A S S I F I E D
SIC LGZ/Z6F
(SIC Z6F INSERTED BY DCC)
A 041910L OCT 86/ONE SIGHTING TWO MINUTES
B ONE OBJECT, HALF MOON SHAPE WITH CURVED OUTSIDE UPPERMOST CONE ON
TOP. RED LIGHT ON THE SIDE ONE EIGHTH OF THE LENGTH, WHITE GLOW FROM
THE OBJECT. BIGGER IN SIZE THAN A LARGE PASSENGER AIRCRAFT
C STATIONARY IN Section 40   BRANSHOLME, HULL
D BY THE NAKED EYE
E OVER THE EAST PARK AREA
F 15 DEGREES
G ONE AND ONE HALF MILES
H FM EAST TO WEST RETURNED EAST AND THEN DISAPPEARED AFTER HOVERING
FOR A WHILE
J DUSK WITH NO CLOUD
K POLICE STATION
L BRANSHOLME POLICE

PAGE 2 RBDDXA 824 UNCLAS
M Section 40   ON BEHALF OF HIS TEN
YEAR OLD SON Section 40
N NONE
O TWENTY OTHER PEOPLE INCLUDING TWO ADULTS
P 041925L OCT 86
BT

DISTRIBUTION   LGZ
F
NO SDL

DISTRIBUTION   Z6F
F
CAB   1 Se   ION (CXJ   1 AFDO)
CAM   1 ACS(P)
CYD   1 DD GE/AEW
CAV   1 DI 55
CAV   2 DSTI

142

U N C L A S S I F I E D

CAB188 03/2159 276C4788

FOR CAB

ROUTINE 031950Z OCT 86

FROM   RAF WEST DRAYTON
TO   MODUK AIR

U N C L A S S I F I E D
SIC Z6F
SUBJECT AERIAL PHENOMENA
A. 031950A OCT 86, 2 MINS
B. ONE, VERY BIG STAR SHAPE, BRIGHT WHITE, NO SOUND OR SMELL
C. OUTDOORS, HOME, STATIONARY
D. NAKED EYE
E. TOWARDS PUDSEY
F. HIGH BEFORE DESCENDING AND DISAPPEARING
G. RELATIVELY LOCAL IN PUDSEY DIRECTION
H. HOVERED FOR APPROX 90 SECS THEN DESCENDED OVER WEADON
J. CLEAR NIGHT
K. OPEN ASPECT
L. ATC LEEDS/BRADFORD AIRPORT
M.
BRA███████████████████████████████████████, DRIGHLINGTON,
FORD, ████████

PAGE 2 RBDAID 011 UNCLAS
N. NONE
O. HUSBAND
P. 032040A OCT 86
BT

DISTRIBUTION   Z6F
F
CAB   1   Sec (AS) ACTION (CXJ   1   AFDO)
CAM   1   ACS(P)
CYD   1   DD GE/AEW
CAV   1   DI 55
CAV   2   DSTI

REPORT OF UNIDENTIFIED FLYING OBJECTS   MATS 6 - 18

MINISTRY OF DEFENCE
Sec.(AS)2
23 OCT 1986
FILE

A. DATE, TIME, AND DURATION OF SIGHTING
   LOCAL TIMES TO BE QUOTED.

   5/10/86, 1950, 2 minutes

B. DESCRIPTION OF OBJECT
   NUMBER OF OBJECTS, SIZE, SHAPE, COLOURS, BRIGHTNESS, SOUND,
   SMELL ETC.

   1 object, white bright light like a very big star
   no sound or smell

C. EXACT POSITION OF OBSERVER
   GEOGRAPHICAL LOCATION, INDOORS OR OUTDOORS, STATIONARY
   OR MOVING.

   outdoors at home

D. HOW OBSERVED
   NAKED EYE, BINOCULARS, OTHER OPTICAL DEVICE, STILL OR
   MOVIE CAMERA.

   naked eye

E. DIRECTION IN WHICH OBJECT WAS FIRST SEEN
   A LANDMARK MAY BE MORE USEFUL THAN A BADLY ESTIMATED BEARING.

   Towards Pudsey

F. ANGULAR ELEVATION OF OBJECT
   ESTIMATED HEIGHTS ARE UNRELIABLE.

   high before descending and disappearing

G. DISTANCE OF OBJECT FROM OBSERVER
   BY REFERENCE TO KNOWN LANDMARK WHEREVER POSSIBLE.

   relatively local in the Pudsey direction

H. MOVEMENTS OF OBJECT
   CHANGES IN E, F AND G MAY BE OF MORE USE THAN ESTIMATES
   OF COURSE AND SPEED.

   hovered for about 90 seconds before descending towards Yeadon

U N C L A S S I F I E D

QAB047 02/1250 27501525

ROR CAB

ROUTINE 020925Z OCT 86

FROM   RAF VALLEY
TO: MODUK AIR
       HQRAFSC

U N C L A S S I F I E D
SIC Z4F
SUBJECT UNIDENTIFIED FLYING OBJECT
A. 29 SEP 86 2030(A) FOR QUOTE LONGTIME UNQUOTE
B. ONE VERY BRIGHT OBJECT LIKE COMET
C. OUTSIDE, CAERNARFON
D. NAKED EYE
E. TO NORTHEAST, TRAVELLING SOUTHWEST
F. 45 DEG ABOVE HORIZON
G. NO ESTIMATE
H. AS IN PARA E
J. CLEAR NIGHT
K. CAERNARFON AIRFIELD
L. RAF VALLEY ONLY
M. Section 40   RHOS TRYFAN, CAERNARFON

PAGE 2 R90BV8 006 UNCLAS
N. NO
O. NO
P. 292115A SEP
BT

DISTRIBUTION   Z4F
F
CAB   1 Sec (AS) ACTION (DXJ   1 AFDC)
CAB   1 ACS(P)
CYO   1 DD GE/AEW
CAV   1 DI 55
CAV   2 DSTI

Section 40

U N C L A S S I F I E D

CWD071 02/1247 27SC1523

FOR CAB

ROUTINE 020925Z OCT 86

FROM   RAF VALLEY
TO   MODUK AIR
       HQRAFSC

U N C L A S S I F I E D
SIC Z6F
SUBJECT UNIDENTIFIED FLYING OBJECT
A. 29 SEP 86 2030(A) FOR 3 MIN
B. ONE SINGLE BRIGHT LIGHT
C. OUTDOORS, STATIONARY. AT CAERNARFON LOOKING TOWARDS SNOWDONIA.
D. NAKED EYE
E. TO NORTH EAST
F. HIGH ANGLE BUT NOT DIRECTLY OVERHEAD
G. DISTANCE UNKNOWN
H. OBJECT WAS IN STRAIGHT STEADY CLIMB
J. VERY CLEAR NIGHT
K. NONE
L. RAF VALLEY (ATC)
M. Section 40   PORT DINORWIC, CAERNARFON. TEL

PAGE 2 R9DBV6 005 UNCLAS
Section 40
N. NIL
O. Section 40
P. 2030(A) 29 SEP 86
DT

DISTRIBUTION   Z6F
F
CAB   1 Sec (AS) ACTION (DXJ   1 AFBG)
CAM   1 ACS(F)
CYD   1 DD SE/AEW
CAV   1 DI 55
CAV   2 DSTI

UNCLASSIFIED

CAB205 30/2340 27305274

FOR CAB

ROUTINE/ROUTINE 301945Z SEP

FROM   RAF LEUCHARS
TO   MODUK
INFO   HQSTC
        UKRADC

UNCLASSIFIED
SIC IGZ/Z99 (SIC Z99 INS - DCC USE ONLY)
MODUK FOR AFOR(RAF). SUBJECT UFO REPORT
A 301100Z SEP FOR APPROX 60 MINS
B ONE SILVER COLOURED OVAL-SHAPED OBJECT APPROX THE SIZE OF A LIGHT
AIRCRAFT. THE OBJECT REFLECTED THE BRIGHT SUNLIGHT AND MADE NO
NOISE
C POSN OF OBJECT: 2 MILES NORTH OF CRAIGOWL HILL IN THE SIDLAW HILLS
APPEARED TO BE MOTIONLESS
D FIXED EYE
E AS ABOVE
F HEIGHT: APPROX 15000FT
G 2 MILES FROM OBSERVER
H NIL, AS OBSERVER ATTEMPTED TO CLOSE WITH THE OBJECT, HE LOST SIGHT

PAGE 2 RBDUXJ 053 UNCLAS
OF IT BEHIND SOME TREES. OBJECT DID NOT REAPPEAR
J NIL. CLEAR BLUE SKIES, NO CLOUDS, BRIGHT SUNLIGHT
K NIL. OPEN PARKLAND
L WING OPS RAF LEUCHARS
M INFORMANT: Section 40
N O.G NIL
O 301730Z SEP 86

DISTRIBUTION   IGZ

BY SDL

DISTRIBUTION   Z99

XXXX 1 DS WA ACTION (GTK 1 RED CLERK)

147

Sec.(AS)2
30 SEP 1986

FILE

Section 40

ANNEX A TO
SOP 502

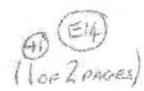
(1 OF 2 PAGES)

REPORT OF AN UNIDENTIFIED FLYING OBJECT

A.	Date, Time & Duration of Sighting	29 Sep 86 1900Z onwards
B.	Description of Object (No of objects, size, shape, colour, brightness)	Flashing red green white light, irregular pattern
C.	Exact Position of Observer Location, indoor/outdoor, stationary/moving	Indoors Section 40 Wellington Salop
D.	How Observed (naked eye, binoculars, other optical device, still or movie)	Naked eye
E.	Direction in which object first seen (A landmark may be more useful than a badly estimated bearing)	To right of Church tower - south
F.	Angle of Sight (Estimated heights are unreliable)	Half way up Church Tower
G.	Distance (By reference to a known landmark)	N/K
H.	Movements (Changes in E, F & G may be of more use than estimates of course and speed)	Stationary
J.	Met Conditions during Observations (Moving clouds, haze, mist etc)	Clear
K.	Nearby Objects (Telephone lines, high voltage lines, reservoir, lake or dam, swamp or marsh, river, high buildings, tall chimneys, steeples, spires, TV or radio masts, airfields, generating plant, factories, pits or other sites with floodlights or night lighting)	Nil

L.	To whom reported (Police, military, press etc)	Orderly Officer For A Section 40 RAF Shawbury.
M.	Name & Address of Informant	Section 40
N.	Background of Informant that may be volunteered	Normal
O.	Other Witnesses	Section 40 (son in law)
P.	Date, Time of Receipt	2000Z 29 Sep
Q.	Any Unusual Meteorological Conditions	NR
R.	Remarks	

Section 40

Duty Operations Officer
AF Ops

Date 29 Sep 86......

Copies to:
Sec(AS)2
AEW/GE
DI 55
File AF Ops/2/5/1

U N C L A S S I F I E D

CAB077 27/2132 27OC1455

FOR CAB

ROUTINE 272110Z SEP 86

FROM   RAF WEST DRAYTON
TO   MODUK AIR

U N C L A S S I F I E D
SIC Z6F
SUBJECT: AERIAL PHENOMOENA
A. 272100A SEP 86, 25 MINS
B. 4 BALL SHAPED OBJECTS, 1 LARGE, 2 SMALL, 2 ORANGE AND 1 GREEN
WITH A WHITE SURROUND
C. CADDINGTON, WEST OF LUTON, INDOORS, STATIONARY
D. NAKED EYE AND BINOCULARS
E. WEST OF LUTON
F. NOT KNOWN
G. 2 TO 3 MILES APPROX
H. CHANGING
J. SKY CLEAR CAVOK
K. T.V. MASTS
L. LUTON POLICE, AIRPORT DUTY OFFICER, AIR TRAFFIC CONTROL
M. Section 40

PAGE 2 RBDAID 001 UNCLAS
N. NONE
O. OTHERS, NO NAMES
P. 272200A SEP 86
BT

DISTRIBUTION   Z6F
F
CAB   1 Sec (AS) ACTION (CX)   1 AFDO)
CAM   1 ACS(P)
CYD   1 DD OE/AEW
CAV   1 GI 55
CAV   2 DSTI

MINISTRY OF DEFENCE
Sec.(AS)2
- 6 OCT 1986
FILE

Section 40
(E12/1)

AIR TRAFFIC CONTROL UNIT

FORM OF REPORT OF UNIDENTIFIED FLYING OBJECT

A. DATE, TIME AND DURATION OF SIGHTING   27·09·86

Local times to be quoted 2100 - 2125

B. DESCRIPTION OF OBJECT
1 LARGE ORANGE BALL   1 GREEN BALL WITH WHITE SURROUND
Number of objects, size, shape, colours, brightness, sound, smell etc.
2 SMALL ORANGE BALLS

C. EXACT POSITION OF OBSERVER
CADDINGTON   NR LUTON   HOVERING
Geographical location, indoors or outdoors, stationary or moving.

D. HOW OBSERVED
NAKED EYE + BINOCULARS
Naked eye, binoculars, other optical device, still or movie camera.

E. DIRECTION IN WHICH OBJECT WAS FIRST SEEN
WEST OF LUTON
A landmark may be more useful than a badly estimated bearing.

F. ANGULAR ELEVATION OF OBJECT

Estimated heights are unreliable.   NO   INFO

G. DISTANCE OF OBJECT FROM OBSERVER

By reference to a known landmark wherever possible. 2-3 MILES AWAY

H. MOVEMENT OF OBJECT
HOVERING   MOST OF THE TIME - LITTLE SIDEWAY
Changes in E, F and G may be of more use than estimates of course MOVEMENT
and speed.

J. METEOROLOGICAL CONDITIONS DURING OBSERVATIONS

Moving clouds, haze, mist, etc. CAVOK   VIS 10KM

K. NEARBY OBJECTS

Telephone or high-voltage lines; reservoir, lake or dam; swamp or marsh;
river; high buildings; chimneys; steeples; spires; TV or radio masts; airfields;
generating plant; factories; pits or other sites with floodlights or other
lighting.

L. TO WHOM REPORTED
POLICE   ADD   LIA
Police military organisations, the press, etc.

M. NAME AND ADDRESS OF INFORMANT Section 40

N. ANY BACKGROUND INFORMATION ON THE INFORMANT THAT MAY BE VOLUNTEERED NIL

O. OTHER WITNESSES MORE THAN 1 WITNESS

P. DATE AND TIME OF RECEIPT OF REPORT

21.35

Air Traffic Control Officer

The details are to be telephoned immediately to AIS (Military), LATCC.

The completed form (with one photocopy) is to be placed in the S.A.T.C.O's
basket in the general office.

U N C L A S S I F I E D

CWB900 22/1792 265C3374

FOR CAB

ROUTINE 221400Z SEP 86

FROM   RAF WEST DRAYTON
TO   MODUK AIR

U N C L A S S I F I E D
STC Z6F
SUBJECT AERIAL PHENOMENA
A. 221400L SEP 86, SEVERAL MINUTES
B. ONE RED DISC SHAPED OBJECT TRAILING VERY BRIGHT SILVER CORD,
LENGTH NOT KNOWN
C. OUTDOORS IN GARDEN AT ▮▮▮▮▮▮▮▮▮▮ LUTON
D. NAKED EYE THEN USED BINOCULARS
E. FROM THE NORTH WEST HEADING SOUTH
F. DIRECTLY ABOVE HIM
G. HIGH
H. MOVING VERY FAST
J. CLEAR SKY
K. NIL
L. LUTON AIR TRAFFIC SUPERVISOR
M. ▮▮▮▮▮▮▮▮▮▮▮▮▮▮▮▮▮▮▮▮

PAGE 2 RBDAID 010 UNCLAS
N. NIL
O. SISTER ▮▮▮▮▮▮▮▮▮▮▮▮▮
P. 221430L SEP 86
BT

DISTRIBUTION   Z6F
I F
CAB   1   Sec (AS) ACTION (CXJ   1   ATIG)
CAM   1   ACS(F)
CYD   1   DI GE/AEW
CAV   1   DI 55
CAV   2   DSTI

LUTON AIRPORT

AIR TRAFFIC CONTROL UNIT

FORM OF REPORT OF UNIDENTIFIED FLYING OBJECT

A. DATE, TIME AND DURATION OF SIGHTING

Local times to be quoted   22/9/86 : 2.00pm : 2mins

B. DESCRIPTION OF OBJECT

Number of objects, size, shape, colours, brightness, sound, smell etc.
RED DISC, TRAILING CORDS, GLINTED SILVER,

C. EXACT POSITION OF OBSERVER   'LIKE PARACHTE WITH NO-ONE ON IT

Geographical location, indoors or outdoors, stationary or moving.
HEADING SE.

D. HOW OBSERVED

Naked eye, binoculars, other optical device, still or movie camera.

E. DIRECTION IN WHICH OBJECT WAS FIRST SEEN

A landmark may be more useful than a badly estimated bearing.
NW → SE

F. ANGULAR ELEVATION OF OBJECT

Estimated heights are unreliable. ALMOST DIRECTLY ABOVE, APPEARED TO BE FALLING

G. DISTANCE OF OBJECT FROM OBSERVER

By reference to a known landmark wherever possible. 'HIGH AS HIGH JETS'

H. MOVEMENT OF OBJECT

Changes in E, F and G may be of more use than estimates of course
and speed   'MOVING VERY FAST'

J. METEOROLOGICAL CONDITIONS DURING OBSERVATIONS

Moving clouds, haze, mist, etc. 2/8 @ 3000', 10km viz

K. NEARBY OBJECTS

Telephone or high-voltage lines; reservoir. lake or dam; swamp or marsh;
river; high buildings; chimneys; steeples; spires; TV or radio masts; airfields;
generating plant; factories; pits or other sites with floodlights or other
lighting.

L. TO WHOM REPORTED

Police military organisations, the press, etc.

M. NAME AND ADDRESS OF INFORMANT Section 40   HIGHTOWN, LUTON.

N. ANY BACKGROUND INFORMATION ON THE INFORMANT THAT MAY BE VOLUNTEERED

O. OTHER WITNESSES Section 40

P. DATE AND TIME OF RECEIPT OF REPORT   22/9/86 : 2.30pm

Section 40 ASSISTANT
Air Traffic Control Officer

The details are to be telephoned immediately to AIS (Military), LATCC ✓ 2.40 pm

The completed form (with one photocopy) is to be placed in the S.A.T.C.O's
basket in the general office.

153

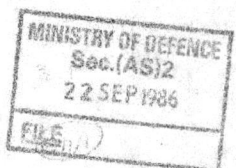

U N C L A S S I F I E D

CAB447 20/1528 263C1368

FOR CAB

ROUTINE 201430Z SEP 86

FROM   RAF WEST DRAYTON
TO   MODUK AIR

U N C L A S S I F I E D
SIC Z6F
SUBJECT AERIAL PHENOMENA
A. 20 SEP 86 1430 LOCAL FOR 30 MINS
B. NUMEROUS BRIGHT PINK LIGHTS POPPING VERY HIGH IN THE SKY, LOUD
POPPING NOISES
C. IN HOUSE GARDEN AT HOME
D. FIRSTLY WITH NAKED EYE THEN MORE CLOSELY WITH 10 X 50 BINOCULARS
E. N/A
F. NOT KNOWN
G. VERY HIGH
H. APPEARED AS STEADY OBJECTS WHICH THEN FELL AWAY FROM NW TO SE
DIRECTION
J. CLEAR SKIES, NIL CLOUDS
K. N/A
L. REPORTED TO AISM LATCCMIL RAF WEST DRAYTON

PAGE 2 RDDAID 002 UNCLAS
M. Section 40   BLETCHLEY, MILTON KEYNES (TEL M.K.
Section 40
N. NONE
O. OTHER FAMILY MEMBERS
P. 201501 LOCAL SEP 86
BT

DISTRIBUTION Z6F
F
CAB   1 Sec (AS) ACTION (CXJ   1 AFDO)
CAM   1 ACS(P)
CYR   1 DD GE/AEW
CAV   1 DI 55
CAV   2 DSTI

UNCLASSIFIED

CAB014 20/0654 263C0710

FOR CAB

ROUTINE 200630Z SEP 86

FROM   RAF WEST DRAYTON
TO   MODUK AIR

UNCLASSIFIED
SIC Z6F
SUBJECT AERIAL PHENOMENA
A. 200015Z SEP 86\
B. ONE SINGLE SPOTLIGHT
C. OUTDOORS MOVING, NEAR FIDDLERS FERRY POWER STATION
D. NAKED EYE
E. OVER MARSHES TOWARDS POWER STATION
F. NOT KNOWN
G. NOT KNOWN
H. STEADY
J. CLEAR SKY
K. NONE   Section 40
L. POLICE WOMAN ████ WARRINGTON POLICE STATION Section 40 ████
M. Section 40 ████████ WARRINGTON
N. NIL

PAGE 2 RBDAID 001 UNCLAS
O. NONE
P. 200045Z SEP 86
BT

DISTRIBUTION   Z6F
F
CAB   1 Sec (AS) ACTION (CXJ   1 AFDO)
CAM   1 ACS(F)
CYO   1 DD CE/AEW
CAV   1 DI 55
CAV   2 D8TI

155

REPORT OF AN UNIDENTIFIED FLYING OBJECT

A.	Date, Time & Duration of Sighting	18 Sep 86 2208 Local
B.	Description of Object (No of objects, size, shape, colour, brightness)	one, small & lights round it, bright green
C.	Exact Position of Observer Location, indoor/outdoor, stationary/moving	Indoors, Section 40 Banbury.
D.	How Observed (naked eye, binoculars, other optical device, still or movie)	Telescope
E.	Direction in which object first seen (A landmark may be more useful than a badly estimated bearing)	To right of moon above Technical College
F.	Angle of Sight (Estimated heights are unreliable)	-
G.	Distance (By reference to a known landmark)	No Idea
H.	Movements (Changes in E, F & G may be of more use than estimates of course and speed)	Moved about
J.	Met Conditions during Observations (Moving clouds, haze, mist etc)	Clear
K.	Nearby Objects (Telephone lines, high voltage lines, reservoir, lake or dam, swamp or marsh, river, high buildings, tall chimneys, steeples, spires, TV or radio masts, airfields, generating plant, factories, pits or other sites with floodlights or night lighting)	Moon

L.	To whom reported (Police, military, press etc)	Thames Valley Police, Banbury.
M.	Name & Address of Informant	Section 40
N.	Background of Informant that may be volunteered	Unknown
O.	Other Witnesses	Section 40
P.	Date, Time of Receipt	182209 Local Sep 86
Q.	Any Unusual Meteorological Conditions	
R.	Remarks	

Section 40
....

Squadron Leader
Duty Operations Officer
AF Ops

Date... 18 Sep 86 ....

Copies to:
Sec(AS)2
AEW/GE
DI 55
File AF Ops/2/5/1

U N C L A S S I F I E D

CAB120 18/1707 251C3433

FOR CAB

ROUTINE 180930Z SEP 86

FROM   RAF WEST DRAYTON
TO   MODUK AIR

U N C L A S S I F I E D
SIC Z6F
SUBJECT AERIAL PHENOMENA
A. 072000Z SEP 86, 7 MINS DURATION
B. INTERMITTENT BEAMS OF LIGHT, CENTRE BEAM EXTREMELY BRIGHT, LENGTH
OF BEAM APPROX 200 YARDS
C. Section 40   BANKS, SOUTHPORT
D. NAKED EYE
E. COMING FROM SOUTH-EAST
F. VERY LOW IN SKY
G. N/K
H. STRAIGHT LINE VERY SOLOW
J. LOW CLOUD
K. PYLONS IN VICINITY OF CARAVAN PARK
L. WIGAN POLICE 17 SEP 86
M. Section 40   WIGAN. TELNO WIGAN Section 40

PAGE 2 RBDAID 001 UNCLAS
N. LATE REPORT OF SIGHTING DUE TO INFORMATION BEING ON HOLIDAY TILL
16 SEP
O. HUSBAND
P. 180920Z FROM MANCHESTER SUB-CENTRE
BT

DISTRIBUTION   Z6F
F
CAB   1 Sec (AS) ACTION (CXJ   1 AFDO)
CAM   1 ACS(P)
CYD   1 DD GE/AEW
CAV   1 DI 55
CAV   2 DSTI

U N C L A S S I F I E D

CAB011 15/0707 258C0425

FOR CAB

ROUTINE 150630Z SEP 86

FROM   RAF WEST DRAYTON
TO   MODUK AIR

U N C L A S S I F I E D
SIC Z6F
SUBJECT: AERIAL PHENOMENA.
A. 142330L SEP 86, 3 MINS
B. TRIANGULAR IN SHAPE WITH THREE WHITE LIGHTS AND A NOSE CONE ON
THE LEFT HAND SIDE
C. OUTDOORS STATIONARY NEAR HOME ADDRESS
D. NAKED EYE
E. NORTH
F. 300FT
G. HALF A MILE
H. MOVED SLOWLY AND THEN ZOOMED OFF
J. CAVOK
K. NIL
L. SUNDERLAND WEST CONSTABULARY PC Section 40
M. Section 40   SPRINGWELL, SUNDERLAND

PAGE 2 RBDAID 001 UNCLAS
N. EX-RAF
O. Section 40
P. 141105Z SEP 86
BT

DISTRIBUTION   Z6F
F
CAB   1 Sec (AS) ACTION (CXJ   1 AFB0)
CAR   1 AC8(F)
CYD   1 DD CE/AEW
CAV   1 DI 55
CAV   2 DBTI

UNCLASSIFIED
RESTRICTED

CBD150 09/1733 252C3213 CORRECTED VERSION

FOR CBD

F816.
Try NAS
ATC people?
AD

ROUTINE 091033Z SEP 86

FROM   CBFASI
TO   MODUK AIR
       HQSTC

R E S T R I C T E D
SIC KQJ/K2B
SUBJECT AIRMISS WITH UNIDENTIFIED OBJECT. REF ASMA TOTE DCON 17
PAGE 1 DTG 41832 SEP
1. REPEAT OF REF AS FOLLOWS CLN QUOTE FROM CAPT ████ (IN COMPANY
WITH ████ 40WISH TO REPORT THAT AT 041128Z AT PSN 2020S 2250W AN
UNIDENTIFIED OBJECT—PASSED CLOSE TO PORT SIDE OF A/C. POSSIBLITIES
CONSIDERED A) ASTEROID B) RETURNING SPACE DEBRIS OR C) RE-ENTERING
MISSILE. IF IT IS ESTABLISHED THAT C) IS THE CASE THEN CPT AND CREW
VERY UNIMPRESSED AS A/C WAS AT F190- OBJECT TRACKED 270 DEG M (AC
TRACKING 245 DEG M) ESTIMATED DISTANCE OF 1.5NM- BURN OUT- ABOUT
F190. UNQUOTE
2. AT PRESENT UNABLE TO FOLLOW UP BY ASMA DUE TO UNSERVICEABILITY
WOULD APPRECIATE INVESTIGATION AND REPORT ON INCIDENT
3. BECAUSE OF NATURE OF INCIDENT F765A NOT RAISED

PAGE 2 RBVAA 019 R E S T R I C T E D UNCLASSIFIED
BT

DISTRIBUTION   KQJ
F
CBD   4   IFS(RAF) ACTION (CXJ   1   JOC AFDO)
CAV   1   CE (RAF)
CAT   1   DD Air Eng 1(RAF)
CAT   1   DD Air Eng 2(RAF)
CAM   2   DD Wpn Eng(RAF)
CBD   1   DT(F)(RAF)
CAM   1   D TES (RAF)
CAB   1   ACAS

DISTRIBUTION   K2B
F
CWU   1   C(G)9 ACTION (CXJ   1   JOC AFDO)

U N C L A S S I F I E D

CAB001 09/0006 252C0023

FOR CAI

ROUTINE 082100Z SEP 96

FROM   RAF NEATISHEAD
TO   MODUK AIR
        UKRADC
        HQ 11 GP

U N C L A S S I F I E D
SIC I3F/ZAF
FOLLOWING SIGNAL TEXT OF U.F.O. REPORT PASSED TO SOC NEATISHEAD BY
EASTERN RADAR SUPERVISOR 082159Z SEP 96
A. 8 SEP-2040 LOCAL-5-8 MINUTES
B. 1, 4 BY SIZE JUMBO JET, NO SHAPE, COLOUR, SMELL OR SOUND, JUST A
VERY BRIGHT LIGHT
C. 5400N 00110E, MOVING
D. VISUAL AND RADAR CONTACT
E. SOUTH EASTERN SKY-OBSERVING A/C ALSO HEADING SOUTH EAST
F. SAME LEVEL-OBSERVING A/C FL330
G. 40 MILES (RADAR) ON INITIAL CONTACT
H. ACCELERATED AWAY, APPROX 10 NM IN 10 SECS. ESTIMATED HEADING 115
MAGNETIC

PAGE 2 RHUDWL 006   UNCLAS
J. CLEAR SKY (FL330). OTHER A/C IN AREA REPORTED CLOUD TOPS APPROX
FL100
K. AHEAD BY 80 NM, BUT NOT IN RADAR CONTACT BY OBSERVING A/C, 1 BY
DAN AIR BAC111 4000FT LOW
L. A/C REPORTED TO CIVIL CONTROLLER, CIVIL CONTROLLER TO EASTERN
SUPERVISOR, EASTERN SUPERVISOR TO SOC NEATISHEAD DUTY CONTROLLER
M. CAPTAIN OF ▇Section 40▇ ▇▇▇▇▇ NEWCASTLE TO LGKR,
EASTERN SUPERVISOR FLT LT ▇Section 40▇ EASTERN RADAR
N. NON KNOWN
O. NIL EXTERNAL, INTERNAL A/C UNKNOWN
P. 082140Z SEP 96, RECEIVED SOC NEATISHEAD 082158Z SEP 96
COMMENT BY SOC NEATISHEAD DUTY FA. AT THE TIME OF THE REPORT THERE
WAS NO AIR DEFENCE NIGHT FLYING IN PROGRESS AT SOC NEATISHEAD,
CRC BOULMER OR CRP STAXTON WOLD. BORDER RADAR AND EASTERN MILITARY
HAD NO A/C IN THE AREA. THERE WERE NO NOTAMED RELEASES OF BALLOONS
OR FLARES, HOWEVER ON CHECKING WITH THE D AND B CELL AT WEST DRAYTON,
THEY INFORMED ME THAT THERE ARE RIGS AT APPROX POSITION 5330N-00140E
WHO CAN RELEASE FLARES OR BURN CHEMICALS WITHOUT WARNING. NFTR

To:- SEC(AS)2 MOD.
with compliments

Herewith copy of cfo
report as received AIS.
on 16/9/86

Aeronautical Information Section (Military)

London Air Traffic Control Centre (Military)
Royal Air Force
West Drayton
Middlesex   UB7 9AU

Section 40   Ext: Section 40
Section 40

DUTY AISO (M)

162

REPORT FORM

UNIDENTIFIED FLYING OBJECT

A. 2200 — 8TH SEPTEMBER 1986 — RADAR 2½ MINS

B. RADAR RETURN ¼" OVAL SHAPED

C. 33,000' 60 MILES SE OF DOGGER BANK.

D. RADAR.

E. 12' o'clock 40 MILES RANGE. THE PILOT WAS TRACKING 127°.

F. APPEARED AT SAME LEVEL RADAR AT 0 TILT

G. 40 MILES.

H. CONSTANT TRACK 125° IN EXCESS OF MACH 4.

J. VMC NIGHT.

K. NOTHING.

L. SECTOR CONTROLLER NORTH SEA.

M. ████████████████████ Section 40 ████████████████████

N. Pilot reported :— Nothing seen by handover or Manorbier Radar

████████ Section 40 ████████

O. CATTERALL ████████████

P. 1440 — 15.8.1982.

Q.

Copy sent to NAIS ████████ ...... date/time 15 1515 ⚡

CXJ138 08/2132 251C4212

FOR CXJ

ROUTINE 081840Z SEP 86

FROM   UKRAOC
TO   MODUK AIR

S E C R E T
SIC I3F
MOD FOR AFOR
SUSPECT UFO REPORT
A. 041128Z SEPT 86
B. POSSIBLE ASTEROID, RETURNING SPACE DEBRIS, RE-ENTERING MISSILE
C. CAPTAIN OF AIRCRAFT, POSITION 2020 DEGREES SOUTH, 02250 DEGREES
WEST
D. NAKED EYE
E. OBJECT TRACKED 270 DEGREES, AIRCRAFT TRACKING 245 DEGREES
F. NOT KNOWN
G. ESTIMATED 1.5 N.M. FROM AIRCRAFT
H. PASSED CLOSE TO PORT SIDE OF AIRCRAFT
J. NOT KNOWN
K. TWO AIRCRAFT IN COMPANY
L. ASCENSION ISLAND OPS TO UKRAOC OPS

PAGE 2 RBDOYI 245 S E C R E T
M. CAPTAIN OF AIRCRAFT CALLSIGH Section 40
N. NONE
O. NOT KNOWN
P. 081706Z SEPT 86
BT

DISTRIBUTION   I3F
F
CXJ   1 JOC AFDO ACTION < CXJ   1   JOC AFDO >

END

U N C L A S S I F I E D

CA9033 07/2213 259C1160

FOR CAB

ROUTINE 072143Z SEP 86

FROM RAF WEST DRAYTON
TO   MODUK AIR

U N C L A S S I F I E D
SIC 26F
SUBJECT AERIAL PHENOMENA
A. 072030Z SEP 86 45 MINUTES
B. ONE BRIGHT WHITE LIGHT, CHANGED TO RED AND BLUE WHEN IN HOVER
C. IN CAR AT HOME ADDRESS
D. NAKED EYE AND BINOCULARS
E. TRAVELLING N. E. OVER DORNOTH AT HI SPEED AND THEN CAME BACK IN LAND
F. NOT KNOWN
G. NOT KNOWN
H. VERY FAST AND AT A STEEP ANGLE AND THEN APPEARED TO HOVER
J. CAVOK
K. NIL
L. LOSSIEMOUTH OPERATIONS
M. Section 40   INVERGORDON, ROSSHIRE

PAGE 2 REDAID 002 UNCLA
N. NIL
O. WIFE AND MOTHER-IN-LA
P. 072117Z SEP 86
BT

DISTRIBUTION 26F
#
CAB   1 Sup (AS) ACTION (DXJ   1 JSC MI90)
CAN   1 ACB(F)
CYD   1 DD GE/AEW
CAU   1 DI 55
CAV   2 DSTI

UNCLASSIFIED

CAB024 07/1524 25800795

FOR CAB

ROUTINE 071500Z SEP 86

FROM   RAF WEST DRAYTON
TO   MODUK AIR

UNCLASSIFIED
SIC Z6F
SUBJECT AERIAL PHENOMENA
A. 071455(L) SEP 86 15 SECONDS
B. ONE LARGE SILVER FAST MOVING OBJECT
C. Section 40   NEWQUAY. OUTDOORS IN GARDEN
D. NAKED EYE
E. HDG. SOUTH EAST OUT TO SEA OVER NEWQUAY COASTLINE.
F. VERY HIGH
G. NIL
H. STEADY THEN SHOT ACROSS THE SKY VERY FAST
J. CLEAR SKY
K. NIL
L. SGT. Section 40 BASE OPERATIONS, RAF ST. MAWGAN
M. Section 40
N. NIL

PAGE 2 RBDAID 001 UNCLAS
O. NIL
P. 071520(L) SEP 86
BT

DISTRIBUTION Z6F
F
CAB   1 Sec (AS) ACTION (CXJ   1 JGC AFDO)
CAM   1 ACS(P)
CYD   1 DD GE/AEW
CAV   1 DI 55
CAV   2 DSTI

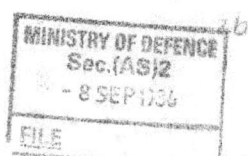

U N C L A S S I F I E D

CAS019 06/0704 269C0653

FOR CAS

ROUTINE 060610Z SEP 86

FROM   RAF WEST DRAYTON
TO   MODUK AIR

U N C L A S S I F I E D
SIC Z6F
SUBJECT: AERIAL PHENOMANA
A. 052325A SEP 86, 3 MINS
B. ONE, VERY LARGE, NOT KNOWN, RED, GREEN, WHITE, VERY BRIGHT,
NONE (VERY STRANGE AS OBJECT WAS SO CLOSE AND SO LARGE), NOT KNOWN
C. OUTDOORS STATIONARY
D. NAKED EYE
E. FROM SOUTH
F. 20 TO 25 DEGREES
G. 2 MILES APPROX
H. VERY FAST
J. SKY CLEAR
K. HOUSE
L. AIR(N)
N. Section 40   SHERFIELD ON LODDON, NR

PAGE 2 RSDAID 001 UNCLAS
BASINGSTOKE
N. NIL
O. Section 40
P. 052340A SEP 86
BT

DISTRIBUTION   Z6F
F
CAB   1 Sec (AS) ACTION (CX)   1 JDC AFDO
CAM   1 ACS(P)
CYD   1 DD GE/AEW
CAV   1 DI 55
CAV   2 DSTI

MOD Form 329D
(Revised 3/83)

MINISTRY OF DEFENCE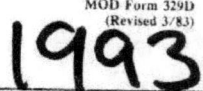

1993

Date opened		DIVISION/ESTABLISHMENT/UNIT/BRANCH
23 Aug 87	1. Attention is drawn to the notes on the inside flap	
Registered file number	2. Enter notes of related files on page 2 of this jacket.	Sec (AS) 2A

D / Sec (AS) 12/2   Part No. D

SUBJECT UNIDENTIFIED FLYING OBJECTS
U.F.O.s

REPORTS

Referred to	Date	Min/Encl	Referred to	Date	Min/Encl	Referred to	Date	Min/Encl	Referred to	Date	Min/Encl
						MOD DR1 21 DEC 1999 SECOND REVIEW					
						2013			Section 40		

Section 40

File Ref SEC(AS)12/C
Part   D

FOR DRO USE ONLY

1st Review date

RCU000342988

2nd Review date

PA ACTION

(MOD Form 262F
must be completed)

Printed for Her Majesty's Stationery Office by R.P.W. Ltd Dd 841/83

Registered File Disposal Form

FILE TITLE: (Main Heading - Secondary Heading - Tertiary Heading etc)

UFOs- Reports

Reference:
(Prefix and Number):
DISEC(AS) 12/2
Part: D

PROTECTIVE MARKING (including caveats & descriptors): UIC

Date of last enclosure: 7.2.88

Date closed: 7.2.88

PART 1. DISPOSAL SCHEDULE RECOMMENDATION
(To be completed when the file is closed)

SCB CS(R) USE ONLY

MOD
DR 1
21 DEC 1999
SECOND REVIEW

Destroy after _____ years

Forward to CS(RM) after _____ years

No recommendation

Date of 1st review: 21 DEC 1999   Date of 2nd review: _____   Forward Destruction Date

Reviewer's Signature: _____   Reviewer's Signature: _____

2013

PART 2. BRANCH REVIEW
(To be completed not later than 4 years after the date of the last enclosure)
(Delete as appropriate)

Section

a. Of no further administrative value and not worthy of permanent preservation - DESTROY IMMEDIATELY (Remember that TOP SECRET and Codeword material cannot be destroyed locally but must be for...)

b. (i) To be retained for _____ years from date of last enclosure) for the following reason(s):

LEGAL	☐	DEFENCE POLICY - OPERATIONS	☐
CONTRACTUAL	☐	ORIGINAL COMMITTEE PAPERS	☐
FINANCE/AUDIT	☐	MAJOR EQUIPMENT PROJECT	☐
DIRECTORATE POLICY	☐	OTHER (Specify)	☐

PPQ = 100

(Continued overleaf)

(ii) Key enclosures which support the recommendation are:

(iii) At the end of the specified retention period the file is to be:

Destroyed ☐

Considered by CS(RM) for
permanent preservation ☐

c. Of no further administrative value but worthy of consideration by CS(RM) for permanent preservation. ☑

PART 3. BRANCH REVIEWING OFFICER	PART 4 DESTRUCTION CERTIFICATE
Signature: Section 40	It is certified that the specified file has been destroyed.
	Signature:
Name:	Name:
(Block Capitals)	(Block Capitals)
Grade/Rank: HEO Date: 22/19/99	Grade/Rank: Date:
(Not below HEO/equivalent)	Witnessed by (TOP SECRET and SECRET only)
Branch Title and Full Address: MINISTRY OF DEFENCE	Signature:
SEC (AS) 2	
ROOM Section 40	Name:
MAIN BUILDING	(Block Capitals)
WHITEHALL	Grade/Rank: Date:
LONDON SW1 2HB	*(FOR CS(RM) USE ONLY)
Tel No: Section 40	

Produced by Ministry of Defence, CS (Pr) 2. Tel. Section 40

ANNEX A TO
SOP 502

REPORT OF AN UNIDENTIFIED FLYING OBJECT

A.	Date, Time & Duration of Sighting	072220 Feb 88 2 Mins
B.	Description of Object (No of objects, size, shape, colour, brightness)	Red & White Lights
C.	Exact Position of Observer Location, indoor/outdoor, stationary/moving	Outdoors on foot in Smethick High Street ? Smethwick ?
D.	How Observed (naked eye, binoculars, other optical device, still or movie	Naked eye
E.	Direction in which object first seen (A landmark may be more useful than a badly estimated bearing)	Overhead
F.	Angle of Sight (Estimated heights are unreliable)	/
G.	Distance (By reference to a known landmark	/
H.	Movements (Changes in E, F & G may be of more use than estimates of course and speed)	Upwards into clouds
J.	Met Conditions during Observations (Moving clouds, haze, mist etc)	Cloudy no rain
K.	Nearby Objects (Telephone lines, high voltage lines, reservoir, lake or dam, swamp or marsh, river, high buildings, tall chimneys, steeples, spires, TV or radio masts, airfields, generating plant, factories, pits or other sites with floodlights or night lighting	Built up area

L.   To whom reported (Police,   West Midlands Police
      military, press etc)   Control Room

M.   Name & Address of Informant   Section 40

N.   Background of Informant that   Nil
may be volunteered

O.   Other Witnesses   Nil

P.   Date, Time of Receipt   0722582 Feb 88

Q.   Any Unusual Meteorological   /
      Conditions

R.   Remarks

                        Sqn Ldr
                        Duty Ops Officer
Date: 7 Feb 88   AF Ops

Distribution:

Sec(AS)2
HEW/GE
Hr 36
File/AF Ops/2/5/1

Sec (AS) c.c.

D/Sc3c (Av)

U N C L A S S I F I E D

CAB029 07/1347 03BC0590

FOR CAB

ROUTINE 071320Z FEB 88

FROM   RAF WEST DRAYTON
TO   MODUK AIR

U N C L A S S I F I E D
SIC Z6F
SUBJECT: AERIAL PHENOMENA
A. 6 FEB 88, 1830, SIX HOURS
B. ONE, LARGE, CONE
C. OUTDOORS, STATIONARY
D. NAKED EYE AND BINOCULARS
E. KILVEY HILL MAST SWANSEA
F. NOT GIVEN
G. THREE AND A HALF MILES
H. FROM 1830 TO 2000 STEADY THEN MOVED WESTWARDS
J. GOOD CLEAR
K. NOT GIVEN
L. COCKETT POLICE STATION SWANSEA
M. Section 40   TEL SWANSEA Section
N. NONE

PAGE 2 RBDAID 002 UNCLAS
O. NEIGHBOUR
P. 061845 FEB 88
BT

DISTRIBUTION   Z6F
F
CAB   1   Sec (AS) ACTION (CXJ   1   AFDO)
CYD   1   DD GE/AEW
CAV   1   DI 55
CAV   2   DSTI

173

U N C L A S S I F I E D

CWD002 07/1407 038C0619 CORRECTED VERSION   (E101)

FOR CAB

ROUTINE 070815Z FEB 88

FROM   RAF WEST DRAYTON
TO   MODUK AIR

U N C L A S S I F I E D
SIC Z6F
SUBJECT: AERIAL PHENOMENA
A. 061845 FEB 88
B. ROUND, GREEN YELLOW AND BLUE LIGHTS
C. DAWLEY TELFORD INDOORS MOVING
D. TELESCOPE
E. NOT GIVEN
F. NOT GIVEN
G. 8000FT GUESS
H. FAST THEN HOVERED CAME TO REST OVER TOWN CENTRE
J. CLEAR
K. NOT GIVEN
L. TELFORD CONSTABULERY Section 40
M. Section 40   DAWLEY TELFORD TEL Section 40
O. FIVE POLICE OFFICERS

PAGE 2 RBDAID 001   UNCLAS
P. 061910 FEB 88
BT

DISTRIBUTION   Z6F
F
CAB   1 Sec (AS) ACTION (CXJ   1 AFDO)
CYB   1 DD GE/AEW
CAV   1 DI 55
CAV   2 DSTI

174

U N C L A S S I F I E D

CAB030 05/0128 035C5356

FOR CAB

ROUTINE 041935Z FEB 88

FROM   RAF WEST DRAYTON
TO   MODUK AIR

U N C L A S S I F I E D
SIC Z6F
SUBJECT: AERIAL PHENOMENA
A. 041750 FEB, 25 MINUTES ALSO MONDAY 011900 FEB DURATION NOT GIVEN
B. THREE WHITE BRIGHT LIGHTS TURNING TO RED PLUS ONE OBJECT NO LIGHTS
ROUND BROWN VERY LOW
C. NEAR M61, OUTDOORS MOVING SLOWLY
D. NAKED EYE PLUS STILL CAMERA
E. NOT GIVEN
F. TWENTY FIVE DEGREES
G. NOT GIVEN
H. SLOWLY
J. CLOUD PLUS RAIN
K. NOT GIVEN
L. MANCHESTER ATCC
M. Section 40   FARNWORTH MANCHESTER

PAGE 2 RBDAID 011   UNCLAS
N. NO
O. PARENTS PLUS NEXT DOOR NEIGHBOUR
P. 041855 FEB
BT

DISTRIBUTION   Z6F
F
CAB   1   Sec (AS) ACTION (CXJ   1   AFDO)
CYD   1   DD GE/AEW
CAV   1   DI 55
CAV ,   2   DSTI   /

Sec (AS) distribution :

  b/ Sc 3c (Air)

U N C L A S S I F I E D

CWD146 04/1206 035C0993

FOR CAB

ROUTINE 040730Z FEB 28

FROM   RAF WEST DRAYTON
TO   MODUK AIR

U N C L A S S I F I E D
SIC Z6F
SUBJECT: AERIAL PHENOMENA
A. 032325 FEB 88 FOR 5 MINS
B. ONE BRIGHTLY LIT WHITE OBLONG SHAPED OBJECT WITH NO SOUND AN$_D$
NO SMELL
C. BETWEEN EWSHOTT AND CRONDAL HAMPSHIRE
D. NAKED EYE
E. UNSURE
F. PASSED OVERHEAD
G. VERY LOW
H. STEADY PASSED QUICKLY
J. WINDY LIGHT DRIZZLE
K. NOTHING OPEN COUNTRY
L. REPORTED TO HEATHROW AIRPORT
M. Section 40

PAGE 2 RBDAID 001 UNCLAS
Section 40
P. 040020Z FEB 88
BT

DISTRIBUTION Z6
F
CAB   1 Sec (AS) ACTION (CXJ   1 AFDO)
CYD   1 DD GE/AEW
CAV   1 DI 53
CAV   2 DSTI

      Sec (AS) distribution
        d/Sc 3 c (Air)

U N C L A S S I F I E D

CWD024 03/0437 033C5537

FOR CAB

ROUTINE 021955Z FEB 88

FROM   RAF WEST DRAYTON
TO   MODUK AIR

U N C L A S S I F I E D
SIC Z6F
SUBJECT: AERIAL PHENOMENA
A. 021645Z FEB, SIX TO SEVEN MINUTES
B. LARGE OBJECT, CYLINDRICAL, NARROW AND LONG, ORANGEY YELLOW IN
COLOUR. THOUGHT AT FIRST IT WAS A CRASHING AIRCRAFT. DESCENDED
DIRECTLY OVERHEAD BRACKNELL VERY FAST THEN SLOWED WITH A PUFF OF
BLACK SMOKE AT REAR THEN DEPARTED TO SOUTHWEST
C. SEEN FIRST FROM CAR W   DRIVING FROM WARFIELD TO BRACKNELL
D. NAKED EYE
E. N/K
F. N/K
G. DIFFICULT TO JUDGE BUT QUITE HIGH
H. CHANGING HEADING
J. VERY FEW CLOUDS LOW WINTERY SUNSHINE
K. TOWN OF BRACKNELL

PAGE 2 RBDAID 008 UNCLAS
L. AIS(M), WEST DRAYTON
M. Section 40
N. FELT FOOLISH REPORTING UFO
O. STEP DAUGHTER
P. 021935 FEB
BT

DISTRIBUTION   Z6F
F
CAB   1   Sec (AS) ACTION (CXJ   1   AFDO)
CYD   1   DD CE/AEW
CAV   1   DI 55
CAV   2   DSTI

Sec (AS) distribution :
     b/ Sc 3c (Air)

MINISTRY OF DEFENCE
Sec.(AS)2
-3 FEB 1988

FILE 12/2

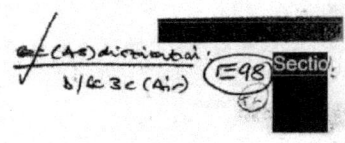

U N C L A S S I F I E D

CAB220 02/2231 03JC4826

FOR CAB

ROUTINE 021500Z FEB 88

FROM   HQRAFSC
TO   MODUK AIR

U N C L A S S I F I E D
SIC Z6F
MODUK AIR FOR SEC AS2A. SUBJECT UNIDENTIFIED FLYING OBJECT REPORT.
ALPHA. 29 JAN 88 FROM 1845HRS UNTIL 1940HRS AND 30 JAN 88 FROM ,
1915 HRS UNTIL 1925HRS
BRAVO. EXTREMELY BRIGHT WHITE LIGHT CONICAL IN SHAPE WITH A TAIL
OF LACY APPEARANCE. SECOND SIGHTING SIMILAR BUT MANOEUVRED
SIDEWAYS TO GIVE SIGHT OF ORANGE BAR COVERING APPROX ONE EIGHTH
OF OVERALL AREA
CHARLIE. STATIONARY OUTDOORS BY BACK DOOR OF HOME AT HOLYBOURNE,
ALTON
DELTA. NAKED EYE AND POWERFUL BINOCULARS
ECHO. DUE WEST
FOXTROT. NOT KNOWN
GOLF. NOT KNOWN
HOTEL. FIRST SIGHTING OBJECT STATIONARY FOR APPROX 35 MINUTES THEN

PAGE 2 RBDBYH 103 UNCLAS
DESCENDED VERTICALLY AND TURNED SOUTH. DISAPPEARED MOMENTARILY
BEHIND CLOUD THEN REAPPEARED REMAINING STATIONARY UNTIL DISAPPEARING
INTO CLOUD AT 1940HRS. SECOND SIGHTING SAME POSITION REMAINING
STATIONARY APART FROM SIDEWAYS MANOEUVRE AT 1925HRS. CHANGED SHAPE
WITH A RING OF LIGHT AND DISAPPEARED
JULIET. FIRST NIGHT PARTLY CLOUDY, SECOND NIGHT CLEAR
KILO. NIL
LIMA. SGT Section RAF POLICE RAF OAKHANGER
Section PC Section 40   ALTON
NOVEMBER. SUBJECT CIVIL POLICE OFFICER CONTACTABLE AT ALTON POLICE
STATION TELEPHONE Section 2 LOCAL NEWSPAPER OVERHEARD CONVERSATION
BETWEEN SUBJECT AND COLLEAGUES
OSCAR. WIFE AND DAUGHTER
PAPA. TO HQRAFSC AT 021100Z FEB 88
B

MINISTRY OF DEFENCE
Sec.(AS)2
- 3 FEB 1988
FILE 12/2

DISTRIBUTION   Z6F

CAB   1 Sec (AS) ACTION (CXJ   1 ARDO)
CYD   1 DD GE/AEW

U N C L A S S I F I E D

CWD013 01/1039 032C0939

FOR CAB

ROUTINE 011000Z FEB 88

FROM   RAF WEST DRAYTON
TO   MODUK AIR

U N C L A S S I F I E D
SIC Z6F
SUBJECT: AERIAL PHENOMENA
A. 010100 FEB 88
B. ONE VERY LARGE NO PARTICULAR SHAPE WINE RED 4 VERY LARGE BRIGHT
LIGHTS LATER MERGED TO ONE SOUND OF POSSIBLE AIRCRAFT NO SMELL
C. SOUTH OF WINDSOR CASTLE NEAR SAFARI PARK SEEN FROM INDOORS AND
OUTDOORS STATIONERY FOR FIVE TO SIX SECONDS THEN MOVED OFF
D. NAKED EYE
E. SOUTH OF WINDSOR CASTLE
F. NOT KNOWN
G. NOT KNOWN
H. STEADY THEN MOVED OFF
J. MOVING CLOUDS HIGH WINDS
K. WINDSOR CASTLE
L. WINDSOR POLICE

PAGE 2 RBDAIR 007 UNCLAS

M. Section 40
N. INFORMANT VERY FRIGHTENED
O. NONE
P. 010902Z FEB 88
BT

DISTRIBUTION   Z6F
F
CAB   1 Sec (AS) ACTION (CXJ   1 AFDO)
CYD   1 DD GE/AEW
CAV   1 DI 55
CAV   1 DSTI

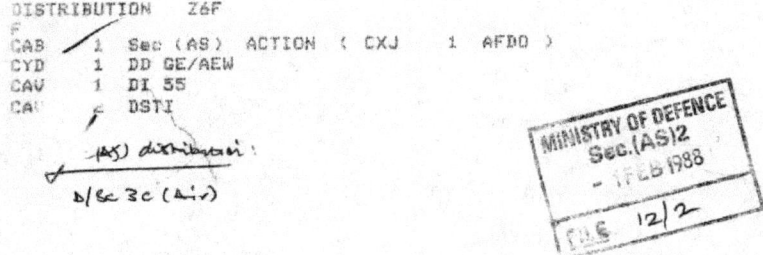

(AS) distribution:
D/Sc 3c (Air)

MINISTRY OF DEFENCE
Sec.(AS)2
- 1 FEB 1988
FILE   12/2

U N C L A S S I F I E D

CWD004 01/0836 032C0511

FOR CAB

ROUTINE 0107442 FEB 89

FROM   RAF WEST DRAYTON
TO   MODUK AIR

U N C L A S S I F I E D
SIC Z6F
SUBJECT: AERIAL PHENOMENA
A. 311730Z JAN 88, 2 TO 3 MINUTES
B. 1 OBJECT OF UNKNOWN SIZE OR SHAPE WITH 2 BRIGHT PARALLEL LIGHTS
C. Section 40   HAMPSTEAD, INDOORS, STATIONARY
D. NAKED EYE
E. MOVING DOWNWARDS
F. N/K
G. 100 YARDS
H. STEADY
J. CAVOK
K. RESIDENTIAL AREA
L. POLICE
M. Section 40
N. NONE

PAGE 2 RBDAID 003   UNCLAS
O. SMALL DAUGHTER
P. 311744 JAN 88
BT

DISTRIBUTION   Z6F
F
CAB   1   Sec (AS) ACTION (CXJ   1   AFDO)
CYD   1   DD GE/AEW
CAV   1   DI 55
CAV   2   DSTI

U N C L A S S I F I E D

CAB007 01/0826 032C0485

FOR CAB

ROUTINE 010745Z FEB 88

FROM   RAF WEST DRAYTON
TO   MODUK AIR

U N C L A S S I F I E D
SIC Z6F
SUBJECT: AERIAL PHENOMENA
A. 310620 JAN 88
B. 1 VERY BRIGHT STATIONARY OBJECT
C. OVER BEACH AT MANCHESTER AIRPORT, OUTDOORS, STATIONARY
D. NAKED EYE
E. WEST
F. N/K
G. N/K
H. STATIONARY
J. N/K
K. NONE
L. MANCHESTER POLICE
M. PC Section 40 CHEADLE HUME POLICE
N. NONE

PAGE 2 RBDAID 002 UNCLAS
O. NONE
P. 010200Z JAN
BT

DISTRIBUTION   Z6
F
CAB   1 Sec (AS) ACTION (CXJ   1   AFDO)
CYD   1 DD GE/AEW
CAV   1 DI 55
CAV   2 DSTI

UNCLASSIFIED

CAB009 01/0836 032C0510

FOR CAB

ROUTINE 010738Z FEB 88

FROM   RAF WEST DRAYTON
TO   MODUK AIR

UNCLASSIFIED
SIC Z6F
SUBJECT: AERIAL PHENOMENA
A. 280645Z JAN 88
B. ALTERNATING WHITE AND GREEN
C. Section 40   SKETTY SWANSEA, INDOORS
D. NAKED EYE
E. STRAIGHT ABOVE
F. UP
G. N/K
H. N/K
J. DAWN
K. N/K
L. BRIDEND POLICE
M. Section 40
O. N/K

PAGE 2 RBDAID 001   UNCLAS
P. 300800Z JAN 88
BT

DISTRIBUTION   Z6F
F
CAB   1   Sec (AS) ACTION (CXJ   1   AFDO
CYD   1   DD GE/AE
CAV   1   DI 55
CAV   2   DSTI

MINISTRY OF DEFENCE
Sec(AS)2
- 11 FEB 1988
D16 12/2

12/2

182

ANNEX A TO
SOP 502

REPORT OF AN UNIDENTIFIED FLYING OBJECT

A.	Date, Time & Duration of Sighting	30 Jan 88 20 Mins
B.	Description of Object (No of objects, size, shape, colour, brightness)	One bright star shaped object multi coloured — mauve, green and yellow
C.	Exact Position of Observer Location, indoor/outdoor, stationary/moving	Indoors
D.	How Observed (naked eye, binoculars, other optical device, still or movie	Naked eye and Binoculars
E.	Direction in which object first seen (A landmark may be more useful than a badly estimated bearing)	Over Stanmore Golf course
F.	Angle of Sight (Estimated heights are unreliable)	Approx 20 to 30 degrees
G.	Distance (By reference to a known landmark	Not known
H.	Movements (Changes in E, F & G may be of more use than estimates of course and speed)	Bobbing up and down
J.	Met Conditions during Observations (Moving clouds, haze, mist etc)	Clear sky
K.	Nearby Objects (Telephone lines, high voltage lines, reservoir, lake or dam, swamp or marsh, river, high buildings, tall chimneys, steeples, spires, TV or radio masts, airfields, generating plant, factories, pits or other sites with floodlights or night lighting)	None.

L   To whom reported (Police,   RAF Bentley Priory then
     military, press etc)   UKRAOC

M.   Name & Address of Informant
        NB. However the telephone number was
                                         unattainable. RAOC checked with
                                         directory enquiries and found there
                                         were 2 Section 40   and that
                                         the one at Section 40   was Ex Directory

N.   Background of Informant that   Had not been drinking
may be volunteered

O.   Other Witnesses   Informants wife.

                                              Details taken by RAOC
P.   Date, Time of Receipt   300250Z Jan 88

Q.   Any Unusual Meteorological   NIL
     Conditions

R.   Remarks   Informant rang the Guardroom
     -------   at Stanmore and Bentley
                                              Priory to ask them to check
                                              if any other reported sightin
                                              The answer given was none.,

                                    Section 40

                                    Sqn Ldr
                                    Duty Ops Office
Date: 30 Jan 88   AF Ops

Distribution:

Sec(AS)2
AEW/GE
DI 55
File AF Ops/2/5/1

U N C L A S S I F I E D

CWD330 28/2324 028C5214

FOR CAB

ROUTINE 281925Z JAN 88

FROM   RAF WEST DRAYTON
TO   MODUK AIR

U N C L A S S I F I E D
SIC Z6F
SUBJECT: AERIAL PHENOMENA
A. 28 JAN 88, 1730 SEEN FOR 30 SECS
B.1. SHAPED LIKE UPTURNED SAUCER LIP GREEN TOP DOMED WITH FLASHING
YELLOW LIGHTS. STARTED TO ROTATE THEN WENT UP AND DISAPPEARED, MADE
NOISE SIMILAR TO AIRSHIP
C. STANWELL, INDOORS CONSERVA
D. NAKED EYE
E. TOWARDS HEATHROW
F. NOT GIVEN
G. NOT KNOWN
H. STEADY
J. CLOUD BASE AT HEATHR... 600 FT
K. HOUSES
L. AIS(M) RAF WEST DRAYTON

PAGE 2 RBDAID 007 UNCLAS
M. Section 40   (AGED 10) Section 40
N. HAS BEEN VERY QUIET SINCE SEEING OBJECT
O. NOISE HEARD BY BOYS MOTHER AND GRAND MOTHER
P. REPORT RECEIVED BY AIS(M) AT 1900
BT

DISTRIBUTION   Z6F
F
CAB   1 Sec (AS) ACTION (CXJ   1 AFDD)
CYD   1 DD GE/AEW
CAV   1 DI 55
CAV / 2 DSTI

 b SC 2a (Air)

MINISTRY OF DEFENCE
Sec.(AS)2
29 JAN 1988

FILE 12/2

U N C L A S S I F I E D

CAB072 28/1233 028C2337

FOR CAi

ROUTINE 291040Z JAN 88

FROM   RAF WEST DRAYTON
TO   MODUK AIR

U N C L A S S I F I E D
SIC Z6F
SUBJECT: AERIAL PHENOME...
A. 270735Z FOUR MINS
B. ONE, MAISONETTE SIZED OBJECT. 3 LIGHS ON TOP WITH 2 LIGHTS
BELOW
C. Section 40   PYLE, NEAR BRIDGEND, GLAMORGAN, OUTDOORS
D. NAKED EYE
E. FACING EAST, OBJECT POSITIONED OVER SOUTH CONNEILY
G. HALF A MILE AWAY
H. LOW IN SKY, DEPARTED IN A NORTHERLY DIRECTION
J. CLEAR SKY, DARK
L. SOUTH WALES CONSTABULARY, SGT Section 40
M. Section 40
N. WISHES TO REMAIN ANONYMOUS
O. NONE

PAGE 2 RBDAID 001 UNCLAS
P. 272042Z JAN 88
BT

DISTRIBUTION   Zor
F
CAB   1   Sec (AS) ACTION (CXJ   1   AFDO
CYD   1   DD GE/AEW
CAV   1   DI 55
CAV   2   DSTI

     ~~Distribui~~:

        D Sc Sc (Air)

STAFFORDSHIRE POLICE

𝓔𝓕 (AS) C.C.
GES
D I SS
D Q.3c (Air)

E90/2

phone: Section 40
Telex: Section 40

Our Ref. RT/JP

Your Ref.

Chief Constable's Office.
Cannock Road.
Stafford.
ST17 0QG.

27TH JANUARY, 1988.

Dear Sir,

REPORT OF AN UNIDENTIFIED FLYING OBJECT

A. **DATE, TIME AND DURATION OF SIGHTING**

9TH DECEMBER, 1987 AT 17.05 AND 17.10 HRS.
FOR APPROX. 3 MINUTES DURATION.

Section 40 — sounds like an aircraft to me. Is this one of our usual B'ham air port routes?

B. **DESCRIPTION OF OBJECT** ONE LARGE, STEADY BRIGHT LIGHT
WITH FIVE SMALLER OVAL WHITE LIGHTS ALONGSIDE IN LINE
ABREAST FORMATION, FOLLOWED ALONG BY TWO SMALL WHITE
LIGHTS ACCOMPANIED BY A LOW PITCHED ROARING SOUND.

Section 40 — 22/2

C. **EXACT POSITION OBSERVED** THE FIRST SIGHTING WAS SEEN TO
APPROACH FROM CANNOCK AT A HIGH ALTITUDE, PASS OVERHEAD AND
GRADUALLY DISAPPEAR FROM VIEW AS IT TRAVELLED TOWARDS LICHFIELD.
THE SECOND SIGHTING WAS EXACTLY THE SAME BUT WAS NOT SEEN
AS IT APPROACHED BUT SEEN AS IT WENT OVERHEAD.

D. **HOW OBSERVED**

NAKED EYE.

E. **DIRECTION IN WHICH OBJECT WAS FIRST SEEN**

DESCRIBED AS TRAVELLING IN A STRAIGHT UNIFORM
PATH AT SPEED FROM CANNOCK TOWARDS LICHFIELD.

F. **ANGLE OF SIGHT**

VIEWED LOOKING VERTICALLY UPWARDS.

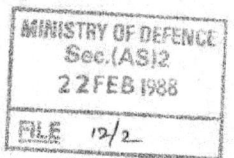

MINISTRY OF DEFENCE
Sec.(AS)2
22 FEB 1988
FILE 12/2

The person dealing with this correspondence is:

P.C. Section 40

G. **DISTANCE**

SEEN TO APPROACH, PASS OVERHEAD AND THEN GRADUALLY DISAPPEAR FROM VIEW.

H. **MOVEMENTS**

TRAVELLED IN A STRAIGHT LINE WEST TO EAST.

J. **METEOROLOGICAL CONDITIONS DURING OBSERVATIONS**

FINE CLEAR NIGHT. SEVERE FROST. HALF MOON VISIBILITY GOOD.

K. **NEARBY OBJECTS**

AREA OF WATER KNOWN AS CHASEWATER. TELEVISION MAST WITH NIGHT LIGHTS AT SUTTON COLDFIELD AND A POWER STATION AT RUGELEY. NOT VISIBLE FROM THE SCENE.

L. **TO WHOM REPORTED**

P.C.  CHASETOWN POLICE STATION

M. **NAME AND ADDRESS OF INFORMANT**

N. **ANY BACKGROUND ON THE INFORMANT THAT MAY BE VOLUNTEERED**

APPEAR REASONABLE, RATIONAL PEOPLE AND NO REASON CAN BE SEEN FOR THEM TO FABRICATE THEIR ACCOUNTS OF WHAT THEY HAD SEEN.

O. **OTHER WITNESSES**

P. DATE AND TIME OF RECEIPT OF REPORT

9TH DECEMBER, 1987 AT 17.25HRS.

Q. IS A REPLY REQUESTED?

No.

AIR TRAFFIC CONTROL ACTION

INFORMED AT TIME OF SIGHTINGS.

Yours faithfully

Section 40

Chief Constable

Section 40

Department of Trade and Industry,
National Air Traffic Control Services.
1, Victoria Street,
LONDON,
SW1H OET

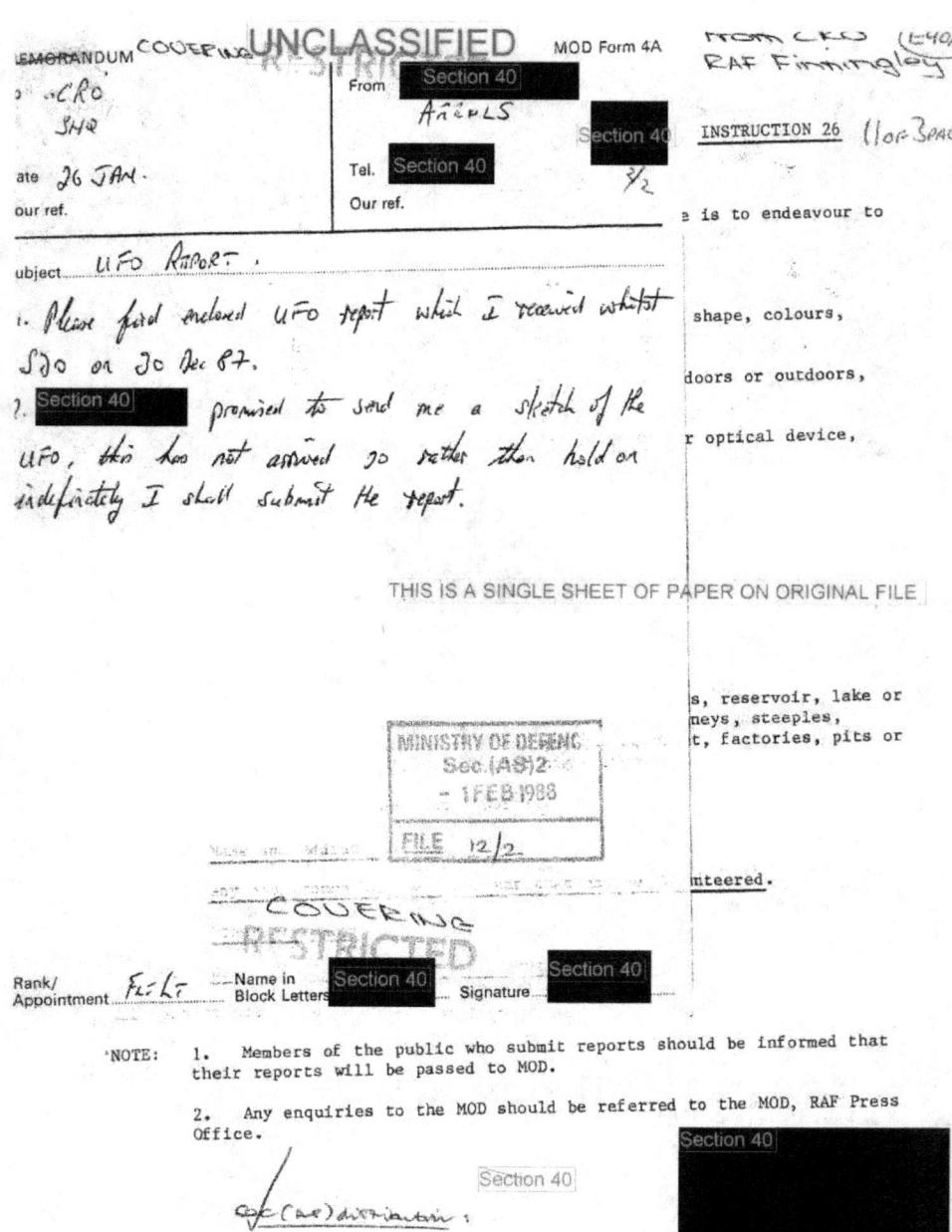

MEMORANDUM COVERING

CRO
SHQ

Date 26 JAN.

our ref.

MOD Form 4A

From Section 40

Aî&rLS

Section 40

Tel. Section 40

Our ref.

FROM CRO (E40/1)
RAF Finningley

INSTRUCTION 26 (1 OF 3 PAGES)

2/2

subject   UFO RAPORT.

1. Please find enclosed UFO report which I received whilst
SDO on 30 Dec 87.

2. Section 40   promised to send me a sketch of the
UFO, this has not arrived so rather than hold on
indefinitely I shall submit the report.

is to endeavour to

shape, colours,

doors or outdoors,

r optical device,

THIS IS A SINGLE SHEET OF PAPER ON ORIGINAL FILE

MINISTRY OF DEFENC
Sec.(AS)2
- 1 FEB 1988
FILE 12/2

s, reservoir, lake or
neys, steeples,
t, factories, pits or

nteered.

COVERING
RESTRICTED

Rank/   FL-LT   Name in   Section 40   Section 40
Appointment   Block Letters   Signature

'NOTE: 1.   Members of the public who submit reports should be informed that
their reports will be passed to MOD.

2.   Any enquiries to the MOD should be referred to the MOD, RAF Press
Office.

Section 40

Section 40

C.C (AS) distribution :

GE (AEN) GPS
D155   note: I have spoken to RAFPC
D/SCRC(Air)   about the classification.
                   i.e. THAT it should be unclassified.

Flt Lt
OC GD Flt
ext Section 40

Dec 85

COVERING

Section 40
2/2

REPORTS OF UNIDENTIFIED FLYING OBJECTS (UFOs)

1. Should the SDO or the OO received a report of a UFO he is to endeavour to obtain the following information:

    a. Date, Time and Duration of Sighting. (Local).

    b. Description of Object. Including number, size, shape, colours, brightness, sound, smell etc.

    c. The exact position of the observer. Whether indoors or outdoors, stationary or moving.

    d. How it was seen, ie, naked eye, binoculars, other optical device, still or movie camera.

    e. The direction in which object was first seen.

    f. The height of the object.

    g. How far away.

    h. Whether it changed direction.

    i. Weather.

    j. Landmarks. (Telephone lines, high voltage lines, reservoir, lake or dam, swamp or marsh, river, high buildings, tall chimneys, steeples, spires, TV or radio masts, airfields, generating plant, factories, pits or other sites with floodlights or other night lighting.

    k. To whom the incident was reported

    l. Name and Address of Informant.

    m. Any background of the Informant that may be Volunteered.

    n. Other Witnesses.

    o. Date and Time of Receipt of Report.

All reports are to be submitted to Station Ops Off.

NOTE: 1. Members of the public who submit reports should be informed that their reports will be passed to MOD.

        2. Any enquiries to the MOD should be referred to the MOD, RAF Press Office.

Section 40

Flt Lt
OC GD Flt
ext Section 40

Dec 85

UNIDENTIFIED FLYING OBJECT REPORT

a.   29 Dec 87, 2020, 5 mins.

b.   Bell shaped, one, no noise, one bright white light + 2 others football size.
Red light, blue. Orange one on top. Bottom of UFO revolving, no smell?

c.   Outdoors, middle of Section 40 Rotherham, moving
pedestrian.

d.   Naked eye.

e.   Doncaster travel towards Sheffield.

f.   Low, 40 ft above houses, pylon height.

g. $\frac{1}{4}$-$\frac{1}{2}$ mile.

h.   Same direction.

i.   Clear, moonlight, no rain, good visibility.

j.   Pylons, 4 dams, no pit lights on.

k.   Rotherham police - PC Section 40 (Rotherham Main Police Stn - Section 40

l.   Section 40

m.   Police say seems reliable witness.

n.   Wife of Section 40

o.   29 Dec 87, 2040.

Possible a/c heading for Manchester ties in with flight path. No press, confidential
please.

U N C L A S S I F I E D

CAB009 25/0912 025C0636

FOR CAB

ROUTINE 250815Z JAN 88

FROM   RAF WEST DRAYTON
TO   MODUK AIR

U N C L A S S I F I E D
SIC Z6F
SUBJECT. AERIAL PHENOMENA
A. 242340Z JAN 10 MINS
B. ONE BRIGHT OBLONG SHAPE WITH TWO FLASHING RED FLIGHTS
C. HOME ADDRESS
D. NAKED EYE
E. FROM DIRECTION OF ARRAN
F. APPEARED QUITE HIGH
G. 15-20 MILES
H. MOVED TO LEFT THEN APPEARED TO MOVE TOWARDS THEM
J. CLOUDY QUITE BRIGHT
K. NIL
L. ATC PRESTWICK AND SCATCC CAB SUPERVISOR WHO SAID THAT SCATCC
DID HAVE AN AIRCRAFT OUTBOUND FROM GLASGOW TO BELFAST AT ABOUT THAT
TIME

PAGE 2 RBDAID 001 UNCL..
M. Section 40   KILDA BANK IRVINE AYRSHIRE
N. N/A
O. INFORMANTS WIF
P. 2500212 JAN 8?
BT

DISTRIBUTION Z6F
F
CAB   1 Sec (AS) ACTION CXJ   1 AFDO
CYB   1 DD GE/
CAV   1 DI 55
CAV   2 DSTI

cof (AS) Aviation

D)ec 3 (A/n).

MINISTRY OF DEFENCE
Sec.(AS)2
2 5 JAN 1988
FILE 12/2

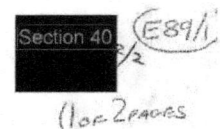

Section 40 E89/1

FIN/2286/Org

(1 of 2 PAGES)

REPORT OF AN UNIDENTIFIED FLYING OBJECT

A. Date, Time and Duration of Sighting. 24 JAN 88. 2045 HRS

B. Description of Object. VERY BRIGHT LIGHT.

C. Exact Position Observer. Section 40
SHEFFIELD

Sc (AS) DISTRIBUTION:
GE (AEW) GE2
D1 58
D/Sc 3c (Air)

D. How Observed. NAKED EYE

E. Direction in which Object was first seen.
FROM SOUTH TO NORTH.
WEST OF MOSBOROUGH VILLAGE

any knowledge of military aircraft trailing an unidentified object?

F. Angle of Sight.
NK.

G. Distance.
NK
Section 40 2/-

H. Movements.
VERY FAST MOVING IN STRAIGHT LINE

J. Meteorological conditions during observation.
GOOD CLEAR SKY

K. Nearby objects.
NO.

L. To whom reported.
SHEFFIELD POLICE
SHEFFIELD STAR

M. Name and Address of informant. Section 40
Section 40

N. Any background on the informant that may be volunteered.
FIRST TIME SHE'S EVER SEEN UFO

O. Other witnesses.
HUSBAND + OTHERS

P. Date and time of receipt of report.
25 JAN 88 1637 HRS

MINISTRY OF DEFENCE
Sec.(AS)2
- 1 FEB 1988
FILE 12/2

Q. Is a reply requested.
YES.   (PC Section 40 SSE HACKENTHORPE POLICE
SHEFF Section 40

Other Information: Section 40 saw object followed by '6 military aircraft'. A/c following object had flashing lights on them. Object increased speed leaving a/c behind.

RESTRICTED

194

The Community Relations Officer

ROYAL AIR FORCE
FINNINGLEY
DONCASTER, SOUTH YORKSHIRE DN9 3LQ
Tel. DONCASTER Section 40

FIN/2286/Org

Section 40

2 January 1988

Dear Section 40

REPORT OF UNIDENTIFIED FLYING OBJECT

I have been contacted by PC Section 40 of Mackenthorpe Police Station concerning your sighting of an Unidentified Flying Object.

I have passed details of the sighting to the Ministry of Defence Department concerned, who will contact you should they need further information.

Yours sincerely

Section 40

Flight Lieutenant
for Officer Commanding

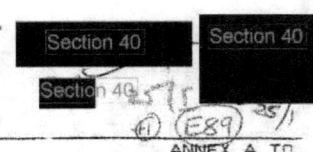
REPORT OF AN UNIDENTIFIED FLYING OBJECT

A.	Date, Time & Duration of Sighting	221815ZJAN 88 15-20 Mins
B.	Description of Object (No of objects, size, shape, colour, brightness)	One object, Bright yellow rising from Park.
C.	Exact Position of Observer Location, indoor/outdoor, stationary/moving	Outdoors walking
D.	How Observed (naked eye, binoculars, other optical device, still or movie	Naked eye
E.	Direction in which object first seen (A landmark may be more useful than a badly estimated bearing)	Over Abington Park Northampton.
F.	Angle of Sight (Estimated heights are unreliable)	Approx 45 degrees
G.	Distance (By reference to a known landmark	100-200 ft of ground.
H.	Movements (Changes in E, F & G may be of more use than estimates of course and speed)	200 to 1000 ft variable slight angle
J.	Met Conditions during Observations (Moving clouds, haze, mist etc)	Clear sky
K.	Nearby Objects (Telephone lines, high voltage lines, reservoir, lake or dam, swamp or marsh, river, high buildings, tall chimneys, steeples, spires, TV or radio masts, airfields, generating plant, factories, pits or other sites with floodlights or night lighting)	Houses/Trees in park

| L. | To whom reported (Police, military, press etc) | Northampton Police |

| M. | Name & Address of Informant | |

| N. | Background of Informant that may be volunteered | Has seen a UFO in the past |

| O. | Other Witnesses | one female, details not given. |

| P. | Date, Time of Receipt | Details taken by AF Ops 222011Z Jan 88 |

| Q. | Any Unusual Meteorological Conditions | NIL |

| R. | Remarks | Informant at first thought it was an aircraft in distres Satellite burning up. |

Sqn Ldr
Duty Ops Officer
AF Ops

Date: 22 Jan 88

Distribution:

Sec(AS)2
AEW/GE
DI 55
File AF Ops/2/5/1
Sec (AS) distribution:

D/Sc 3 (Air)

Section 40

FIN/2286/Org

REPORT OF AN UNIDENTIFIED FLYING OBJECT

A. Date, Time and Duration of Sighting. 19 JAN 88

    2015 HRS. 90 SECONDS

B. Description of Object.

    LIGHT ORANGE BALL OF LIGHT (NAKED EYE)
    DO-NUT SHAPE (THROUGH BINOCULARS)

C. Exact Position Observer.

    KEPLES COLUMN, THORPE HESLEY
    LOUDEN ROAD

D. How Observed.

    NAKED EYE + BINOCULARS

E. Direction in which Object was first seen.

    NE

F. Angle of Sight.

    40°

G. Distance.

    (OVER WENTWORTH AREA) 1 mile?

H. Movements.

    FLYING IN SLIGHT CURVE TO SW

J. Meteorological conditions during observation.

    PATCHY CLOUD

K. Nearby objects.

    KEPLES COLUMN (40FT TOWER)

L. To whom reported.

    ROTHERHAM POLICE
    YORKS UFO SOCIETY

M. Name and Address of informant.

    Section 40

    HEELINGTHORPE, ROTHERHAM.

N. Any background on the informant that may be volunteered.

    YORKS UFO SOCIETY

O. Other witnesses.

    3 OTHERS (IN SAME LOCATION)

P. Date and time of receipt of report.

    20 JAN 88. 1452 HRS.

Q. Is a reply requested.

    YES - Attached copy + gpd.

MINISTRY OF DEFENCE
AS/2
2 0 JAN 1988
FILE 12/2
and 12/3

Sec (AS) distribution :

    GE(ASN) GE3
    D I 55
    D/Sc 3c (Air)

RESTRICTED
UNCLASSIFIED

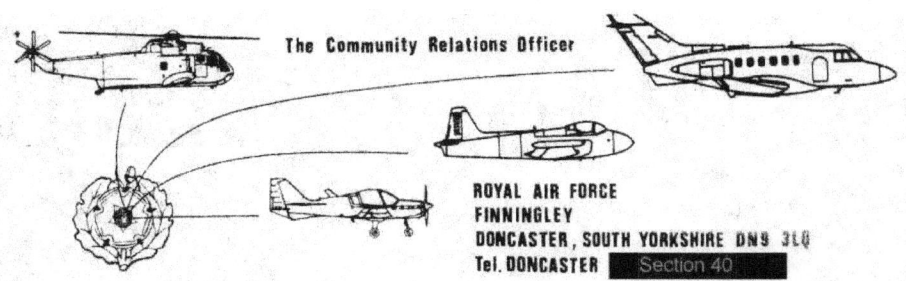

The Community Relations Officer

ROYAL AIR FORCE
FINNINGLEY
DONCASTER, SOUTH YORKSHIRE DN9 3LG
Tel. DONCASTER

FIN/2286/Org

2/ January 1988

Dear Section 40

REPORT OF UNIDENTIFIED FLYING OBJECT

Further to our telephone conversation, I can confirm that I have passed details of your sighting of an Unidentified Flying Object to the Ministry of Defence Department concerned. I have informed them of your address and they will contact you if they wish to obtain more details.

Yours sincerely

Section 40

Flight Lieutenant
for Officer Commanding

199

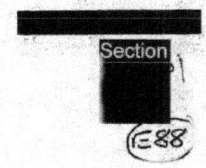

U N C L A S S I F I E D

CWD187 19/2242 019C5327

FOR CAB

ROUTINE/ROUTINE 191135Z

FROM   RAF VALLEY
TO   MODUK
INFO   HQRAFSC

U N C L A S S I F I E D
SIC Z6F/Z99
MODUK FOR DS8, HQRAFSC FOR CPSYO
REPORT OF UNIDENTIFIED FLYING OBJECT
A. 152045A JAN 88, APPROX 1 HOUR
B. SINGLE OBJECT DIAMOND LIKE, MANY AND VARIED COLOURS EMANATING
FROM OBJECT, VERY BRIGHT, NO SOUND
C. OUTDOORS, SEEN OVER JUBILLEE MOUNTAIN NR PENMAENMAWR, N WALES
COAST. OBJECT REMAINED STATIONARY THROUGHOUT 1 HOUR PERIOD BEFORE
MOVING SLOWLY EASTWARD
D. INITIALLY VVIEWED WITH NAKED EYE THEN BINOCULARS
E. APPROX 1 MILE SW OF DWYGYFYLCHI
F. UNABLE TO PROVIDE ANGLE OF SIGHT
G. APPROX 1 TO 1 1/2 MILES DISTANT
H. EASTWARDS

PAGE 2 RBDDVS 011   UNCLAS
J. CLEAR SKY, BRIGHT MOON
K. NONE
L. COLWYN BAY POLICE
M. Section 40
N. NONE
O. NEIGHBOURS AND COLWYN BAY POLICE
P. 152100A JAN 88
BT

DISTRIBUTION
G
NO SDL

DISTRIBUTION (Z99
Z
CAB 1/ SEC(AS) ACTION (CYR 1 RES CLERK)
    & (AS) distribution
    ∆ E 8 (Air)
    ∆ 1 55

MINISTRY OF DEFENCE
Sec.(AS)2
20 JAN 1988
FILE 12/2

200

MOD Form 4A

MEMORANDUM

To MOD D/Sec/AS (AIR)

From CRO
RAF FINNINGLEY

Ref. FIN/2286/ORG

Date 18 JAN 88

Tel.   Ext. Section

Subject REPORT OF UFO - 14 JAN 88

1. Find enclosed a copy of a UFO report received on 14 Jan 88.

2. A letter acknowledging receipt of the report has been sent to the informant.

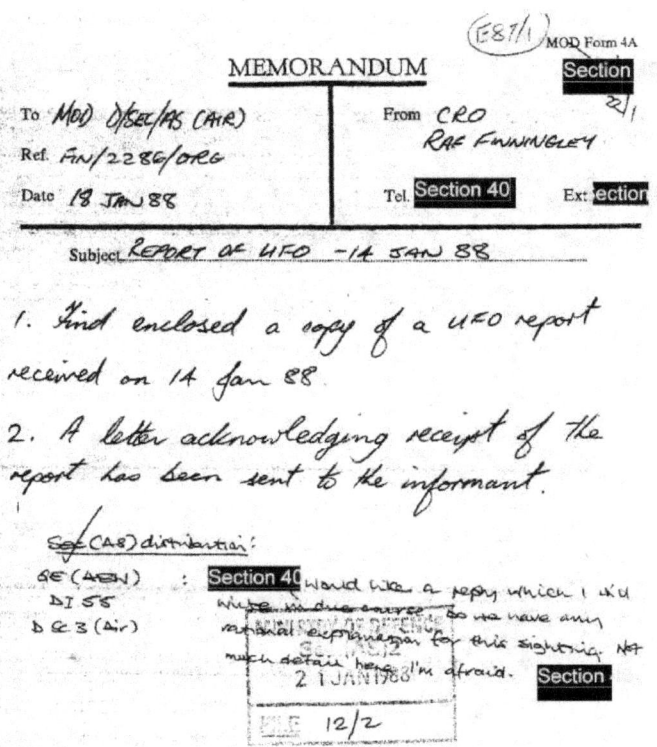

Sec (AS) distribution:

Sec (AS)   :   Would like a reply which I will write in due course so we have any material explanation for this sighting. Not much detail here I'm afraid.   Section

DI 55

D Ec 3 (Air)

MINISTRY OF DEFENCE

2 1 JAN 1988

FILE 12/2

Rank/
~~Appointment~~ Plt Off   Name in block letters   Signature

Complete this form in manuscript unless there are special reasons for typing.

910378 56-5249 6/71 J.P.L.

FIN/2286/Org

REPORT OF AN UNIDENTIFIED FLYING OBJECT

A. Date, Time and Duration of Sighting.
   7 JAN 88. 1930 - 2030 HRS
B. Description of Object.
   OVAL SHAPED LIGHTS. 4 OBJECTS (1 LARGE).

C. Exact Position Observer.
   OLD HALL ROAD
   OLD BRAMPTON, CHESTERFIELD
D. How Observed.
   NAKED EYE AND THROUGH BINOCULARS

E. Direction in which Object was first seen.
   NNW (STATIONERY)

F. Angle of Sight.
   25°

G. Distance.
   —

H. Movements.
   3 STILL. 1 MOVING SLIGHTLY
J. Meteorological conditions during observation.
   PERFECT. VERY CLEAR

K. Nearby objects.
   1 AIRCRAFT PASSED NEARBY.
   OTHERWISE NONE
L. To whom reported.
   POLICE, CHESTERFIELD
   DERBYSHIRE TELEGRAPH
M. Name and Address of informant.

N. Any background on the informant that may be volunteered.
   (EX RAF REGT) 40EKS UFO SOCIETY FOR
                    SOME YEARS
O. Other witnesses.
   7 PEOPLE IN TOTAL

P. Date and time of receipt of report.
   14 JAN 88. 1045 HRS

Q. Is a reply requested.
   YES PLEASE

Similar sighting seen over Eckel
in evening.

U N C L A S S I F I E D

CA8051 18/1537 018C2840

FOR CAS

ROUTINE 181415Z JAN 88

FROM   RAF WEST DRAYTON
TO   MODUK AIR

U N C L A S S I F I E I
SIG Z6F
SUBJECT: AERIAL PHENOMENA
FIRST REPORT A. 171730 JAN FOR A FEW SECONDS
B. WHITE BALL OF LIGHT WITH A BLUE FLAME
C. A243 KINGSTON RD, LEATHERHEAD, SURREY QUARTER OF A MILE NORTH OF
JUNCTION J9 OF THE M25, OBSERVER DRIVING A PRIVATE CAR
D. NAKED EYE
E. TO THE EAST TRAVELLING TOWARDS THE WEST
F. ESTIMATE BELOW 1000 FT (SKY OBSCURED/FOG)
G. NO REFERENCE
H. STEADY EAST TO WEST
J. FOGGY
K. OPEN COUNTRY
L. LEATHERHEAD POLICE
M. Section 40

PAGE 2 RBDAID 008   UNCLAS
N. NIL
O. NONE
P. 181320 JAN 88
SECOND REPORT A. 171730 JAN FOR A FEW SECONDS
B. LARGE GREEN AND YELLOW OBJECT, NO SOUND
C. Section 40   BOOKHAM VILLAGE NEAR LEATHERHEAD, JUST OFF THE
HIGH STREET
D. NAKED EYE
E. FROM DORKING AREA TRAVELLED TOWARDS THE WEST
F. NO ESTIMATE
G. NONE
H. STRAIGHT LINE VERY VERY FAST
J. FOGGY
K. RESIDENTIAL AREA
L. LEATHERHEAD POLICE
M. Section 40
N. NONE
O. NONE
P. 181325 JAN 88
BT

(E88)

U N C L A S S I F I E D

CAB051 18/1537 018CE040

FOR CAB

ROUTINE 181415Z JAN 88

FROM   RAF WEST DRAYTON
TO   MODUK AIR

U N C L A S S I F I E D
SIG Z4F
SUBJECT: AERIAL PHENOMENA
FIRST REPORT A. 171730 JAN FOR A FEW SECONDS
B. WHITE BALL OF LIGHT WITH A BLUE FLAME
C. A243 KINGSTON RD, LEATHERHEAD, SURREY QUARTER OF A MILE NORTH OF
JUNCTION J9 OF THE M25, OBSERVER DRIVING A PRIVATE CAR
D. NAKED EYE
E. TO THE EAST TRAVELLING TOWARDS THE WEST
F. ESTIMATE BELOW 1000 FT (SKY OBSCURED/FOG)
G. NO REFERENCE
H. STEADY EAST TO WEST
J. FOGGY
K. OPEN COUNTRY
L. LEATHERHEAD POLICE
M. Section 40

PAGE 2 RBDAID 008   UNCLAS
N. NIL
O. NONE
P. 181320 JAN 88
SECOND REPORT A. 171730 JAN FOR A FEW SECONDS   (E88)
B. LARGE GREEN AND YELLOW OBJECT, NO SOUND
C. Section 40   BOOKHAM VILLAGE NEAR LEATHERHEAD, JUST OFF THE
HIGH STREET
D. NAKED EYE
E. FROM DORKING AREA TRAVELLED TOWARDS THE WEST
F. NO ESTIMATE
G. NONE
H. STRAIGHT LINE VERY VERY FAST
J. FOGGY
K. RESIDENTIAL AREA
L. LEATHERHEAD POLICE
M. Section 40
N. NONE
O. NONE
P. 181325 JAN 88
BT

U N C L A S S I F I E D

CWD017 18/0905 018C0417

FOR CAB

ROUTINE 180730Z JAN 88

FROM   RAF WEST DRAYTON
TO   MODUK AIR

U N C L A S S I F I E D
SIC Z6F
SUBJECT AERIAL PHENOMENA
A. 11 OR 18 DEC 87
B. ONE GREY OCTAGANAL SHAPED OBJECT WITH LIGHTS AT EACH POINT. VERY
BRIGHT, SIX CAR WIDTHS LONG (APPROX. 40 FT SQUARE)
C. OUTDOORS MOVING, TRAVELING ALONG THE A12 ROAD EAST 5 MILES FROM
CHELMSFORD TURN OFF
D. NAKED EYE THROUGH CAR SUNROOF
E. LEFT TO RIGHT ACROSS ROAD
F. HEIGHT OF POST OFFICE TOWER
J. LATE AFTERNOON SUN GOING DOWN
L. MILITARY ORGANISATION
M. Section 40
N. FIGHTER PILOT
O. PASSENGER IN CAR

PAGE 2 RBDAID 001 UNCLAS
P. 172000 JAN 88
BT

DISTRIBUTION   Z6F
F
CAB   1 Sec (AS) ACTION (CXJ   1 AFDO
CYD   1 DD GE/AEW
CAV   1 DI 55
CAV   2 DSTI

Sec (AS) distribution
D/Sc3 (Air)

MINISTRY OF DEFENCE
Sec.(AS)2
18 JAN 1988

FILE 2/2

With Compliments

National Air Traffic Services
Control Tower, Gatwick Airport, West Sussex, RH6 0LD
Telephone
A joint Civil Aviation Authority — Ministry of Defence Service

19/1/88

REPORT OF AN UNIDENTIFIED FLYING OBJECT

A Date, time and duration of sighting (Local times to be quoted)

17/1/88 . 1715 local about 2 seconds.

B Description of object (Number of objects, size, shape, colours, brightness, sound, smell, etc).

1 very bright object, lime green colour with rocket. like orange trail. Bullet shaped about the size of medium twin Beech AK. No sound or smell detected

C Exact position observer (Geographical location. Indoors or outdoors. Stationary or moving).

Indoors at address below.

D How observed (Naked eye, binoculars, other optical device, still or movie camera).

Naked eye.

E Direction in which object was first seen (A landmark may be more useful than a badly estimated bearing).

First observed to the south. 180° bearing from observer.

F Angle of sight (Estimated heights are unreliable).

20° above horizontal. Approx. 7000ft altitude.

G Distance (By reference to a known landmark wherever possible).

overhead Epsom Common, around 1 mile.

H Movements (Changes in E, F and G may be of more use than estimates of course and speed).

Object moved from south of observer and disappeared from observer bearing around 260°. Object moved horizontally at around 800 m.p.h. Last seen N. side of Epsom Common.

J Meteorological conditions during observations (Moving clouds, haze, mist etc).

3/8 cloud approx. Surface visibility 1-2 miles. Height not known.

K Nearby objects (Telephone lines; high voltage lines; reservoir, lake or dam; swamp or marsh; river; high buildings, tall chimneys, steeples, spires, TV or radio masts; airfields; generating plant; factories, pits or other sites with flood-lights or other night lighting).

Houses & trees none more than 25feet tall. The area is residential only and very dark at night.

L To whom reported (Police, military organisations, the press etc).

Epsom Police

M Name and address of informant

Section 40   EPSOM, SURREY.

N Any background on the informant that may be volunteered (EPSOM Section 40

Section 40   Biggin Hill airport.

O Other witnesses Note. Section 40 stated that he holds a PPL.

NONE

P Date and time of receipt of report 1805 approx same day.

Q Is a reply requested? YES.

SEC (AS) 2

REPORT OF AN UNIDENTIFIED FLYING OBJECT

A.	Date, Time & Duration of Sighting	171706ZJAN 88 6-7 seconds.
B.	Description of Object (No of objects, size, shape, colour, brightness)	One object, similar to a flare - brilliant white with a long tail.
C.	Exact Position of Observer Location, indoor/outdoor, stationary/moving	Outdoors walking close to home - stood stationary to observe object.
D.	How Observed (naked eye, binoculars, other optical device, still or movie	Naked eye
E.	Direction in which object first seen (A landmark may be more useful than a badly estimated bearing)	South of observer.
F.	Angle of Sight (Estimated heights are unreliable)	Approx 20 degrees (CHANGE)
G.	Distance (By reference to a known landmark	4 - 5 km
H.	Movements (Changes in E, F & G may be of more use than estimates of course and speed)	Constant speed and directio... East to West. Through an 80 Degree arc. (ADDITION)
J.	Met Conditions during Observations (Moving clouds, haze, mist etc)	Clear sky
K.	Nearby Objects (Telephone lines, high voltage lines, reservoir, lake or dam, swamp or marsh, river, high buildings, tall chimneys, steeples, spires, TV or radio masts, airfields, generating plant, factories, pits or other sites with floodlights or night lighting)	None.

To whom reported (Police, military, press etc)   West Byefleet Police.

M.   Name & Address of Informant
                                                         West Byefleet
                                                         Tel: West Byefleet

N.   Background of Informant that   Has seen a UFO in the past
may be volunteered   but was some time ago.

O.   Other Witnesses   Informants wife.

                                                         Details taken by AF Ops
P.   Date, Time of Receipt   211500Z Jan 88

Q.   Any Unusual Meteorological   NIL
       Conditions

R.   Remarks   Change to report filed earlie

                                                         Sqn Ldr
                                                         Duty Ops Officer
Date: 28 Jan 88   AF Ops

Distribution

Sec(AS)2
AEW/GE
DI 55
File AF Ops/2/5/1

REPORT OF AN UNIDENTIFIED FLYING OBJECT

A.	Date, Time & Duration of Sighting	171706Z Jan 88 6-7 seconds
B.	Description of Object (No of objects, size, shape, colour, brightness)	One object, similar to a flare - brilliant white with a long tail
C.	Exact Position of Observer Location, indoor/outdoor, stationary/moving	Outdoors walking close to home - stood stationary to observe object
D.	How Observed (naked eye, binoculars, other optical device, still or movie	Naked eye
E.	Direction in which object first seen (A landmark may be more useful than a badly estimated bearing)	South of observer
F.	Angle of Sight (Estimated heights are unreliable)	Approx 45 degrees
G.	Distance (By reference to a known landmark	4-5 km
H.	Movements (Changes in E, F & G may be of more use than estimates of course and speed)	Constant speed and direction East to West
J.	Met Conditions during Observations (Moving clouds, haze, mist etc)	Clear sky
K.	Nearby Objects (Telephone lines, high voltage lines, reservoir, lake or dam, swamp or marsh, river, high buildings, tall chimneys, steeples, spires, TV or radio masts, airfields, generating plant, factories, pits or other sites with floodlights or night lighting)	None

L.	To whom reported (Police, military, press etc)	West Byefleet Police

M.	Name & Address of Informant	West Byefleet Tel: West Byefleet

N.	Background of Informant that may be volunteered	Has seen a UFO in the past but was some time ago

O.	Other Witnesses	Informant's wife

P.	Date, Time of Receipt	Details taken by AF Ops 211500Z Jan 88

Q.	Any Unusual Meteorological Conditions	NIL

R.	Remarks	NIL

Sqn Ldr
Duty Ops Officer
AF Ops

Date: 21 Jan 88

Distribution:

Sec(AS)2
AEW/GE
DI 55
File AF Ops/2/5/1

REPORT OF AN UNIDENTIFIED FLYING OBJECT

A.	Date, Time & Duration of Sighting	17 January 1988 1703 hours 2 seconds
B.	Description of Object (No of objects, size, shape, colour, brightness)	Ball of white light with blue trail. Very bright.
C.	Exact Position of Observer Location, indoor/outdoor, stationary/moving	A car travelling from London towards Leatherhead before M25.
D.	How Observed (naked eye, binoculars, other optical device, still or movie)	Naked eye
E.	Direction in which object first seen (A landmark may be more useful than a badly estimated bearing)	Going from East to West. Very quickly.
F.	Angle of Sight (Estimated heights are unreliable)	40° (half way up car windscreen)
G.	Distance (By reference to a known landmark)	Not known — could not estimate
H.	Movements (Changes in E, F & G may be of more use than estimates of course and speed)	Straight line.
J.	Met Conditions during Observations (Moving clouds, haze, mist etc)	clear starry night but low fog. Object above base
K.	Nearby Objects (Telephone lines, high voltage lines, reservoir, lake or dam, swamp or marsh, river, high buildings, tall chimneys, steeples, spires, TV or radio masts, airfields, generating plant, factories, pits or other sites with floodlights or night lighting)	None of interest

L.	To whom reported (Police, military, press etc)	Phoned local police at Leatherhead Police Station.
M.	Name & Address of Informant	
N.	Background of Informant that may be volunteered	—
O.	Other Witnesses	None
P.	Date, Time of Receipt	1230 pm 18 Jan 88
Q.	Any Unusual Meteorological Conditions	None
R.	Remarks	

This is another report which corresponds to several I have had to-day. Was it a meteorite or was it a martian crash landing? Anybody know ?!

(S) 1

Sec (AS)2a
Squadron Leader
Duty Operations Officer
AF Ops

Date... 18/1/88 ....

Copies to
Sec(AS)2
AEW/GE
DI 55
File AF Ops/1/11
D/Sec 3 (Air)

213

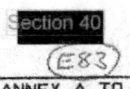

REPORT OF AN UNIDENTIFIED FLYING OBJECT

A.	Date, Time & Duration of Sighting	171700Z Jan 88 2 secs
B.	Description of Object (No of objects, size, shape, colour, brightness)	Shooting Star – Bursting in Flames and Vapour Trail
C.	Exact Position of Observer Location, indoor/outdoor, stationary/moving	A12 Travelling Colchester to Chelmsford – just East of Hatfield Peverell turn off, inside a car
D.	How Observed (naked eye, binoculars, other optical device, still or movie	Naked eye
E.	Direction in which object first seen (A landmark may be more useful than a badly estimated bearing)	See C and G
F.	Angle of Sight (Estimated heights are unreliable)	$40^{0} - 50^{0}$
G.	Distance (By reference to a known landmark	5-10 miles away over Chelmsford.
H.	Movements (Changes in E, F & G may be of more use than estimates of course and speed)	Steady, but slight descent East to West
J.	Met Conditions during Observations (Moving clouds, haze, mist etc)	Misty patches but clear sky above
K.	Nearby Objects (Telephone lines, high voltage lines, reservoir, lake or dam, swamp or marsh, river, high buildings, tall chimneys, steeples, spires, TV or radio masts, airfields, generating plant, factories, pits or other sites with floodlights or night lighting)	No

	To whom reported (Police, military, press etc)	Police – Section 40 Section 40 Welham
M.	Name & Address of Informant	Section 40
N.	Background of Informant that may be volunteered	Not given
O.	Other Witnesses	Wife Section 40 and Section 40
P.	Date, Time of Receipt	171850Z Jan 88
Q.	Any Unusual Meteorological Conditions	NIL
R.	Remarks	NIL

Section 40

Sqn Ldr
Duty Ops Officer
AF Ops

Date: 17 Jan 88

Distribution:

Sec(AS)2
AEW/GE
DI 55
File AF Ops/2/5/1
& Sc 3 (Air)

Section 40

NOTE

I have also received telephone calls today which correspond to the details given here but seen in different areas of the country. The sighting looks like it could well have seen a meteorite. Can we confirm? Section 40 (S).

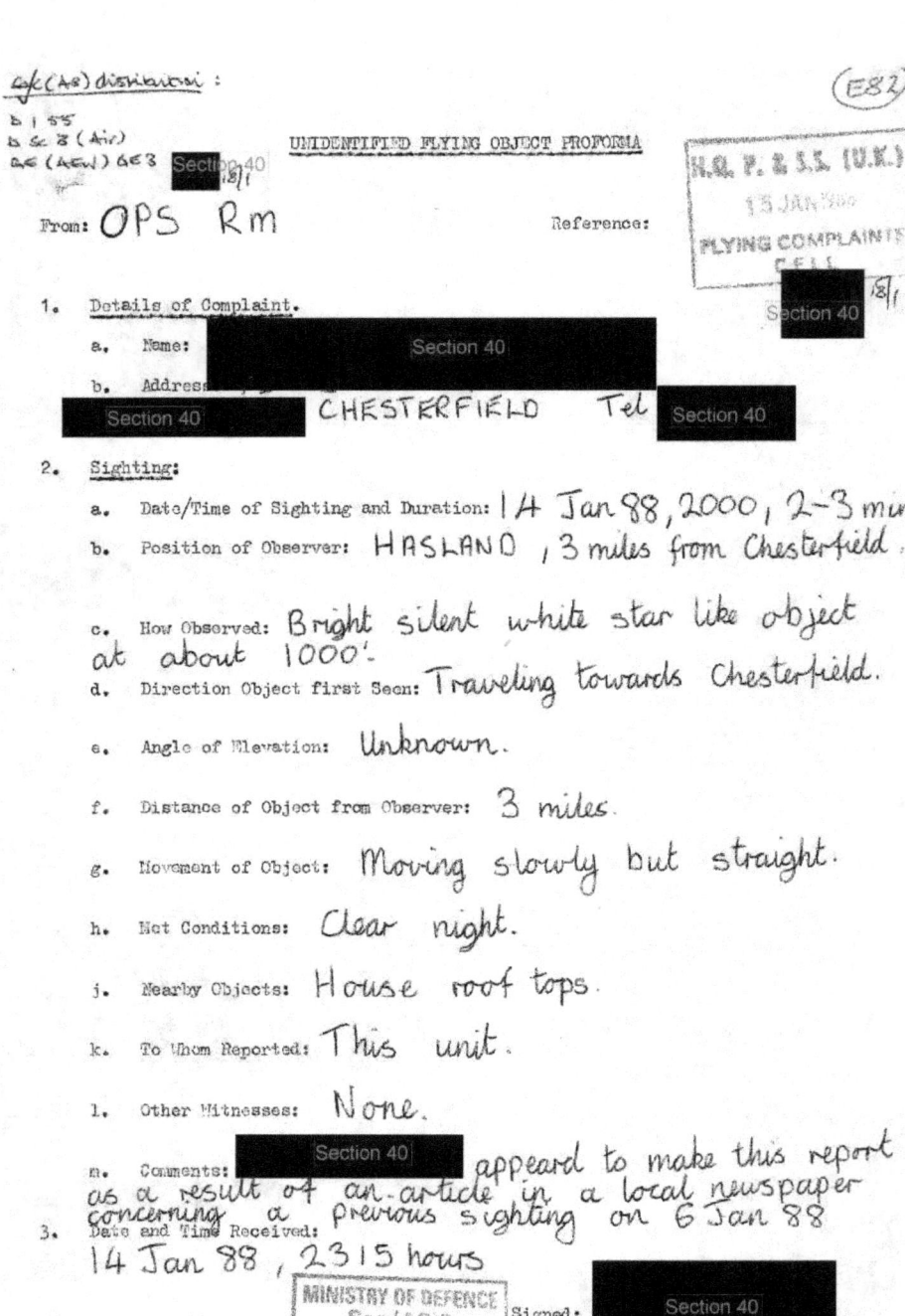

c/c (A8) distribution:
b 1 55
b Sc 8 (Air)
c/c (AEW) GE3   Section 40
                 18/1

(E82)

UNIDENTIFIED FLYING OBJECT PROFORMA

From: **OPS Rm**   Reference:

H.Q. P. & S.S. (U.K.)
15 JAN 1988
FLYING COMPLAINTS
CELL
Section 40   18/1

1. Details of Complaint.

   a. Name: Section 40

   b. Address
      Section 40   CHESTERFIELD   Tel   Section 40

2. Sighting:

   a. Date/Time of Sighting and Duration: 14 Jan 88, 2000, 2-3 mins

   b. Position of Observer: HASLAND, 3 miles from Chesterfield.

   c. How Observed: Bright silent white star like object at about 1000'.

   d. Direction Object first Seen: Traveling towards Chesterfield.

   e. Angle of Elevation: Unknown.

   f. Distance of Object from Observer: 3 miles.

   g. Movement of Object: Moving slowly but straight.

   h. Met Conditions: Clear night.

   j. Nearby Objects: House roof tops.

   k. To Whom Reported: This unit.

   l. Other Witnesses: None.

   m. Comments: Section 40 appeard to make this report as a result of an article in a local newspaper concerning a previous sighting on 6 Jan 88

3. Date and Time Received: 14 Jan 88, 2315 hours

MINISTRY OF DEFENCE
Sec.(AS)2
18 JAN 1988
FILE 12/2

Signed: Section 40
Name:

Date: 14 Jan 88   Rank Cpl   Tel No: Section 40

U N C L A S S I F I E D

CWD024 14/1131 014C1761

FOR CAB

ROUTINE/ROUTINE 141026Z JAN 88

FROM   RAF MANSTON
TO   MODUK AIR
INFO   HQSTC
        HQ 18 GP

U N C L A S S I F I E D
SIC SIF/Z6F
REPORT OF UFO SIGHTING.
A. 6 JAN 1988 2140 TILL 2150
B. VERY LITTLE SHAPE SEEN HOWEVER FOUR BRIGHT LIGHTS 2 BLUE STROBE
OUTER. RED PULSATING AND WHITE CONTINUOUS BETWEEN
C. MAP REF 731721 SHEET 1/1
D. NAKED EYE
E. NEAR GROUND APPROX 1 MILE NE FROM OBSERVER POSITION
F. 30 DEG
G. 1 MILE
H. FROM FIRST SIGHTED POSITION BANKED TO SOUTH AND CLIMBED RAPIDLY
TRAVELLING OVER OBSERVER POSITION AT A HEIGHT 200 TO 300FT THEN
CONTINUED NW ACROSS THAMES AT SIMILAR HEIGHT UNTIL OUT OF SIGHT

PAGE 2 RBDTRS 002 UNCLAS
J. FINE AND DRY CLEAR SKY GOOD VIS
K. NOT KNOWN
L. RAF MANSTON
M. Section 40
N. SERVING POLICE CONSTABLE Section
O. Section 40
P. 11 JAN 88
BT

DISTRIBUTION   SIF
F
NO SDL

DISTRIBUTION   Z6F
F
CAB   1   Sec (AS) ACTION (CXJ   1 AFDO) -
CYD   1   DD GE/AEW
CAV   1   DI 55
CAV / 2   DSTI
    ef (AS) distribution

MINISTRY OF DEFENCE
Sec.(AS)2
14 JAN 1988
FILE 12/2

217

U N C L A S S I F I E D

CWD008 15/0933 015C1150

FOR CAB

ROUTINE 140850Z JAN 88

FROM   RAF WEST DRAYTON
TO   MODUK AIR

U N C L A S S I F I E I
SIC Z6F
SUBJECT: AERIAL PHENOMENA. A. 141845Z JAN, 5 MINS. B. RED, BLUE
GREEN AND WHITE LIGHTS FOLLOWED BY 4 TO 5 FOOTBALL SIZED RED LIGHT.
C. Section 40   , SEAFORD, OUTDOORS. D. NAKED
EYE. E. SOUTH EAST TOWARDS SEAFORD HEAD. F. OVERHEAD. G. 50 FEET
H. STEADY AND FAST. J. CLEAR AND DRY. K. RESIDENTIAL AREA. L. POLICE
M. Section 40   SEAFORD
SUSSEX. N. DAUGHTER OF Section 40 WHO IS IN INTELLIGENCE SERVICE
CONSIDERED RELIABLE, AND RESIDES IN ASHFORD KENT. O. NONE. P. 142040
JAN
BT

DISTRIBUTION Z6F

CAB   1 Sec (AS) ACTION (CXJ   1 AFDO)
CYD   1 DD GE/AEW
CAV   1 DI 55
CAV   2 DSTI
Sec (AS) distribution.
   & Sc (Air) 3b

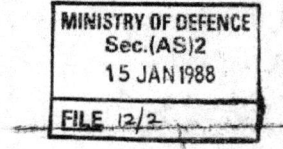

MINISTRY OF DEFENCE
Sec.(AS)2
15 JAN 1988
FILE 12/2

218

REPORT OF AN UNIDENTIFIED FLYING OBJECT

A.	Date, Time & Duration of Sighting	18 January 1987 at 1030 pm
B.	Description of Object (No of objects, size, shape, colour, brightness)	Pulsating purple light with pink overtones. Circular - disc like - but like a disembodied light. Very bright
C.	Exact Position of Observer Location, indoor/outdoor, stationary/moving	At home. Saw it outside the window. Went outside when it went below the level of next row of houses.
D.	How Observed (naked eye, binoculars, other optical device, still or movie)	Naked Eye only.
E.	Direction in which object first seen (A landmark may be more useful than a badly estimated bearing)	To the east towards woods.
F.	Angle of Sight (Estimated heights are unreliable)	Shallow angle.
G.	Distance (By reference to a known landmark)	Seemed very close but don't know exactly.
H.	Movements (Changes in E, F & G may be of more use than estimates of course and speed)	Dropped slowly behind the houses, across the road.
J.	Met Conditions during Observations (Moving clouds, haze, mist etc)	Still wet from rain. but little cloud. Saw Stars.
K.	Nearby Objects (Telephone lines, high voltage lines, reservoir, lake or dam, swamp or marsh, river, high buildings, tall chimneys, steeples, spires, TV or radio masts, airfields, generating plant, factories, pits or other sites with floodlights or night lighting)	Nothing unusual.

219

L.	To whom reported (Police, military, press etc)	Nobody.
M.	Name & Address of Informant	Plumstead SE2
N.	Background of Informant that may be volunteered	Office worker
O.	Other Witnesses	Family
P.	Date, Time of Receipt	1000 hours on 14 January 1988
Q.	Any Unusual Meteorological Conditions	None
R.	Remarks	Felt ecstatic when he saw it which he thought was unusual !

Sec (AS) 2a
Squadron Leader
Duty Operations Officer
AF Ops

Date. 14.01.88 ....

Copies to:
Sec(AS)2
AEW/GE
DI 55
File AF Ops/1/11
D Sc (Air) 3

220

UNCLASSIFIED

ROYAL AIR FORCE NEWTON

NOTTINGHAM NG13 8HL

Tel. East Bridgford Section 40

MOD (Sec(AS)2b)

Please reply to
Officer Commanding
Your reference

Our reference
NEW/2/3/Air
Date
13 Jan 88

SIGHTING OF UFO OVER RAF NEWTON

Please find, attached, a copy of a report received from
one of the Cpl's based at RAF Newton regarding the
sighting of UFOs in the Nottinghamshire area which is
enclosed for your information.

You will wish to know that many national newspapers
carried reports of a very large UFO over Nottingham
on that night.

Section 40

```
MINISTRY OF DEFENCE
    Sec.(AS)2
    2 2 JAN 1988
FILE 12/2
```

Flt Lt
for OC

Sec(AS) distribution.
GE (AEW) GE3
D I 55
D Sc (Air)

We appear to have ten reports which
relate to this sighting. The object travelled from Notts through to Staff.
then to Suffolk. Timings and reports appear to fit together. Do we
know of any rational explanation which could account for this flying
football pitch?

Section 40 221

UNCLASSIFIED

SIGHTING OF UFO OVER RAF NEWTON

On Wednesday the 9th Dec 1987, around 1710 hrs I had just locked Bld 29, Supply
Flt, and was carrying out an external security check. While carrying out my
check, on the barrack stores side of supply, my attention was drawn to a large
formation of lights in the sky.

The lights were in two lines. The front line being larger than the rear line.
They were about a mile apart, the rear line being slightly off set. I would
estimate that there was between 12 to 16 lights in the front and 8 to 10 in the
rear, outside lights being red, inside lights white, all being of equal distance
from each other. They appeared in the north west and headed towards the south
east.

I noted that there was too many lights for a large transport aircraft and moving
too slow for fast jets. The speed of the formation was slow, more of a glide, when
the formation was directly above me I heard jet engine noise, but not very loud,
if there was a number of aircraft involved.

Two or three minutes later I noticed a second large formation. I thought it was
odd seeing two large formations, one after the other.

The formation was smaller than the first, but with the same sequence of lights, the
outside being red and inside white. I counted these lights - 8 in the front line
and 4 in the rear line. The rear lights not so off set as in the first formation.
The lights were also of equal distance apart, same speed and heading in the same
direction. There was also jet engine noise when the formation was directly above
me. A minute or so later the formation banked to the east keeping perfect
formation.

I did not think any more about what I saw because of the engine noise, thinking
it was a large formation of aircraft. I mentioned it to my wife when I got home
and on Thursday morning I mentioned it to Cpl ████ who was in the Guardroom
on Wednesday evening who said that the Nottingham Police had rang asking if we
had any aircraft flying at the time, because of reports of UFOs from the Public.

Cpl ███████ gave me the Policeman's name which was ███ PC ████████. I rang
PC ████████ on Thursday evening when I got home and told him what I saw.

ORIGINAL SIGNED BY
████████
Supply Flt
RAF Newton

D155 rung on 25/1

████████ said that he had plotted
the sightings and suggested that they
could well have been an RAF Fast jets or jets
[Humberside, Lincoln, Nottingham, Birmingham]
and a commercial airliner [B'ham — Suffolk].
████████
25/1

Formation N°1

‖‖‖‖‖‖‖‖‖

‖‖‖‖‖‖‖‖‖‖‖‖‖‖‖‖

Formation N° 2.

‖‖‖‖

‖‖‖‖‖‖‖

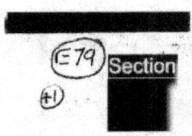

U N C L A S S I F I E D

CAB205 12/2121 012C3825

FOR CAB

ROUTINE/ROUTINE 121547Z JAN 88

FROM   RAF SHAWBURY
TO   MODUK AIR
INFO   HQRAFSC

U N C L A S S I F I E D
SIC Z6F
MODUK AIR FOR S4F, HQRAFSC FOR CBYO. SUBJECT UNIDENTIFIED FLYING
OBJECT REPORT
A WED 6 JAN 88 2345Z TILL 2350Z
B ONE OBJECT, SIZE UNKNOWN, CIRULAR WITH A SKIRT CONICAL UPPER
STRUCTURE, GREEN, VERY BRIGHT, NO SOUND NO SMELL
C Section 40   TELFORD, OUTDOORS, STATIONARY
D NAKED EYE
E OVERHEAD THE WREKIN NEAR TELFORD
F ANGLE OF SIGHT VARIED TILL OVER HEAD ESTIMATED HEIGHTS 5000FT
G FROM THE WREKIN TO ST GEROGES THEN STOPPED, FILTED LEFT THEN
RIGHT. THEN WENT TOWARD THE CREWE AREA, THE OBJECT THEN BEGAN TO
ROVOLVE AND ACCELERATE TOWARDS CREWE, ESTINATED 200KTS
H AS IN G

PAGE 2 RBDTOE 009 UNCLAS
J CLEAR SKIES, LOTS OF STARS, DRIZZLE ?
K NIL
I RAF SHAWBURY ORDERLY OFFICER PLT OFF Section 40
Section 40   SAINT GEROGES TELFORD SHROPSHIRE
M NIL
O NIL
P 11 JAN 88 2030Z
BT

DISTRIBUTION   Z6F

CAB   1 Sec (AS) ACTION (CXJ   1 AFDO)
CYD   1 DD GE/AEW
CAV   1 DI 55
CAV   2 DSTI

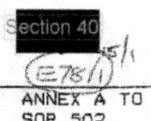
REPORT OF AN UNIDENTIFIED FLYING OBJECT

A.	Date, Time & Duration of Sighting	110955Z Jan 88 for approx 30-60 seconds.
B.	Description of Object (No of objects, size, shape, colour, brightness)	1 x object, size not estimated, cylindrical without wings, primary colou purple and quite bright.
C.	Exact Position of Observer Location, indoor/outdoor, stationary/moving	Outside and stationary.
D.	How Observed (naked eye, binoculars, other optical device, still or movie	Naked eye
E.	Direction in which object first seen (A landmark may be more useful than a badly estimated bearing)	SE over M1 motorway.
F.	Angle of Sight (Estimated heights are unreliable)	Unknown.
G.	Distance (By reference to a known landmark	Below ht of ac approaching London Heathrow airport.
H.	Movements (Changes in E, F & G may be of more use than estimates of course and speed)	No apparent change. Speed increase from slow to very high speed in matter of secs
J.	Met Conditions during Observations (Moving clouds, haze, mist etc)	Clear blue sky and sunny.
K.	Nearby Objects (Telephone lines, high voltage lines, reservoir, lake or dam, swamp or marsh, river, high buildings, tall chimneys, steeples, spires, TV or radio masts, airfields, generating plant, factories, pits or other sites with floodlights or night lighting)	Object observed across area known locally as Arrandene Recreation ground (Barnett).

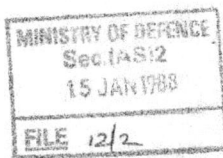

| L. | To whom reported (Police, military, press etc) | MOD Air Force Operations only. |

| M. | Name & Address of Informant | |

| N. | Background of Informant that may be volunteered | Occupation: Property Investment Consultant. |

| O. | Other Witnesses | None |

| P. | Date, Time of Receipt | 141915Z Jan 88 |

| Q. | Any Unusual Meteorological Conditions | None |

| R. | Remarks | Reporter was out walking dog on Arrandene Recreational ground |

Sqn Ldr
Duty Ops Officer
AF Ops

Date: 14 Jan 88

Distribution:

Sec(AS)2
AEW/GE
DI 55
File AF Ops/2/5/1

Sec (AS) distribution:

D Sc (Air) 3b

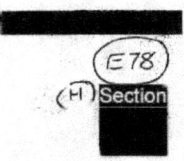

UNCLASSIFIED

CAB051 09/0309 008C5514

FOR CAB

ROUTINE/ROUTINE 081342Z JAN 88

FROM   RAF VALLEY
TO   MODUK AIR
INFO   HQRAFSC

UNCLASSIFIED
SIC Z6F
MODUK FOR DS8, HQRAFSC FOR CPSYO REPORT OF UNIDENTIFIED FLYING
OBJECT
A. 022210Z JAN 88, FIFTEEN MINUTES
B. 43 WHITE LIGHTS IN A RANDOM GROUPING
C. PENYFFORDD NR CHESTER, OUTDOORS, STATIONARY
D. NAKED EYE
E. OVERHEAD SPREAD BETWEEN 25 DEGREE LEFT AND RIGHT OF THE VERTICAL
F. OBSERVER COULD ONLY SAY HIGH ALTITUDE FIRST SEEN AT APPROX 45
DEGREE
G. COULD NOT BE RELIABLY BE ESTIMATED

H. HEADING SOUTH WEST
J. BROKEN CLOUD COVER WITH CLOUD BASE BETWEEN 1000-1500 FEET, GOOD
VISIBILITY WHEN CLOUD COVER BROKE, HIGH WINDS, MOON NEARLY FULL

PAGE 2 RBDBVS 024 UNCLAS
K. NIL
L. LIVERPOOL PLANETARIUM
M. Section 40
N. NIL
O. CONFIRMED BY NEIGHBOUR

P. 051400Z JAN 87
Q. REPORTED THAT A SIMILAR SIGHTING OCCURRED A COUPLE OF WEEKS
EARLIER BUT OBJECTS TRAVELLING ON RECIPROCAL HEADING
BT

DISTRIBUTION Z6F
F
CAB   1 Sec (AS) ACTION (CXJ   ,1 AFDO)
CYD   1 DD GE/AEW
CAV   1 DI 55
CAV, 2 DSTI

Sec (AS) distribution   b) Sec 3 (Air)

UNCLASSIFIED

CAB162 07/2010 007C4764

FOR CAP

ROUTINE 071902Z JAN 88

FROM   RAF WEST DRAYTON
TO   MODUK AIR

UNCLASSIFIED
SIC Z6F
SUBJECT: AERIAL PHENOMENA
A. 051810 JAN 88 1 MINUTE
B. ONE RED OBJECT DULL BECAME BRIGHTER THEN FADED
C. DIAL HILL, CLEVEDON, AVON
D. NAKED EYE
E. EAST
F. APPROX 70 DEGREES
G. N/K
H. STEADY HEADING EAST
JM MOVING CLOUDS
K. TREES 400 METRES NORTH
L. BRISTOL AIRPORT
M. Section 40
TEL: Section 40

PAGE 2 RBDAID 013   UNCLAS
O. NIL
P. 071520 JAN 88
BT

DISTRIBUTION   Z6F
F
CAB   1   Sec (AS) ACTION (CXJ   1   AFDO
CYD   1   DD GE/AEW
CAV   1   DI 55
CAV   2   DSTI

Sec (AS) distribution
D/Sc 3 (Air).

228

U N C L A S S I F I E D

CAB034 88/0333 0p8C0347

FOR CAB

ROUTINE 071130Z JAN 88

FROM   RAF BINBROOK
TO   MODUK AIR

U N C L A S S I F I E D
SIC L6Z/Z6F
(Z6F IN8 BY DCC)
A 062315Z JAN 88, FOR FOURTY FIVE MINUTES
B A LIGHT IN THE SKY, FIVE TIMES THE SIZE OF A STAR, CONSTANTLY
CHANGING SHAPE, WHITE/SILEVER COLOUR WITH A BLUE HAZE AND IRREGULAR
RED FLASHES
C AT HER HOME IN GRIMSBY THROUGH A REAR ROOM WINDOW FACING WEST
D NAKED EYE
E THE OBJECT WAS SEEN IN A WESTERLY DERECTION OVER THE VILLAGE OF
COTTINGHAM AND MOVED STEADILY NORTH EAST FROM COTTINGHAM
F ESTIMATED 45 DEGREE ANGLE FROM THE GROUND
G ESTIMATED THREE MILES
H THE OBJECT STAYED AT ROUGHLY THE SAME ANGLE AND DISTANCE BUT MOVED
STEADILY NORTH EAST
J A RELATIVELY CLEAR NIGHT WITH A MOON AND MOVING CLOUDS. THE CLOUD
DID NOT OBSCURE THE OBJECT AT ALL, WHICH APPEARED TO BE BELOW THE

CLOUD COVER
K NO NEARBY OBJECTS
L HUMBERSIDE POLICE
M Section 40
N A PRACTICAL AND UNIMAGINATIVE WOMAN
O Section 40   OF THE SAME ADDRESS
P 062335Z JAN 88
BT

DISTRIBUTION   L6Z
F
NO SDL

DISTRIBUTION   Z6F
F
CAB   1   Sec (AS) ACTION (CXJ   1 AFDO
CYD   1   DB GE/AEW
CAV   1   DI 55
CAV   2   DSTI
cof (AE) distribution
b/Sc 3 (Air)

U N C L A S S I F I E D

CWD067 07/1413 007C2746

FOR CAB

ROUTINE 071015Z JAN 88

FROM   RAF WEST DRAYTON
TO   MODUK AIR

U N C L A S S I F I E D
SIC Z6F
SUBJECT: AERIAL PHENOMEN
A. 070645Z JAN 88 FOR 3 TO 4 MINUTES
B. ONE LONG OBJECT WITH FLASHING LIGHTS
C. INDOORS AT HOME ADDRESS
D. NAKED EYE
E. FROM BATH CITY CENTRE TOWARDS WARMINSTER WILTS
H. STEADY
J. CLEAR DRY
K. BATH ABBEY CITY CENTRE
L. REPORTED TO CITY OF BATH POLICE TELEPHONE BATH Section 40
M. Section 40
P. 071005Z JAN 88
BT.

(E76)

DISTRIBUTION   Z6F
F
CAB   1 Sec (AS) ACTION (CXJ   1 AFDO)
CYD   1 DD GE/AEW
CAV   1 D1 55
CAV   2 DSTI

Cof (AS) on circulation:
   Sc 3 (Air)

FLYING COMPLAINT FORM

(DO NOT STATE THAT AN INVESTIGATION WILL ATTEND)

From: HQ P&SS (UK)   TO: MOD Sec (AS) 2b

1. Details of Complaint.

    a. Name & Initials . Section 40 ....

    b. Address .... Section 40 ....

        .... HERRINGTHORPE ...... SOUTH YORKS ....

    c. Nearest Large Town .... ROTHERHAM ....

    d. Telephone No with code . Section 40 ....

2. Details of Incident.

    a. Date ... 6.8.7. Jan. 88 ....

    b. Time (Local or Zulu) .1945 . 2000 ....

    c. No of ac involved .... UFO ....

    d. Height ...... NOT KNOWN ....

    e. Direction .... MOVING SOUTH ....

3. Description of Aircraft.

    ~~Jet~~ ~~Propellor~~ ~~Military~~ ~~Civil~~ ~~Fighter~~ ~~Bomber~~ ~~Helicopter~~ ~~Light ac~~

    ~~Camouflaged~~ ~~Silver~~ ~~White~~ ~~Any noticeable Colours/markings~~

4. Location of Complaint (if Different from 1b)(with telephone No if applicable.)

    ....

    ....

5. Claims. (Do not prompt complainant). Is there any injury/damage to persons/
    livestock/property which will result in a claim? Complainants claiming injury to
    livestock should report the incident to their local NFU, producing a veterinary
    report. Or for any of the above claims that may occur they can write to MOD Claims,
    First Avenue House, High Holborn, London, WC1V 6HE. Tel Section 40

    Details ....

    ....

    ....

6. Full Details of Complaint. .. UFO described as 3 orange balls....
    .... of light ... stationary ... then moving south ....
    .. On .. 16.1.88 .. same .. UFO .. was .. chased .. by .. a ....
    .. military .. jet .. no .. details .. available ....

    Is this likely? Any news?

    ....

    Date/Time Report Received .. 7.1.88 .. 2010 hours .

                                                        Signed Section 40

                                                        Name .

                                                        Rank .. Sgt... Tel Section 40

NB Section 40 is an
    investigator with the
    Yorkshire UFO Society.

Sec(AS) distribution:
    GE (AE-1) SE3
    D1 55
    D SC 3 (Air)

MINISTRY OF DEFENCE
Sec.(AS)2
13 JAN 1988

FILE 12/2

UNCLASSIFIED

CAB183 06/2130 006C4594

FOR CAB

ROUTINE 061915Z JAN 88

FROM RAF WEST DRAYTON
TO   MODUK AIR

UNCLASSIFIED
SIC Z6F

SUBJECT AERIAL PHENOMENA
A. 6 JAN 88 0644 HRS. B. ONE LARGE WHITE BALL WITH A TALE OF LIGHT
(VERY BRIGHT). C. DRIVING A CAR TOWARDS GUILFORD ON THE HOGS BACK
NEAR THE PUTTENHAM TURN OFF. D. NAKED EYE. E. TO THE NORTH MOVING
SOUTH, DESCENDING, DISAPPEARED BELOW THE TREE LINE. F. 45 DEGREES
G. 100 YARDS AHEAD. H. VERTICAL DOWNWARDS MOVEMENT. J. CLEAR SKY
JUST BEFORE DAWN, HAD BEEN RAINING, ROAD WAS WET. K. TRAFFIC ON
ROAD. L. FARNHAM POLICE STATION AND SUN NEWSPAPER. M. Section 40
Section 40   N. Section 40
INFORMED DUTY ALSO HE HAD HAD A PREVIOUS UFO SIGHTING ABOUT 6 YEARS
AGO NEAR GATWICK, HE REPORTED THAT ONE ALSO. O. NO OTHER WITNESS
BUT HIS BOSS WAS IN THE CAR READING THE NEWSPAPER AT THE TIME.
RECEIVED THIS REPORT 6 JAN 1830 HRS
9T

PAGE 2 RBDAID 011 UNCLAS

DISTRIBUTION Z6F
F
CAB   1 Sec (AS) ACTION (CXJ   1 AFDO)
CYD   1 DD GE/AEW
CAV   1 DI 55
CAV   2 DSTI

UNCLASSIFIED

CY0028 07/0727 006C4705

FOR CAB

ROUTINE 061910Z JAN 88

FROM   RAF WEST DRAYTO
TO   MODUK AIR

U N C L A S S I F I E D
SIC Z6F
SUBJECT. AERIAL PHENOMENA. A. 022359 45 MINS. B. ONE, MYRIAD
OF DIFFERENT COLOURED LIGHTS MADE VERY LOUD ROARING NOISE. C. AT
HOME ADDRESS. D. NAKED EYE. E. OVER THE THAMES ESTURAY. F. NOT
KNOWN. H. AND THEN DISSAPPEARED. J. CAVOK. L. RADIO LONDON
M. Section 40   N. HEARD UFO
REPORT ON RADIO NEWS WHICH GAVE HIM THE IDEA TO INFORM THE
AUTHORITIES
O. Section 40 WIFE. P. 061830Z
BT

DISTRIBUTION Z6F
F
CAB   1   Sec (AS) ACTION (CXJ   1 AFDO)
CYD   1   DD GE/AEW
CAV   1   DI 55
CAV   2   DSTI

12/2

MINISTRY OF DEFENCE
Sec.(AS)2
- 7 JAN 1988

FILE 12/2

233

UNCLASSIFIED

CAB139 06/1834 006C3699

FOR CAB

ROUTINE 061605Z JAN 88

FROM   RAF WEST DRAYTON
TO   MODUK AIR

UNCLASSIFIED
SIC Z6F
SUBJECT AERIAL PHENOMENA
A. 4 JAN 88 2130 HRS FOR A FEW SECONDS B. ONE OBJECT SAME SIZE AS
A CESSNA AIRCRAFT, TADPOLE SHAPE, HEAD BRILLIANT AND ROTATING, BL
FLAMES FROM THE TAIL. NO SMELL NO SOUND AS OBSERVER WAS PASSENGE!
IN A CAR C. ON THE INVERNESS TO ABERDEEN ROAD (A92) 29 MILES NORT
OF ABERDEEN TRAVELLING IN A PRIVATE CAR D. NAKED EYE E. SOUTH
WESTERLY DIRECTION F. OUT OF CAR WINDOW G. NO ESTIMATE (SHORT
SIGHTING) H. STRAIGHT PATH THEN LOST IN CLOUD J. MOVING CLOUDS
K. COUNTRYSIDE L. PC Section 40 ABERDEEN POLICE (NO Section 40 M. Section 40
Section 40 WAS PROMPTED TO REPORTED SIGHTING
AFTER UFO NEWS ITEM ON TV. OBSERVER LIVES AND WORKS IN TEXAS
RETURNING TO USA SOON O. BROTHER WAS IN CAR BUT DID NOT SEE THE UFO
DUE TO SHORT SIGHTING. RECEIVED AT AIS 061500Z JAN 88

DISTRIBUTION   Z6F

CAB   1   Sec (AS) ACTION (CXJ   1   AFDO)
CYB   1   DD GE/AFM
CAC   1   DI 55
CAV   2   DSTI

With the Compliments

of

Officer Commanding

HEADQUARTERS PROVOST AND SECURITY SERVICES
(United Kingdom)
FLYING COMPLAINTS & CUSTOMS LIAISON FLIGHT

Royal Air Force
Rudloe Manor
Hawthorn
Wiltshire
SN13 0PQ

Telephone Hawtho

Section 40

UNIDENTIFIED FLYING OBJECT PROFORMA

From: Sgt    Reference:
DERBY POLICE.

1. Details of Complaint.

    a. Name:

    b. Address

2. Sighting:

    a. Date/Time of Sighting and Duration: 6 Jan 85   1115L

    b. Position of Observer: on Shardlow bridge which is on the A6 approx 6 miles SE of Derby.

    c. How Observed: Naked Eye

    d. Direction Object first Seen: —

    e. Angle of Elevation: Descending straight down

    f. Distance of Object from Observer: 1 mile

    g. Movement of Object: Straight down.

    h. Met Conditions: Clear & bright after a shower.

    j. Nearby Objects: —

    k. To Whom Reported: Derby Police

    l. Other Witnesses: Her daughter.

    m. Comments: No shape, bright light like a beam & aircraft size.

3. Date and Time Received: 061330Z Jan 85

MINISTRY OF DEFENCE
Sec.(AS)2
1 1 JAN 1988

FILE 12/2

Signed

Name:

Date:

Rank AA   Tel No:

U N C L A S S I F I E D

CAB047 05/1055 005C1363

FOR CAB

ROUTINE 051042Z JAN 88

FROM   RAF WEST DRAYTON
TO   MODUK AIR

U N C L A S S I F I E D
SIC Z6F
SUBJECT: AERIAL PHENOMENA
A. 041855Z JAN 88, 10 MINS
B. ONE LARGE CROSSLIKE OBJECT WITH MANY RED AND GREEN LIGHTS,
NO NOISE
C. ▮Section 40▮   DULVERTON SOMERSET
D. NAKED EYE
E. IN VALLEY BELOW HIS HOUSE
F. NOT KNOWN
H. HOVERED STEADILY AND THEN MOVED OFF AT GREAT SPEED
J. CAVOK
L. MOD POLICE RAF LOCKING PC ▮Section 40▮
M. ▮Section 40▮ AS SERIAL C
P. 050915Z JAN 88
BT

PAGE 2 RBDAID 009 UNCLAS

DISTRIBUTION   Z6F

CAB   1 Sec (AS) ACTION (CXJ   1 AFDO)
CYD   1 DD GE/AEW
CAV   1 DI 55
CAV   2 DSTI

REPORT OF AN UNIDENTIFIED FLYING OBJECT

A.	Date, Time & Duration of Sighting	4th January 1988 1700 hours and 2000 hours. (15 minutes) (15 minutes)
B.	Description of Object (No of objects, size, shape, colour, brightness)	Bright white light. Like two triangles or a Christmas tree on its size. Starlight white.
C.	Exact Position of Observer Location, indoor/outdoor, stationary/moving	In house. (1st) In car, (2nd) then stopped to have a look.
D.	How Observed (naked eye, binoculars, other optical device, still or movie)	Naked eye.
E.	Direction in which object first seen (A landmark may be more useful than a badly estimated bearing)	South West (towards) Worcester. Second time in North East.
F.	Angle of Sight (Estimated heights are unreliable)	Just over horizon, very low angle.
G.	Distance (By reference to a known landmark)	Not known. A long way away.
H.	Movements (Changes in E, F & G may be of more use than estimates of course and speed)	Backwards and forwards, side to side, moving to gate quickly.
J.	Met Conditions during Observations (Moving clouds, haze, mist etc)	Full moon. Scattered high cloud. No wind.
K.	Nearby Objects (Telephone lines, high voltage lines, reservoir, lake or dam, swamp or marsh, river, high buildings, tall chimneys, steeples, spires, TV or radio masts, airfields, generating plant, factories, pits or other sites with floodlights or night lighting)	Nothing obvious.

L.	To whom reported (Police, military, press etc)	Air Traffic Control, Birmingham Airport Meteorological Society " " Press, Central TV, Police.
M.	Name & Address of Informant	
N.	Background of Informant that may be volunteered	—
O.	Other Witnesses	His children and other fellow travellers.
P.	Date, Time of Receipt	1600 6 January 1988
Q.	Any Unusual Meteorological Conditions	None
R.	Remarks	Obviously saw something unusual. Similar to other sightings seen in early Jan 88. Any connection?

Sec (AS) 2a
Squadron Leader
Duty Operations Officer
AF Ops

Date. 6 Jan 88 ....

Copies to:
Sec(AS)2
AEW/GE
DI 55
File AF Ops/1/11

239

U N C L A S S I F I E D (ER)

CAB030 04/1053 004C0722

FOR CAB

ROUTINE 041000Z JAN 88

FROM   RAF WEST DRAYTON
TO   MODUK AIR

U N C L A S S I F I E D 88
SIC Z6F
SUBJECT: AERIAL PHENOMENA
A. 030200Z UNTIL 0205Z JAN 88
B. ONE OBJECT NO SOUND SAUCER SHAPED WITH BASE THAT HAD FLASHING
RED LIGHTS
C. A264 ROAD HOLTYE GOLF COURSE TRAVELLING WEST TO EAST GRINSTEAD
D. NAKED
E. ABOVE AND AHEAD THEN HOVERING IN FRONT
F. 30 DEGREES   03 Jan
H. STEADY
J. OVERCAST
K. TREES TO SOUTH OPEN GOLF COURSE TO NORTH
L. POLICE
M. Section 40 ████████████████████████████████████
SUSSEX

PAGE 2 RDDAID 004   UNCLAS
N. WAS EMPLOYED AT EAST GRINSTEAD POLICE STATION FOR A YEAR
ABOUT ONE AND A HALF YEARS AGO
P. 031514Z JAN 88
BT

DISTRIBUTION   Z6F
F
CAB   1 Sec (AS) ACTION (CXJ   1 AFDO)
CYD   1 DD GE/AEW
CAV   1 DI 55
CAV   2 DSTI

U N C L A S S I F I E D

CWD010 04/1045 004C0671

FOR CAB

ROUTINE 040850Z JAN 88

FROM   RAF WEST DRAYTON
TO   MODUK AIR

U N C L A S S I F I E D
SIC Z6F
SUBJECT: AERIAL PHENOMENA
A. 311650Z DEC 87
B. ONE OBJECT OF NO DISTINCT SHAPE WITH 2 RED LIGHT ROTATING AROUND
i WHITE LIGHT
C. Section 40   NEWMALDEN
D. NAKED EYE
E. OVERHEAD
F. 30 DEGREES 1500FT
H. STEADY
J. CLOUD 2 OCTAS AT 3500FT (HEATHROW MET)
K. BUILT UP AREA
L. REPORTED TO LONDON AIR TRAFFIC CONTROL CENTRE CIVIL SUPERVISOR
Section 40
M. Section 40

PAGE 2 RBDAID 003 UNCLAS
N. Section 40   SAW 2 OF ABOVE ABOUT 2 MONTH AGO
O.
P. 311725Z DEC 87

DISTRIBUTION   Z6F
F
CAB   1 Sec (AS) ACTION (CXJ   1 AFDO)
CYD   1 DD GE/AEW
CAV   1 DI 55
CAV   2 DSTI

U N C L A S S I F I E D

CWD008 04/1041 004C0647

FOR CAB

ROUTINE 040840Z JAN 88

FROM   RAF WEST DRAYTON
TO   MODUK AIR

U N C L A S S I F I E D
SIC Z6F
SUBJECT: AERIAL PHENOMENA
A. 022350Z JAN 88 90 MINUTES
B. ONE ROUND, VERY BRIGHT MULTICOLOURED OBJECT
C. INDOORS AT HOME ADDRESS
D. TELESCOPE
E. SOUTH WEST
H. SLOW
J. CLEAR
K. BUILT UP AREA
L. REPORTED TO POLICE
M. Section 40   SW10
O. ALSO SEEN BY 8 POLICEMEN FROM SOUTH KENSINGTON POLICE STATION
P. 030130Z JAN 88
BT

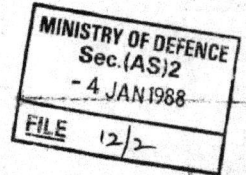

PAGE 2 RBDAID 0000 UNCLAS

DISTRIBUTION   Z6F
F
CAB   1 Sec (AS) ACTION (CXJ   1   AFDO)
CYD   1 DD GE/AEW
CAV   1 DI 55
CAV   2 DSTI

MINISTRY OF DEFENCE
Sec.(AS)2
- 4 JAN 1988

FILE 12/2

242

REPORT OF AN UNIDENTIFIED FLYING OBJECT

A.	Date, Time & Duration of Sighting	031600Z Jan 88 More than 20 Mins
B.	Description of Object (No of objects, size, shape, colour, brightness)	Flat cigar shaped Bright orange , split into two smaller objects 1 higher, 1 lower
C.	Exact Position of Observer Location, indoor/outdoor, stationary/moving	Outdoors on Wimbledon Common near Tooting – moving.
D.	How Observed (naked eye, binoculars, other optical device, still or movie	3 witnesses – naked eye 1 witness – video camera plus 10 other witnesses
E.	Direction in which object first seen (A landmark may be more useful than a badly estimated bearing)	Unknown
F.	Angle of Sight (Estimated heights are unreliable)	Unknown
G.	Distance (By reference to a known landmark	Unknown
H.	Movements (Changes in E, F & G may be of more use than estimates of course and speed)	Slow to medium speed
J.	Met Conditions during Observations (Moving clouds, haze, mist etc)	Clear, wet, but no rain
K.	Nearby Objects (Telephone lines, high voltage lines, reservoir, lake or dam, swamp or marsh, river, high buildings, tall chimneys, steeples, spires, TV or radio masts, airfields, generating plant, factories, pits or other sites with floodlights or night lighting)	Cleared tops of trees on common.

NOTE

Spoke Duty Officer, UK RAOC on 3/1, and asked for him
to ring Section 40 in the evenings as I was having trouble
contacting him. He will try and will let me know results
on Monday 11/1. However, he doesn't hold out much hope
of obtaining the video as he seems to remember that the
camera was held by a witness who didn't know Section 40 (and vice versa).
UKRAOC rang on 11/1. No video Section 40 No further action Section 40 .

243

L.	To whom reported (Police, military, press etc)	Duty controller UKRAOC, HQSTC Ext Section 40 at 2345 on 5 Jan 88

M. Name & Address of Informant

N. Background of Informant that may be volunteered

Nil

O. Other Witnesses

No other Addressess

P. Date, Time of Receipt

052344SZ Jan 88

Q. Any Unusual Meteorological Conditions

No

R. Remarks

Nil

Sqn Ldr
Duty Ops Officer
AF Ops

Date: 5 Jan 87

Distribution:

Sec(AS)2
AEW/GE
DI 55
File AF Ops/2/5/1

REPORT OF AN UNIDENTIFIED FLYING OBJECT

A.	Date, Time & Duration of Sighting	Sunday 3 January 1600 hours. 15/20 mins duration
B.	Description of Object (No of objects, size, shape, colour, brightness)	Bright light covered by haze Yellow colour and pointed shape. Very large but couldn't guess. Triangular.
C.	Exact Position of Observer Location, indoor/outdoor, stationary/moving	Outside car
D.	How Observed (naked eye, binoculars, other optical device, still or movie)	eye then binoculars
E.	Direction in which object first seen (A landmark may be more useful than a badly estimated bearing)	To the west of observer Just above horizon.
F.	Angle of Sight (Estimated heights are unreliable)	Low angle.
G.	Distance (By reference to a known landmark)	Not known. Outside of atmosphere.
H.	Movements (Changes in E, F & G may be of more use than estimates of course and speed)	Main object stayed stationary Part of it sped away. Gradually faded away.
J.	Met Conditions during Observations (Moving clouds, haze, mist etc)	Patchy cloudy and hazy. Sunset.
K.	Nearby Objects (Telephone lines, high voltage lines, reservoir, lake or dam, swamp or marsh, river, high buildings, tall chimneys, steeples, spires, TV or radio masts, airfields, generating plant, factories, pits or other sites with floodlights or night lighting)	Crane and tall building.

245

L.	To whom reported (Police, military, press etc)	Not before reporting to MOD
M.	Name & Address of Informant	Section 40 / Section 40 / Ealing W5
N.	Background of Informant that may be volunteered	Ex-sailor
O.	Other Witnesses	His girlfriend. Section 40
P.	Date, Time of Receipt	1100 6 January, 1988
Q.	Any Unusual Meteorological Conditions	None other sunset.
R.	Remarks	Seems to me that this could be refraction of sun's rays as it occured in west shortly after sunset.

p.s. I note that this corresponds to a
report from AF Ops' dated 5 Jan 87 / for
a Section 40   Any comments?
Section 40
6/1

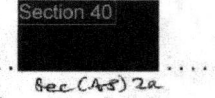

Section 40

Sec (AS) 2a
Squadron Leader
Duty Operations Officer
AF Ops

Date.. 6 Jan 88........

Copies to:
Sec(AS)2
AEW/GE
DI 55
File AF Ops/1/11

U N C L A S S I F I E D

CWD015 27/1610 361C0439

FOR CAB

PRIORITY 271424Z DEC 87

FROM   MOD TELEX REFILE
TO   MODUK AIR

U N C L A S S I F I E D
SIC Z6F

592352 HUMPOL G
0340 HQ TLX 87-12-27 14:24

FROM CC HUMBERSIDE POLICE(BG SUB DIV.)
TO MINISTRY OF DEFENCE
DTO 1217/27/12/87

U.F.O. SIGHTING
==================

A.   0130/27/12/87 FEW SECONDS.

B.   A LARGE OBLONG SHAPE GLOWING BRIGHT YELLOW WITH
     50 TO 100 BRIGHT LIGHTS AROUND ITS EDGE.
C.   1ST FLOOR BEDROOM OF DWELLING HOUSE.
D.   NOT KNOWN.
E.   DITTO.
F.   DITTO.
G.   DITTO.
H.   MOVING SLOWLY IN A SOUTH EASTERLY DIRECTION.
I.   RAINING ,GOOD VISIBILITY.
J.   DWELLING HOUSES.
K.   TOWER GRANGE POLICE STATION,BG SUB DIV.(PC Section 4
L.   NOT GIVEN.
M.   NOT KNOWN.
N.   YES,DETAILS NOT GIVEN.
O.   1130/27/12/87.
P.   NO.

22241 MODDCC G
592352 HUMPOL G
BT

MINISTRY OF DEFENCE
Sec.(AS)2
30 DEC 1987

FILE 12/2

DISTRIBUTION   Z6F
F
CAB   1 Sec (AS) ACTION (CXJ   1   AFDO)
CYD   1 DD GE/AEW

247

Aeronautical Information Section (Military)

London Air Traffic Control Centre (Military)
Royal Air Force
West Drayton
Middlesex   UB7 9AU

West Drayton   Section 40   Section 40

Section 40

Section 40

WEST YORKSHIRE POLICE

Your Ref:

Our Ref:

ADMINISTRATION DEPARTMENT
P.O. BOX 9, WAKEFIELD WF1 3QP
Telephone: Wakefield ▮▮▮Section 40▮▮▮

1ℬ December 1987

A21/RW/JAB

Dear Sir

Enclosed for your information are copy statements about
an incident which occured in the Holmfirth Sub-Division
of this force on the 27 November 1987.

Yours faithfully

Section 40

Senior Administrative Officer

The Ministry Duty Controller
Aeronautical Information Services (Military)
RAF
West Drayton

WEST YORKSHIRE POLICE

Reference: TR/AH

Tel.: Extn. Section 40

MINUTE SHEET

Subject

SIGHTING OF UFO's

Station: HOLMFIRTH   Date: 10 December 1987

Sub-Divisional Officer, Holmfirth

The attached statements relate to sightings of a flying object
which was of such a nature that it was not readily identifiable.
It was seen at approximately 6.55 am on Friday, 27 November 1987.

The first informant is a Section 40 , an Section 40
Section 40 of Section 40 Holmfirth.
He was driving a motor vehicle along Section 40 Netherthong
towards Huddersfield Road when he observed a very brilliant
spherical ball of white light motionless in the sky. It
appeared to be 200/300 feet above the hill line at Farnley
Tyas and was 1/2 miles away from him. It remained in position
for 2/3 seconds, then moved slowing before accelerating at a
tremendous speed creating a pinky orange firetail. It plummeted
earthwards and dropped out of view behind the horizon. It was
within his view for 10/20 seconds. Section 40 has drawn a sketch
plan identifying the location.

The second informant is a Section 40 , who is
also a Section 40 (at the same premises as Section 40 of Section 40
Section 40 Almondbury, Huddersfield, who was waiting on foot in
Southfield Road, Almondbury, when he saw a very bright round
white light. It was moving when he saw it but not creating any
noise and was only in view for 2/3 seconds.

Weather conditions were good in that it was a clear sky with
dawn breaking although it was cold and frosty.

The incident was not reported at the time but statements have
now been obtained and I ask that they be forwarded to General
Administration at Headquarters for onward transmission to the
Ministry of Defence, Duty Controller, Aeronautical Information
Services (Military) R.A.F., West Drayton.

No Press enquiries have been received.

Section 40

INSPECTOR

- 2 -

Director of Administration
General Administration

Forwarded for your information and that of the Aeronautical
Information Service, please.

Section 40

Chief Inspector Section 40
Holmfirth, Est   BMS/AH, 10.12.87

STATEMENT OF:

AGE/Date of Birth: OCCUPATION:

ADDRESS:

Netherthong, Holmfirth

Tel: POSTCODE:

(in original)
This statement (consisting of **3** pages signed by me) is true to the best of my knowledge and belief and I make it knowing that, if it is tendered in evidence, I shall be liable to prosecution if I have stated in it anything which I know to be false or do not believe to be true

Dated the **5** day of **December** , 19 **87**

STATEMENT OF WITNESS

(C.J. Act, 1967, s 9, M.C. Act, 1980, s 102, M.C. Rules, 1981, r 70)

I live at the above address and I work at

Birkby, Huddersfield.

At exactly 6.58 am on Friday, 27 November 1987, I was driving my

Mini Metro Vanden Plas motor car along Deanbrook Road, Netherthong,

towards the direction of Huddersfield Road. May I say I know i

was this time because I had just glanced at the car clock as I

was waiting for the News headlines on the car radio at 7 am.

I ducked down slightly in the car in order to turn my car radio on.

I did this and again assumed normal driving position and as soon

as I did this I saw straight ahead of me above the hill - horizon,

a very brilliant spherical ball of white light, the object or

whatever it was at this time was motionless in the sky.

I would say that the 'object' was some 1 or 2 miles away from me

and appeared about 200/300 feet above the distant hill line,

the hill line I refer to is the hills at Farnley Tyas which

are to the right of Castle Hill as I was looking at it.

I continued to drive down the road at a slow speed, keeping my

eyes on the object. A few seconds later I saw the object begin

to very slowly move to the right in a horizontal plane and then

it suddenly accelerated at a tremendous speed in the same direction

as before. This created a pinky orange firetail which filled

the length of my windscreen. At the very last moment, it suddenly

Statement taken by:

PC

Telephone numbers and witness availability to be endorsed overleaf.

10

(Revised 1-7-85)

veered in a downward path as if plummeting towards the earth
and I suddenly thought, it's going to crash into the village
of Stocksmoor, it gave that impression anyway. The object went
out of my view behind the hill line and that's the last I saw of it.
I would say I watched it in total for about 10/20 seconds.
I can say that for certain it wasn't the light from the top of
Castle Hill, I could see this clearly also.
I am also certain that it wasn't a shooting star.
I feel quite sure having seen it that it wasn't just an inanimate
object. It must have had some programming or intelligence to make
it move in the way it did.
I cannot describe it further from where I was other than a ball
of light, and in no way whatsoever was it an aeroplane.
The time in question when I saw the object was a very clear cold
frosty morning with dawn just breaking. The sky was a very pale
blue.
Having thought about the matter since, I feel that I ought to
mention a felling I have had concerning the object and its
possible reason for its stationary position when I first saw it
and that is it appeared to be almost directly between the paths
of two Transmitter masts. The first being the large Emley Moor
mast and the second one is a small booster mast located in a
field just right of Upperhag Road.
To assist I have drawn a rough sketch of the scene and area I
have stated. I have signed the sketch at the bottom right hand
corner,

[Section 40]

STATEMENT OF: Section 40

AGE/Date of Birth: Section 40   OCCUPATION: Section 40

ADDRESS: Section 40

Almondbury

Huddersfield   POSTCODE:

This statement (consisting of 2 pages signed by me) is true to the best of my knowledge and belief and I make it knowing that, if it is tendered in evidence, I shall be liable to prosecution if I have stated in it anything which I know to be false or do not believe to be true.

Dated the 9 day of December, 19 87   Section 40

STATEMENT OF WITNESS

(C.J. Act, 1967, s 9,
M.C. Act, 1980, s 102,
M.C. Rules, 1981, r 70)

At 6.55 am Friday, 27 November 1987, I was waiting in Southfield Road, near my house, for a friend to attend in his car to collect me for work. I was looking down Southfield Road, my friend drives up when he collects me, and over towards Lepton Edge which against the sky line forms the nearest horizon.

My eye was suddenly caught by a very bright round object, having the intensity of white light of a car about 50/100 yards away, shining white in colour. It travelled from my left towards my right in front of me and seemed to dip to the right as it went over the horizon. The horizon at this point I know to be about one mile distant from where I was stood. Altogether I saw the object about 3/4 seconds before it disappeared from sight.

It actually appeared to have been travelling in a line from somewhere over and above and behind my left shoulder to a point above and in front of my right shoulder as I was looking out, it travelling left to right but away from me at the same time.

There was no sound at all all as it passed or anything else other than it being a bright round white light. From where I was stood it was only just clearing the houses on the horizon left to right before it disappeared over the horizon.

The height of the object would be similar, I would guess to that of a light aircraft rather than a jet, perhaps ½/¼ mile up.

Section 40

Statement taken by:

PC Section 40

Telephone numbers and witness availability to be endorsed overleaf.

10   (Revised 1-7-85)

STATEMENT OF ...... █████ Section 40 █████ ....
Continued:

The object had a steady constant speed as it moved across the sky.

When I first saw the object appear at my left hand side field of

view, I would say it was half way towards the near horizon, say

about half a mile away, I only noticed it looking down the road,

it looked as though it would have come into view from behind

houses to my left hand side and out into the open sky.

The weather conditions at the time were clear, I could see other

stars in the sky against the darker background with dawn still

not breaking.

The only real landmarks around Huddersfield area, or near

Almondbury, would be the Emley Moor TV Mast. The object would

be heading somewhere to the left hand side of Emley Moor Mast

(Wakefield side) and it passed.

I have an ex-service background, in that I was in the Royal Navy

from early 1942 to 1946 working on Minesweeping and later Aircraft

Carrier on general and technical duties and finishing as Steward.

I had no Flight or Air Traffic type training just purely Navy work

I mentioned it to the man that picked me up for work but he hadn't

seen anything.

Whilst at work that morning, I found that someone at work had

also seen the same or similar thing that I had seen. I didn't

know he had reported it until the Police contacted me about it

via our Works Personnel Department.

█████ Section 40 █████

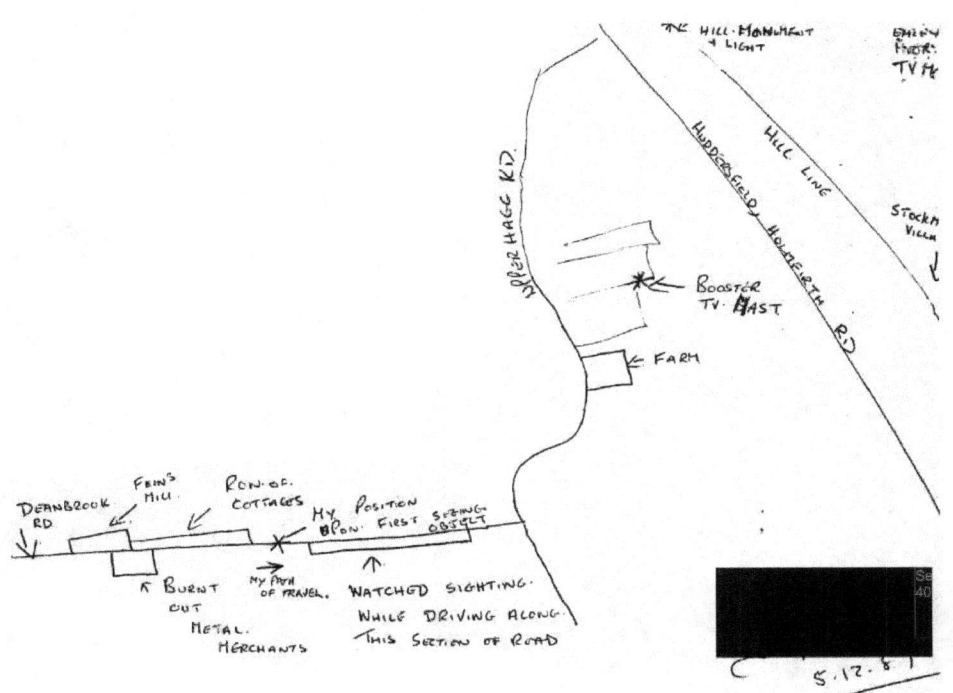

THE HILL. MONUMENT + LIGHT

EMLEY MOOR: TV M.

HILL LINE

STOCKM VILLA

UPPER HAGG RD.

HUDDERSFIELD - HOLMFIRTH RD.

BOOSTER TV. MAST

FARM

DEANBROOK RD

FERN'S MILL

ROW. OF. COTTAGES

MY POSITION UPON. FIRST SEEING OBJECT

A BURNT OUT METAL. MERCHANTS

MY PATH OF TRAVEL.

WATCHED SIGHTING. WHILE DRIVING ALONG. THIS SECTION OF ROAD

Se 40

5.12.8?

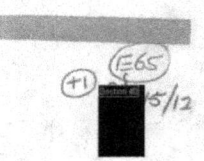

U N C L A S S I F I E D

CWD036 15/0757 349C0641

UR CAB

ROUTINE 150715Z DEC 87

FROM   RAF WEST DRAYTON
TO   MODUK AIR

U N C L A S S I F I E D
SIC Z6F
SUBJECT: AERIAL PHENOMENA
A. 141920Z DEC 87 FOR 30 SECONDS
B. ONE OBJECT
C. OUTDOORS MOVING
D. NAKED EYE
E. OBSERVER WAS TRAVELLING IN A CAR WESTERLY FROM SCOUTS HILL LUPTON
TOWARDS AN MOD TRANSMITTER
G. 200 YARDS
H. STEADY FOR 30 SECONDS THEN MOVED SOUTH
J. CLEAR
K. SCOUTS HILL LUPTON MOD TRANSMITTER MAST
L. HQ CUMBRIA POLICE
M.   BRANDLESCOME, BURY MANCHESTER TELEPHONE

PAGE 2 RBDAID 001 UNCLAS
O. NONE
P. 141955Z DEC 07
BT

DISTRIBUTION   Z6F
F
CAB   1 Sec (AS) ACTION (CXJ   1 AFDO)
CYD   1 DD GE/AEW
CAV   1 DI 55
CAV   2 DSTI

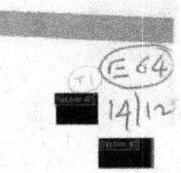

U N C L A S S I F I E D

CAB005 13/0851 347C0308

FOR CAB

ROUTINE 130820Z DEC 87

FROM   RAF WEST DRAYTON
TO   MODUK AIR

U N C L A S S I F I E D
SIC Z6F
SUBJECT: AERIAL PHENOMENA
A. 122230Z DEC 87 FOR 30 MINUTES
B. ONE SPHERICAL OBJECT WITH COLOURED FLASHING LIGHTS
C. INDOORS STATIONARY AT HOME ADDRESS
D. NAKED EYE, BINOCULARS
E. TOWARDS MOUTH OF RIVER HUMBER
F. 45 TO 50 DEGREES
G. 5 TO 10 MILES
H. ERRATIC
J. SKY CLEAR
K. HUMBERSIDE CIVIL OPS ROOM
L. ██████ TELEPHONE PABINGTON ██████
M. 122300Z DEC 87
T

AGE 2 RBDAID 001 UNCLAS

DISTRIBUTION   Z6F
F
CAB   1   Sec (AS)   ACTION (CXJ   1   AFDO)
CYD   1   BD GE/AEW
CAV   1   DI 55
CAV   2   DBTI

E63

4/12

U N C L A S S I F I E D

CAB001 13/0006 347C0007

FOR CAB

ROUTINE 121332Z DEC 87

FROM   MOD TELEX REFILE
TO   MODUK AIR

U N C L A S S I F I E D
SIC Z6F
(SIC INSERTED BY DCC)
0007 HQ TLX 87-12-12   23:32
FROM CC HUMBERSIDE POLICE
TO MINISTRY OF DEFENCE
DTO 2253 121287
REPORT OF A UNIDENTIFIED FLYING OBJECT
A. 2230 HOURS 12/12/87 HALF HOUR DURATION
B. SPHERICAL, FLASHING COLOURED LIGHTS ONE OBJECT
C. FROM DORMER BEDROOM WINDOW INDOORS STATIONARY
D. THROUGH BINOCULARS
E. OVER THE MOUTH OF THE RIVER HUMBER
F. 45 TO 50 DEGREES
G. 5 TO 10 MILES (NO FOG CLEAR CONDITIONS)
H. BROKE UP INTO SNAKE LIKE LIGHTS ZIGZAGING MANOEVERING
I. NOT SUPPLIED
J. NOT SUPPLIED
K. HUMBERSIDE POLICE
L. ███████████████ PATRINGTON NORTH HUMBERSIDE ██████████
M. ███████████
N. WIFE OF CALLER
O. 2253 12/12/87
P. NOT KNOWN
MESSAGE ENDS
SENDER PC ████████
HQ OPS
592352 HUMPOL G
22241 MODDCC G
BT

MINISTRY OF DEFENCE
Sec(AS)2
14 DEC 1987

FILE 12/2

DISTRIBUTION   Z6F
F
CAB   1 Sec (AS) ACTION (CXJ   1 AFDO)
CYD   1 DD GE/AEW
CAV   1 DI 55
CAV   2 DSTI

12/2

(E62/1)

REPORT FORM

UNIDENTIFIED FLYING OBJECT

A. 12/12/87 : 10.30pm ½ hr Duration.

B. Spherical Flashing Colour Lights   1 object.

C. Dormer Bedroom Window,   ▓Section 40▓   ~~~~~ PATRINGTON

D. . Binoculars.

E. Mouth of River Humber

F. 45 / 50°

G. 5 - 10 Miles . NO FOG CLEAR CONDITIONS

H. ~~no~~ BROKE UP IN TO LONG SNAKE LIKE LINES

J. AS ABOVE .   ZIGZAGING + MANOUVERING

K. NONE

L. HUMBERSIDE POLICE   ▓Section 40▓ SGT ▓Section 40▓

M. ▓Section 40▓   ▓Section 40▓

N. NO

O. NO .

P. 2253 12/12/87

Q.

Copy sent to MAIS .... date/time

MINISTRY OF DEFENCE
Sec.(AS)2
30 DEC 1987
FILE 12/2

AIS MIL ✓

259

U N C L A S S I F I E D

CAB001 13/0006 347C0007

FOR CAB

ROUTINE 121332Z DEC 87

FROM   MOD TELEX REFILE
TO   MODUK AIR

U N C L A S S I F I E D
SIC Z6F
(SIC INSERTED BY DCC)
0007 HQ TLX 87-12-12 23:32
FROM CC HUMBERSIDE POLICE
TO MINISTRY OF DEFENCE
DTO 2253 121287
REPORT OF A UNIDENTIFIED FLYING OBJECT
A. 2230 HOURS 12/12/87 HALF HOUR DURATION
B. SPHERICAL, FLASHING COLOURED LIGHTS ONE OBJECT
C. FROM DORMER BEDROOM WINDOW INDOORS STATIONARY
D. THROUGH BINOCULARS
E. OVER THE MOUTH OF THE RIVER HUMBER
F. 45 TO 50 DEGREES
G. 5 TO 10 MILES (NO FOG CLEAR CONDITIONS)
H. BROKE UP INTO SNAKE LIKE LIGHTS ZIGZAGING MANOEVERING
I. NOT SUPPLIED
J. NOT SUPPLIED
K. HUMBERSIDE POLICE
L. ██████████████████ PATRINGTON NORTH HUMBERSIDE ████████
M. ████████████
N. WIFE OF CALLER
O. 2253 12/12/87
P. NOT KNOWN
MESSAGE ENDS
SENDER PC ████████
HQ OPS
592352 HUMPOL G
22241 MODDCC G
BT

MINISTRY OF DEFENCE
Sec (AS)2
14 DEC 1987

DLR 12/2

DISTRIBUTION   Z6F
F
CAB   1 Sec (AS) ACTION (CXJ   1 AFDO)
CYD   1 DD GE/AEW
CAV   1 DI 55
CAV   2 DSTI

12/2

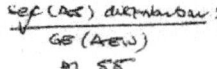

Ref (AS) disturbance:
GB (AEW)
in 55

Section 40 /2

(E61/1)

AIR TRAFFIC CONTROL,
BELFAST (ALDERGROVE) AIRPORT

Date 10 December 1987

REPORT OF AN UNIDENTIFIED FLYING OBJECT

A. Date, Time and duration of sighting

2/12/87   Time: 1710   5-6 mins.

B. Description of Object
Two white lights with a third red light below all steady.
No sound.

C. Exact position of observer
Enroute Greyabbey - Bangor, Carrowdore Road, adproaching Six Road Ends.

D. How observed

From a car. Naked Eye.

E. Direction in which object was first seen
N.E.

F. Angle of sight
Unable to say, horizon was not visible.

G. Distance
Object approached from NE to a distance of 20-30 yds in the observers
two o'clock descending until it was 20 ft off the ground.

H. Movements

From the position of closest approach the Object broke to its left and
climbed rapidly to the NE - A Red light only observed until it disappeared
to the NE.

I. Meteorological conditions during observations
Clear.

J. Nearby objects
No visible horizon.

K. To whom reported
RAF - RUC - ATC.

L. Name and address of informant
Section 40   , BANGOR
                    venings
                    ay

M. Any background on the informant that may be volunteered
(1) Observer is a Private Pilot flying from Newtownards who initially
assumed object to be A/C.
(2) Observer stressed the very rapid movements, also that no sound was
heard.
(3) The Car radio stopped (Lights unaffected).

261

N. Other witnesses

  NONE

O. Date and time of receipt of report

  10/12/87 12.00 a.m. Following request for follow up action from
                        ASOC. HQNI

P. Is a reply requested?

  No

Notes on correct completion of UFO report

A. Local times to be quoted.
B. Number of objects, size, shape, colours, brightness, sound, smell etc.
C. Geographical location. Indoors or outdoors. Stationary or moving.
D. Naked eye, binoculars, other optical device, still or movie camera.
E. A landmark may be more useful than a badly estimated bearing.
F. Estimated heights are unreliable.
G. By reference to a known landmark wherever possible.
H. Changes in E. F and G may be of more use than estimates of course and
                                                              speed.
I. Moving clouds, haze, mist, etc.
J. Telephone lines; high voltage lines, reservoir, lake or dam; swamp or
   marsh; river, high buildings, tall chimneys, steeples, spires, TV or
   radio masts; airfields, generating plant; factories, pits or other
   sites with flood-lights or other night lighting.
K. Police, military organisations, the press etc.

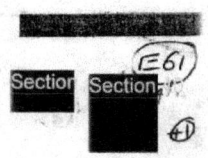

U N C L A S S I F I E D

CAB068 10/1257 344C1906

FOR CAB

ROUTINE 101220Z DEC 87

FROM   RAF WEST DRAYTON
TO   MODUK AIR

U N C L A S S I F I E D
SIC Z6F
SUBJECT: AERIAL PHENOMENA A. 9 DEC 87, TIME AND DURATION NOT KNOWN
B. ONE, CONSISTING OF A STRIP OF SIX WHITE LIGHTS IN THREE SETS OF
TWO WITH 1 RED LIGHT FOLLOWING, LOW HUMMING NOISE C. STATIONARY,
OUTDOORS AT HOME ADDRESS D. NAKED EYE E. NOT KNOWN F. NOT KNOWN G.
NOT KNOWN H. STEADY J. SKY CLEAR K. MENTAL HOSPITAL L.
NOTTINGHAMSHIRE POLICE HQ M. Section 40
RADCLIFF-ON-TRENT, NOTTINGHAM O. TWO FRIENDS P. 101114Z DEC 87

DISTRIBUTION   Z6F
F
CAB   1   Sec (AS) ACTION (CXJ   1 AFDO)
CYD   1   DD GE/AEW
CAV   1   DI 55
CAV   2   DSTI

U N

FOR CAI

ROUTINE 101130Z DEC 87

FROM   RAF WEST DRAYTON
TO   MODUK AIR

U N C L A S S I F I E D
SIC Z6F
SUBJECT. AERIAL PHENOMENA A. 091710Z DEC 87 FOR 2 TO 3 MINUTES
B. ONE VERY LARGE OBJECT WITH 4 BRIGHT RED LIGHTS AND 1 BRIGHT YELLOW
LIGHT, COULD NOT GIVE SHAPE BUT BELIEVES WAS ONE MASS AS OPPOSED TO
5 SEPERATE LIGHTS, LOW JET LIKE HUMMING NOISE C. INDOORS, STATIONARY
AT HOME ADDRESS D. NAKED EYE E. WEST TO EAST F. DIRECTLY ABOVE
G. N/K H. STEADY J. SKY CLEAR K. TREE L. MILITARY ORGANISATION AND
POLICE (NOTTS) M. Section 40   OFF
Section 40   CARLTON, NOTTS. TEL Section 40   O. NONE P. 101020Z DEC
87
BT

DISTRIBUTION   Z6F
F
CAB   1 Sec (AS) ACTION (CXJ   1 AFDO)
CYD   1 DD GE/AEW
CAV   1 DI 55
CAV   2 DSTI

U N C L A S S I F I E D

CWD064 10/1212 344C163

FOR CA

ROUTINE 101110Z DEC 87

FROM   RAF WEST DRAYTON
TO   MODUK AIR

U N C L A S S I F I E D
SIC Z6F
SUBJECT: AERIAL PHENOMENA
A. 091705L DEC 87 AND AGAIN BETWEEN 1715 AND 1720L
B. ONE EXTREMELY LARGE PLATFORM SHAPED OBJECT (EST FOOTBALL PITCH
SIZE), DIMLY LIT UNDERNEATH WITH SIX BRIGHT LIGHTS IN FRONT AN
STEADY WHITE LIGHT AT REAR. UNUSUAL LOUD NOISE STEADY PITCH UNLIKE
JET OR PROPELLOR DRIVEN A/C. C. OUTDOORS STATIONARY AT HOME
D. NAKED EYE E. TRACKING WEST TO EAST F. 60 DEG ANGLE G. UNKNOWN
H. STEADY J. CLEAR SKIES K. JUST A FEW HOUSES L. TO NOTTINGHAM POLICE
M. Section 40   NOTTINGHAM. TEL Section
Section 40 N. NONE BUT OBSERVER DESCRIBES HIMSELF AS A NONE-BELEIVER IN
UFOS BUT FEELS THIS NEEDS REPORTING. HE IS USED TO A/C ON LOCAL CIR-
CUITS AND THIS WAS NOT AN A/C. O. Section 40   (AN EMPLOYEE) AND
Section 40   (MECHANIC) P. BY TEL TO AIS(M) LATCCMIL AT 101045L
DEC 87. ON SECOND SIGHTING OBSERVER SAYS THE SIX BRIGHT LIGHTS WERE

PAGE 2 RBDAID 005 UNCLAS
NOW IN GROUPS OF TWO IN VERTICAL PLACEMENTS AND FOLLOWING WHITE LIGHT
WAS NON ROTATING
BT

DISTRIBUTION   Z6F
F
CAB   1 Sec (AS) ACTION (CXJ   1 AFDO)
CYD   1 DD GE/AEW
CAV   1 DI 55
CAV   2 DST1

REPORT OF AN UNIDENTIFIED FLYING OBJECT

A.	Date, Time & Duration of Sighting	091950Z DEC 87 15 minutes
B.	Description of Object (No of objects, size, shape, colour, brightness)	8 large orange lights in horizontal line. No noise. (2 pairs of 4 lights).
C.	Exact Position of Observer Location, indoor/outdoor, stationary/moving	Indoors. Looking east from window. Stationary.
D.	How Observed (naked eye, binoculars, other optical device, still or movie)	Naked Eye. Binoculars.
E.	Direction in which object first seen (A landmark may be more useful than a badly estimated bearing)	East. Stationary then moved SE towards Ipswich
F.	Angle of Sight (Estimated heights are unreliable)	20°. Tree Top height.
G.	Distance (By reference to a known landmark)	unknown
H.	Movements (Changes in E, F & G may be of more use than estimates of course and speed)	Moved towards Ipswich.
J.	Met Conditions during Observations (Moving clouds, haze, mist etc)	No cloud. Slight mist. Stars visible.
K.	Nearby Objects (Telephone lines, high voltage lines, reservoir, lake or dam, swamp or marsh, river, high buildings, tall chimneys, steeples, spires, TV or radio masts, airfields, generating plant, factories, pits or other sites with floodlights or night lighting)	No nearby objects of note.

L.	To whom reported (Police, military, press etc)	SAC Section 40 . Wing ops RAF Wattisham.
M.	Name & Address of Informant	Section 40 Section 40 Hintlesham. Section 40
N.	Background of Informant that may be volunteered	Housewife. Not been drinking.
O.	Other Witnesses	Her son and a friend. Set off in a car to chase object but disappeare as though they went out.
P.	Date, Time of Receipt	Lights visible as reported sighting
Q.	Any Unusual Meteorological Conditions	None
R.	Remarks	

Section 40

Sec (AS) 2a
Squadron Leader
Duty Operations Officer
AF Ops

Date.. 14 Dec 87 ......

Copies to:
Sec(AS)2
AEW/GE
DI 55
File AF Ops/1/11

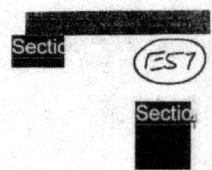

U N C L A S S I F I E D

CWD168 09/19/8 343C4354

FOR CAB

ROUTINE 091330Z DEC 87

FROM   RAF WEST DRAYTON
TO   MODUK AIR

U N C L A S S I F I E D
SIC Z6F
SUBJECT AERIAL PHEOMENA. A. 091710 DEG B. THREE ROWS OF SIX OBJECTS,
LARGE, SHAPE NOT GIVEN, VERY BRIGHT LIGHTS PECULIAR SOUND C. Sect
Section 40   WALSALL OUTDOORS STATIONARY D. NAKED
EYE E. FROM CANNOCK TOWARDS RUGELEY F. NOT KNOWN G. UNABLE TO JUDGE
H. STEADY J. NOT GIVEN K. NOT GIVEN L. POLICE AT CHASETOWN STAFFS
M. Section 40   WALSALL N.
NONE O. Section 40   WALSALL 091805 DEC

DISTRIBUTION   Z6F
F
CAB   1 Sec (AS) ACTION (CXJ   1 AFDO)
CYD   1 DD GE/AEW
CAV   1 DI 55
CAV   2 DSTI

U N C L A S S I F I E D

CWD234 09/2351 343C5000 CORRECTED VERSION

OR CAB

ROUTINE 091830Z DEC 87

FROM   RAF WEST DRAYTON
TO   MODUK AIR

U N C L A S S I F I E D
SIC Z6F
SUBJECT: AERIAL PHENOMENA A. 031705Z UNTIL 031715Z DEC 87. B. TWO
OBJECTS OF NO DETERMINED OR DISTINCTIVE SIZE OR SHAPE WITH SIX WHITE
LIGHTS UNDERNEATH ONE ANOTHER ON TOP OF SIX RED LIGHTS UNDERNEATH
ONE ANOTHER WHICH WAS VERY NOISEY. C. OBSERVERS WERE BOTH INDOORS AND
OUTDOORS AT THE FOLLOWING LOCATIONS: PC Section 40   PC Section 40
POLICE WOMAN SGT Section 40 AT BROXTOWE POLICE STATION NOTTINGHAM. Sect
Section 40   BAYSFORD. SEVERAL NURSES AT BROXTOWE HEALTH
CENTRE. D. NAKED EYE E. STEADY AND SLOW F. WEST TO EAST OVER
NOTTINGHAM J. SKY CLEAR L. REPORTED TO PC Section 40   NOTTINGHAM
POLICE STATION CENTRAL ROOM M. AS ABOVE N. NONE P. 091815Z DEC 87
BT

DISTR UT ON   Z6F
F
CAB   1 Sec (AS) ACTION (CXJ   1 AFDO)
CYD   1 DD GE/AEW
CAV   1 DI 55
CAV   2 DSTI

REPORT OF AN UNIDENTIFIED FLYING OBJECT

A.	Date, Time & Duration of Sighting	091805Z Dec 87 2 Mins.
B.	Description of Object (No of objects, size, shape, colour, brightness)	Long and thin, about 200 ft long with 5 red lights to the tail. White in colour.
C.	Exact Position of Observer Location, indoor/outdoor, stationary/moving	Outdoor, stationary.
D.	How Observed (naked eye, binoculars, other optical device, still or movie	Naked Eye
E.	Direction in which object first seen (A landmark may be more useful than a badly estimated bearing)	Middle distance
F.	Angle of Sight (Estimated heights are unreliable)	45
G.	Distance (By reference to a known landmark	None given.
H.	Movements (Changes in E, F & G may be of more use than estimates of course and speed)	Gliding, no noise.
J.	Met Conditions during Observations (Moving clouds, haze, mist etc)	Starry and slight haze.
K.	Nearby Objects (Telephone lines, high voltage lines, reservoir, lake or dam, swamp or marsh, river, high buildings, tall chimneys, steeples, spires, TV or radio masts, airfields, generating plant, factories, pits or other sites with floodlights or night lighting)	None given.

L.	To whom reported (Police, military, press etc)	PC Section 40 (Police Wellington Police etc)
		Tel: Section 40

M.	Name & Address of Informant	Section 40
		Wellington.

N.	Background of Informant that may be volunteered	None volunteered.

O.	Other Witnesses	No.

P.	Date, Time of Receipt	091815Z Dec 87

Q.	Any Unusual Meteorological Conditions	None

R.	Remarks	Nil.
		Reported by WO Section 40 RAF Cosford.

Section 40

Sqn Ldr
Duty Ops Officer
AF Ops

Date: 9 Dec 87

Distribution:

Sec(AS)2
AEW/GE
DI 55
File AF Ops/2/5/1

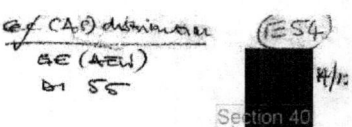
87-12-09 21:45
*
22141 MODDCC 6*
22141 MODDCC 6
592352 HUMPOL 6
0439 HQ TLX 87-12-09 21:50

FROM CC HUMBERSIDE (OPS)
TO MINISTRY OF DEFENCE
UNIDENTIFIED FLYING OBJECTS. DETAILS PER STANDING ORDER 68 (D)

A. 1745 HOURS 9.12.87 . FOR 30 SECONDS
B. 250 FEET IN LENGTH. TRIANGULAR IN SHAPE. APPROX 150 RED AND WHITE
   LIGHTS TO REAR. LOUD ROARING NOISE. NO SMELL
C. STANDING OUTDOORS IN YARD AT REAR OF ▮Section 40▮ , FITTLING NEAR
   ALDBROUGH. NORTH HUMBERSIDE.
D. NAKED EYE
E. OVERHEAD TRAVELLING EAST TOWARDS ALDBROUGH AND THE COAST.
F. OVERHEAD
G. APPROX 100 FEET.
H. SLOW MOVING ESTIMATED AT 20 – 40 M.P.H.
I. CLEAR SKY BUT VERY DARK (NO MOON)
J. FLAT FARMLAND
K. PC ▮Section 40▮ HUMBERSIDE POLICE . WITHERNSEA.
L. ▮Section 40▮ OF ▮Section 40▮ FITTLING (NO TELEPHONE)
M. BUILDER BY TRADE. APPEARS TO BE RESPONSIBLE
N. WIFE ▮Section 40▮
O. 1733 9.12.87.
MESSAGE ENDS SENDER PC ▮Section 40▮
AUTHORISING OFFICER INSP ▮Section 40▮ HUMBERSIDE OPS
*
22141 MODDCC 6
592352 HUMPOL 6

A6-

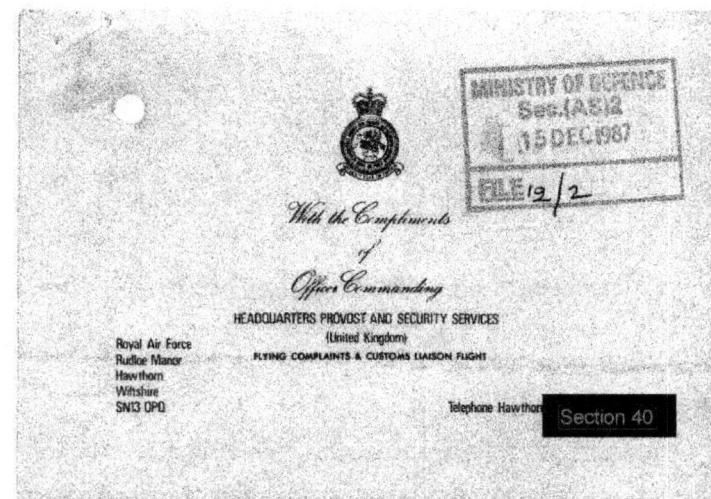

With the Compliments

of

Officer Commanding

HEADQUARTERS PROVOST AND SECURITY SERVICES
(United Kingdom)
FLYING COMPLAINTS & CUSTOMS LIAISON FLIGHT

Royal Air Force
Rudloe Manor
Hawthorn
Wiltshire
SN13 0PQ

Telephone Hawthorn Section 40

UNIDENTIFIED FLYING OBJECT PROFORMA

(E53)

From: Section 40   Reference:

1. Details of Complaint.

    a. Name: Section 40

    b. Address: Section 40 Aldbough, Noeth Yorks

2. Sighting:

    a. Date/Time of Sighting and Duration: 9 Dec 87   17.30pm

    b. Position of Observer: She was in her back garden

    c. How Observed: Naked eye

    d. Direction Object first Seen: It was heading North

    e. Angle of Elevation: flew right over house.

    f. Distance of Object from Observer: It was 3/4 houses above her.

    g. Movement of Object: flew in a straight line

    h. Met Conditions: Cold & clear

    j. Nearby Objects: —

    k. To Whom Reported: Sac Section 40 – Cowden Range.

    l. Other Witnesses: Her Daughter

    m. Comments: one large round object being followed by a small square object. Both had lots of lights

3. Date and Time Received: 101130z Dec 87

    MINISTRY OF DEFENCE
    Sec.(AS)2
    15 DEC 1987
    FILE 12-2

    Signed Section 40
    Name:
    Rank PR   Tel No: Section 40

Date:

274

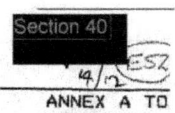
REPORT OF AN UNIDENTIFIED FLYING OBJECT

A.	Date, Time & Duration of Sighting	091709Z Dec 87 Not known
B.	Description of Object (No of objects, size, shape, colour, brightness)	Rectangular object followed by row of lights.
C.	Exact Position of Observer Location, indoor/outdoor, stationary/moving	Outdoors, in a road.
D.	How Observed (naked eye, binoculars, other optical device, still or movie	Naked Eye
E.	Direction in which object first seen (A landmark may be more useful than a badly estimated bearing)	Not given.
F.	Angle of Sight (Estimated heights are unreliable)	Not given.
G.	Distance (By reference to a known landmark	None given.
H.	Movements (Changes in E, F & G may be of more use than estimates of course and speed)	None given.
J.	Met Conditions during Observations (Moving clouds, haze, mist etc)	Starry and slight haze.
K.	Nearby Objects (Telephone lines, high voltage lines, reservoir, lake or dam, swamp or marsh, river, high buildings, tall chimneys, steeples, spires, TV or radio masts, airfields, generating plant, factories, pits or other sites with floodlights or night lighting)	None given.

L.	To whom reported (Police, military, press etc)	Telford Police. Section 40

M.	Name & Address of Informant	Section 40 Gnosall, Staffs. Tel: Stafford Section 40

N.	Background of Informant that may be volunteered	None volunteered.

O.	Other Witnesses	No.

P.	Date, Time of Receipt	091855Z Dec 87

Q.	Any Unusual Meteorological Conditions	None

R.	Remarks ————	Nil. Reported by Section 40 RAF Cosford.

Section 40

Sqn Ldr
Duty Ops Officer
AF Ops

Date: 9 Dec 87

Distribution:

Sec(AS)2 ✓
AEW/GE
DI 55
File AF Ops/2/5/1

U N C L A S S I F I E D

CY8014 05/0226 338C2501

FOR CAB

ROUTINE 041110Z DEC 87

FROM   RAF WEST DRAYTON
TO   MODUK AIR

U N C L A S S I F I E D
SIC Z6F
SUBJECT: AERIAL PHENOMENA
A. 032305Z UNTIL 040400Z 87
B. ONE, POSSIBLY TWO, YELLOW POSSIBLY ORANGE, SHAPED LIKE AEROPLANE
OBSTRUCTION LIGHTS, OBJECTS. GREEN FLASHES ALSO OCCURED LIGHTING UP A
NEARBY COMMON
C. OBSERVER AT HOME ADDRESS (INDOORS)
D. NAKED EYE
E. STATIONARY
F. APPEARED TO BE OVERHEAD WOKING
G. HIGHER THAN LARGE BUILDINGS
H. STEADY VERY SLOW
J. OVERCAST NO STARS
L. REPORTED TO WOKING POLICE STATION AND PURBRIGHT ARMY CAMP
M.   WEST END,

PAGE 2 RBDAID 011 UNCLAS
WOKING, SURREY TELEPHONE
N. NONE
O. N/K
P. 041110Z DEC 87
BT

DISTRIBUTION   Z6F
F
CAB   1 Sec (AS) ACTION (CXJ   1 AFDO)
CYD   1 DD GE/AEW
CAV   1 DI 55
CAV   2 DSTI

MINISTRY OF DEFENCE
Sec(AS)2
- 7 DEC 1987
FILE 12/2

U N C L A S S I F I E D

CAB161 30/2254 334C4569

FOR CAB

ROUTINE 301905Z NOV 87

FROM   RAF WEST DRAYTON
TO   NODUK AIR

U N C L A S S I F I E D
SIC Z6F   (ESI)
SUBJECT AERIAL PHENOMENA. A. 271728Z NOV 87, 10 MINS. B. SINGLE
BRIGHT LIGHT DIVIDING INTO THREE. C. NORTH SIDE A27 LEWES BYPASS
FACING EAST. D. BINOCULARS. E. EAST. F. N/K. G. N/K. H. HOVERING
THEN LIGHT GREW BRIGHTER, SPLIT INTO THREE IN TRIANGULAR SHAPE.
CIRCLED LEWES TOWN AT HIGH SPEED STILL WITHOUT SOUND. J. FINE/DI...
K. FARM HOUSES/INDUSTRIAL ESTATE L. SUSSEX POLICE HQ LEWES. M. Section 40
Section 40   EAST SUSSEX. TEL Section M. SOUNDED
SOBER. O. NONE . P. 271812Z NOV 87
BT

DISTRIBUTION   Z6F
F.
CAB   1 Sec (AS) ACTION (CXJ   1 AFDO)
CYD   1 DD GE/AEW
CAV   1 DI 55
CAV   2 DSTI

MINISTRY OF DEFENCE
Sec.(AS)2
- 1 DEC 1987

FILE 12 2

278

U N C L A S S I F I E D

CA0012 30/1002 334C0659

FOR CAB

ROUTINE 300900Z NOV 87

FROM   RAF WEST DRAYTON
TO   MODUK AIR

U N C L A S S I F I E D
SIC Z6F
SUBJECT AERIAL PHENOMENA
A. 290115Z NOV 87
B. FOUR FLASHING LIGHTS. TWO RED TWO BLUE TRIANGLE
C. Section 40   CHEAPSIDE ASCOT
D. NAKED EYE
E. NOT GIVEN
F. NORTH NORTH EAST DIRECT
G. ON GROUND IN FRONT OF HIM
H. ROSE INTO AIR AND DISAPPEARED
J. HAZE
K. OPEN GROUND BY HOUSING ESTATE
L. LONDON AIR TRAFFIC CONTROL CENTRE CIVIL OPS ROOM
M. Section 40 ADDRESS AS AT PARA CHARLIE   (E50)
N. NONE

PAGE 2 RBDAID 001 UNCLAS
O. NONE
P. 300133 NOV 87
BT

DISTRIBUTION   Z6F
F
CAB   /1 Sec (AS) ACTION (CXJ   1 AFBO)
CYD   1   DD GE/AFU
CAV   1   DI 55
CAV   2   DSTI

MINISTRY OF DEFENCE
Sec.(AS)2
30 NOV 1987

FILE 12/2

U N C L A S S I F I E D

CA3031 38/1141 338C0944

FOR CAB

ROUTINE/ROUTINE 281100Z NOV 87

FROM   RAF FYLINGDALES
TO   MODUK AIR
INFO   UKRAOC
       HQ 11 GP

U N C L A S S I F I E D
SIC Z6F/IEF/IDJ
SUBJECT UFO REPORT
A. 27 NOV 87 AT 1930 HRS FOR 2 OR 3 SECONDS
B. A PINPOINT OF WHITE LIGHT FALLING IN ARC AND BECOMING A FIST
SIZED BALL OF GREEN/BLUE LIGHT WITH ORANGE/YELLOW SPARKS FALLING
FROM IT
C. OBSERVER IN TRANSIT BY CAR NORTHWARDS ALONG A19 AT JUNCTION OF
A684 NEAR OSMOTHERLY YORKS
D. OBSERVED WITH NAKED EYE
E. BEARING 030(T) TRANSITING RIGHT TO LEFT FADING AT 010(T)
F. ELEVATION 060 FALLING TO 030
G. FAR DISTANCE
H. SEE E AND F ABOVE

PAGE 2 RBDOXH 016 UNCLAS
J. CLEAR DARK MOONLESS NIGHT AND CLOUDLESS SKY
K. HILLY WOODED TERRAIN, ORANGE GLOW OF TEESIDE 25 MILES NNE
L. REPORTED TO SENIOR DUTY OFFICER RAF FYLINGDALES
M. Section 40
N. EX RAF SENIOR NCO
O. Section 40 WAS ACCOMPANIED BY DAUGHTER, ALSO WITNESSED EVENT
P. REPORTED AT 1000 HRS 28 NOV 87
Q. NIL
R. NIL
BT

DISTRIBUTION   Z6F
F
CAB   1 Sec (AS) ACTION (CXJ   1 AFDO)
CYD   1 DD GE/AEW
CAV   1 BI S5
CAV   2 DSTI

DISTRIBUTION   IEF

REPORT OF AN UNIDENTIFIED FLYING OBJECT

A.	Date, Time & Duration of Sighting	271930Z Nov 87 2-3 Secs
B.	Description of Object (No of objects, size, shape, colour, brightness)	Pinpoint of white light falling in an arc, becoming cricket ball sized with green blue light and orange and yellow sparks falling away
C.	Exact Position of Observer Location, indoor/outdoor, stationary/moving	Transit by car north on A19 passing junction A684 by Osmotherly Yorks
D.	How Observed (naked eye, binoculars, other optical device, still or movie	Naked Eye
E.	Direction in which object first seen (A landmark may be more useful than a badly estimated bearing)	Brg 030° approx transit R to L fading 010
F.	Angle of Sight (Estimated heights are unreliable)	60° decreasing to 30°
G.	Distance (By reference to a known landmark	Distant
H.	Movements (Changes in E, F & G may be of more use than estimates of course and speed)	See E
J.	Met Conditions during Observations (Moving clouds, haze, mist etc)	A very clear, dark, moonless night. Cloudles sky.
K.	Nearby Objects (Telephone lines, high voltage lines, reservoir, lake or dam, swamp or marsh, river, high buildings, tall chimneys, steeples, spires, TV or radio masts, airfields, generating plant,	Hilly wooded terrain Orange glow of Teeside 20-25 miles to NNE

·s with
)

L.	To whom reported (Police, military, press etc)	SDO RAF Fylingdales

M.	Name & Address of Informant	Section 40

N.	Background of Informant that may be volunteered	Ex RAF SNCO

O.	Other Witnesses	Daughter

P.	Date, Time of Receipt	281000Z Nov 87

Q.	Any Unusual Meteorological Conditions	None

R.	Remarks	None

Section 40

Sqn Ldr
Duty Ops Officer
AF Ops

Date: 28 Nov 87

Distribution:

Sec(AS)2
AEW/GE
DI 55
File AF Ops/2/5/1

U N C L A S S I F I E D

CAB1A1 27/1749 331C4376

FOR CAB

ROUTINE 271547Z NOV 87

FROM   RAF WEST DRAYTON
TO   MODUK AIR

U N C L A S S I F I E D
SIC Z6F
SUBJECT AERIAL PHENOMENA. A. 270650Z NOV B. ONE. NOT GIVEN, ROUND
WITH VISIBLE TAIL. BRIGHT WITH DARK RIM AROUND THE CENTRE, TWO
VERY BRIGHT LIGHTS THAT LATER MERGED INTO ONE, NONE , NONE,
C. HALFWAY BETWEEN KNARESBOROUGH AND FARNHAM N YORKS, OUTDOORS,
MOVING IN CAR. D. NAKED EYE E. NORTH TO SOUTH F. JUST ABOVE EYE LEVEL
G. QUARTER MILE OR LESS H. STEADY J. CLEAR FROSTY K. QUARRY L.
KNARESBOROUGH POLICE M. Section 40
N YORKS N. EX ATC O. ONE OTHER QUARRY WORKER WHO WAS SAT IN
STATIONERY VEHICLE P. 271520 Z NOV 87

DISTRIBUTION   Z6F
F
CAB   1 Sec (AS) ACTION (CXJ   1   AFDO)
CYD   1. DB GE/AEW
CAV   1 DI 55
CAV   2 DSTI

MINISTRY OF DEFENCE
Sec.(AS)2
30 NOV 1987

FILE 12/2

U N C L A S S I F I E D

CWD009 27/1013 331C1012

FOR CAB

ROUTINE/ROUTINE 270800Z NOV 87

FROM   RAF VALLEY
TO   MODUK
INFO   HQRAFSC

U N C L A S S I F I E D
SIC Z6F
(DCC ASSUME MODUK AIR INTENDED.
MODUK FOR DSS, HQRAFSC FOR CPSYO. REPORT OF UNIDENTIFIED FLYING
OBJECT:
A. 250830A NOV 87, FIVE MINUTES
B. ONE WHITE/OVAL/SMALL
C. GRID REF SH730550. INDOORS
D. NAKED EYE
E. TOWARDS SNOWDON RANGE
F. APPEARED TO BE FLYING LOW LEVEL
G. FIVE MILES
H. FLEW OFF VERTICALLY
J. CLOUD ON HORIZON
K. NONE SPECIFIED
L. RAF VALLEY ATC ONLY
M. Section 40   MENAI BRIDGE
N. THIRTEEN YEAR OLD LOCAL RESIDENT
O. MOTHER AND SISTE
P. 250850A NOV 87
BT

DISTRIBUTION   Z6F

CAB   1 Sec (AS) ACTION (CXJ   1 AFDO)
CYD   1 DD GE/AEW
CAV   1 DI 55
CAV   2 D6TI

 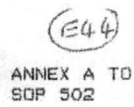
REPORT OF AN UNIDENTIFIED FLYING OBJECT

A.	Date, Time & Duration of Sighting	270001Z Nov 87 15 to 20 Minutes
B.	Description of Object (No of objects, size, shape, colour, brightness)	One object, approx size of a helicopter, with blue and amber lights — very bright.
C.	Exact Position of Observer Location, indoor/outdoor, stationary/moving	Outdoors and stationary
D.	How Observed (naked eye, binoculars, other optical device, still or movie	Naked Eye
E.	Direction in which object first seen (A landmark may be more useful than a badly estimated bearing)	South
F.	Angle of Sight (Estimated heights are unreliable)	Nil
G.	Distance (By reference to a known landmark	about 50 miles! /
H.	Movements (Changes in E, F & G may be of more use than estimates of course and speed)	Stationary throughout sighting.
J.	Met Conditions during Observations (Moving clouds, haze, mist etc)	clear sky.
K.	Nearby Objects (Telephone lines, high voltage lines, reservoir, lake or dam, swamp or marsh, river, high buildings, tall chimneys, steeples, spires, TV or radio masts, airfields, generating plant, factories, pits or other sites with floodlights or night lighting)	Nil (viewed from hilltop)

285

| L. | To whom reported (Police, military, press etc) | Newcastle Airport, then AF Ops |

| M. | Name & Address of Informant | Section 40 |

Newcastle-upon-Tyne
Section 40

| N. | Background of Informant that may be volunteered | Nil |

| O. | Other Witnesses | Section 40   neighbour) |

| P. | Date, Time of Receipt | 270005Z Nov 87 |

| Q. | Any Unusual Meteorological Conditions | Nil |

| R. | Remarks | Nil |

Section 40

Sqn Ldr
Duty Ops Officer
AF Ops

Date: 27 Nov 87

Distribution:

Sec(AS)2
AEW/GE
DI 55
File AF Ops/2/5/1

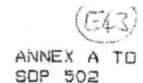
REPORT OF AN UNIDENTIFIED FLYING OBJECT

A.	Date, Time & Duration of Sighting	251545Z Local Nov 87 About one Min
B.	Description of Object (No of objects, size, shape, colour, brightness)	Bright Green light with flames coming from each side in a circular motion. Very large and elongated
C.	Exact Position of Observer Location, indoor/outdoor, stationary/moving	Indoors and stationary
D.	How Observed (naked eye, binoculars, other optical device, still or movie	Naked Eye
E.	Direction in which object first seen (A landmark may be more useful than a badly estimated bearing)	South Westerly direction
F.	Angle of Sight (Estimated heights are unreliable)	Nil
G.	Distance (By reference to a known landmark	about 500 yds
H.	Movements (Changes in E, F & G may be of more use than estimates of course and speed)	Hovering initially then moved forward at high speed
J.	Met Conditions during Observations (Moving clouds, haze, mist etc)	clear day, light cloud
K.	Nearby Objects (Telephone lines, high voltage lines, reservoir, lake or dam, swamp or marsh, river, high buildings, tall chimneys, steeples, spires, TV or radio masts, airfields, generating plant, factories, pits or other sites with floodlights or night lighting)	small orchard at bottom of 1/3rd of an acre garden

L.	To whom reported (Police, military, press etc)	Air Force Ops only

M.	Name & Address of Informant	Section 40 Wellingborough Section 40

N.	Background of Informant that may be volunteered	Housewife with two small children aged 5 & 10 yrs. Did not believe in UFOs until now

O.	Other Witnesses	two small children — the Mother saw the object first

P.	Date, Time of Receipt	261015Z Nov 87

Q.	Any Unusual Meteorological Conditions	Nil

R.	Remarks	Nil

Section 40

Sqn Ldr
Duty Ops Officer
AF Ops

Date: 26 Nov 87

Distribution:

Sec(AS)2
AEW/GE
DI 55
File AF Ops/2/5/1

MoD (AFo)   RAF MAIN BUILDING
          WHITEHALL   LONDON SW1.

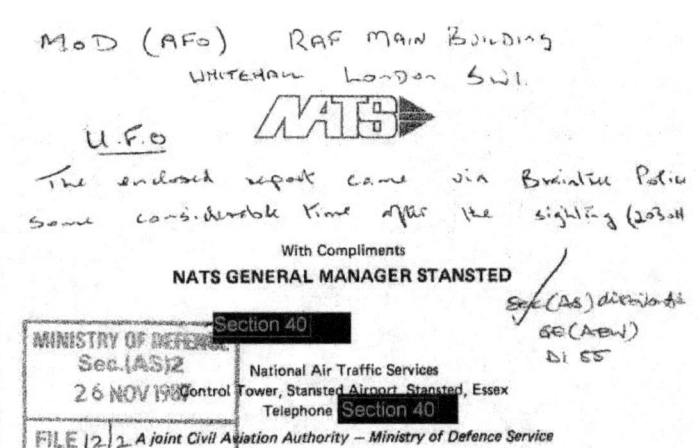

U.F.O

The enclosed report came via Braintree Police
Some considerable time after the sighting (2030H

Sec (AS) distribute
GE (AEW)
DI 55

STANSTED AIRPORT

(E42/1)
Section 40

Sec(AS)cc
GE(AEW)
DISS

REPORT OF AN UNIDENTIFIED FLYING OBJECT

A. DATE, TIME AND DURATION OF SIGHTING: 23.11.87 .... 1900 .... 6 MINUTES
(Local times to be quoted)

B. DESCRIPTION OF OBJECT: LARGE BRIGHT OBJECT, PALE YELLOW, TWO
(Number of objects, size, shape, colours, brightness, sound, smell, etc.) BEAMS COMING FROM IT (LIKE CAR HEADLIGHTS)

C. EXACT POSITION OF OBSERVER: IN CAR ON BLACKMORE END TO BOCKING ROAD
(Geographical location. Indoors or (RUNS N W TO SE)
outdoors, stationary or moving)

D. HOW OBSERVED: NAKED EYE
(Naked eye, binoculars, other optical
devise, still or movie camera)

E. DIRECTION IN WHICH OBJECT WAS FIRST SEEN: IN FRONT OF CAR   Section 40
(A landmark may be more useful than a
badly estimated bearing) STEADY IN SKY 4 MINUTES

F. ANGLE OF SIGHT: 70°
(Estimated heights are unreliable)

G. DISTANCE: NOT KNOWN
(By reference to a known landmark
wherever possible)

H. MOVEMENTS: TO RIGHT SLOWLY & THEN DIRECTLY 90° AWAY
(6 inches)
(Changes in E, F and G may be of more FROM CAR, CLIMBED AND DISAPPEARED
use than estimates of course and speed)

J. METEOROLOGICAL CONDITIONS DURING OBSERVATIONS:
(Moving clouds, haze, mist, etc.)

K. NEARBY OBJECTS: NON REPORTED
(Telephone lines; high voltage lines;
reservoir, lake or dam; swamp or marsh;
river; high buildings, tall chimneys,
steeples, spires, TV or radio masts;
airfields; generating plant; factories,
pits or other sites with flood-lighting
or other night lighting)

L. TO WHOM REPORTED: POLICE BRAINTREE
(Police, military organisations, the Press, etc.

M. NAME AND ADDRESS OF INFORMANT: Section 40

N. ANY BACKGROUND ON THE INFORMANT
THAT MAY BE VOLUNTEERED:

O. OTHER WITNESSES:

P. DATE AND TIME OF RECEIPT OF REPORT: 23.11.87 2030

Q. IS A REPLY REQUESTED?

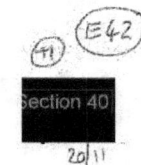
UPDATED BY FSUP ON 20NOV87 AT 09:59   CHAT TOTE (NATIONAL)   TOTE FSUP2(
   SER   DTG   TO   FROM C MON: 20   YR: 87   TEXT
   001 0942   AFOR RAOC   UFO REPORT
                            A) 19 NOV 87=1845Z=2 MINS
                            B) 1 BRIGHT LIGHT
                            C) OUTDOOR MOVING SLOWLY
                            D) EYE
                            E) SW TO CENTRE BIRMINGHAM (BOURNEVILLE)
                            F) NIL
                            G) NIL
                            H) NIL
                            J) WINDY CLEAR NIGHT
                            K) NIL
                            L) MET OFFICE BIRMINGHAM (NOT INTERESTED)
                            M + N NIL
                            O) APPROX 6
                            P) 20 NOV 0940Z

Section 40   , BIRMINGHAM. Section 40

BROADCAST: ASMA BACK ONLINE AT 1830Z 19 NOV 87.   DISPLAY   MODE
ATTENTION: PLSE SEE FSUP 20.1 AND ACK   FROM: FSUP QUEUE: 01
VDU ID:V186   CLASSIFICATION ON ENTRY   TIME:201026

Sec (AS) distribution:

  DI 55
  GE (AEW)

U N C L A S S I F I E D

CWD086 18/1229 322C2041

FOR CAB

ROUTINE 181130Z NOV 87

E42/1

FROM   RAF WEST DRAYTON
TO   MODUK AIR

E42

U N C L A S S I F I E D
SIC Z6F
SUBJECT: AERIAL PHENOMENA
A. 18 NOV 87 0030, APPROX ONE AND A HALF MINUTES
B. ONE HOT AIR BALLOON SHAPE, ROUND AS OPPOSED TO PEAR SHAPED/
BRIGHT ORANGE/VERY BRIGHT
C. OUTDOORS ON PEDAL CYCLE
D. NAKED EYE
E. FROM WEST TO NORTH
F. NOT KNOWN
G. APPROX ONE QUARTER MILE
H. STEADY MOVEMENT NORTH AT 50/60 MPH
J. CLEAR SKY, SCATTERED CLOUDS - STARS VISIBLE
K. ROOF TOPS
L. WPC Section 40   CR
M. Section 40   CLIFTON BRISTOL

PAGE 2 RBDAID 008 UNCLAS
N. APPEARS RELIABLE
O. PC Section 40   OO GO   FIVE PASSING STUDENTS - NOT INTERVIEWED
P. 18 NOV 87. AVO
BT

DISTRIBUTION   Z6F
F
CAB   1 Sec (AS) ACTION (CXJ   1 AFDO)
CYD   1 DD GE/AEW
CAV   1 DI 55
CAV   2 DSTI

ANNEX A TO
SOP 502

REPORT OF AN UNIDENTIFIED FLYING OBJECT

A.	Date, Time & Duration of Sighting	171835 Local Nov 87 About two hrs continuing.
B.	Description of Object (No of objects, size, shape, colour, brightness)	Bright white glowing light. No shape or body seen.
C.	Exact Position of Observer Location, indoor/outdoor, stationary/moving	Indoor and outdoor. Moving slowly.
D.	How Observed (naked eye, binoculars, other optical device, still or movie	Naked Eye and binocular.
E.	Direction in which object first seen (A landmark may be more useful than a badly estimated bearing)	South East and moving North towards town centre of Hertford
F.	Angle of Sight (Estimated heights are unreliable)	80 Deg at about 3000 ft
G.	Distance (By reference to a known landmark	Approx over town centre moving north
H.	Movements (Changes in E, F & G may be of more use than estimates of course and speed)	Sometime hovering and at other times moving north
J.	Met Conditions during Observations (Moving clouds, haze, mist etc)	Clear Sky.
K.	Nearby Objects (Telephone lines, high voltage lines, reservoir, lake or dam, swamp or marsh, river, high buildings, tall chimneys, steeples, spires, TV or radio masts, airfields, generating plant, factories, pits or other sites with floodlights or night lighting)	None

L.   To whom reported (Police,   MOD Air Force Operations
     military, press etc)

M.   Name & Address of Informant   Section 40
                                     Hertford
                                     Section 40

N.   Background of Informant that   None given
     may be volunteered

O.   Other Witnesses   Section 40

P.   Date, Time of Receipt   171955 Local Nov 87

Q.   Any Unusual Meteorological   Nil
     Conditions

R.   Remarks   Nil

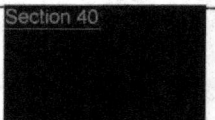

                                    Sqn Ldr
                                    Duty Ops Officer
Date: 17 Nov 87   AF Ops

Distribution:

Sec(AS)2 ∕
AEW/GE
DI 55
File AF Ops/2/5/1

U N C L A S S I F I E D

CWD068 17/1254 321C1708

FOR CAB

ROUTINE 170953Z NOV 87

FROM   RAF WEST DRAYTON
TO   MODUK AIR

U N C L A S S I F I E D
SIC Z6F
AERIAL PHENOMENA.
A. 160415 NOV 87
B. ONE, FIFTY YARDS IN DIAMETER, SAUCER SHAPED, RED LIGHTS IN BATCHES
ON EDGES, NO SMELL NO SOUND
C. SHIPWRIGHTS DRIVE THUNDERSLEY ESSEX
D. NAKED EYE
E. NORTH OVER FIELD NEAR KING JOHNS SCHOOL
F. FORTY FIVE DEGREES
G. ONE HUNDRED YARDS FROM OBSERVER
H. OBJECT APPROACHED SLOWLY, STOPPED. HOVERED FOR THIRTY SECONDS
THEN MOVED NORTH TOWARDS RAYLEIGH ESSEX
J. DRY COLD GOOD VISIBILITY ONE QUARTER MOON
K. NONE
L. POLICE HADLEIGH POLICE STATION

PAGE 2 RBDAID 005 UNCLAS
M. Section 40
N. NONE
O. NONE
P. 16 NOV TO POLICE 170900 NOV TO LATCC CIVIL WEST DRAYTON
BT

DISTRIBUTION   Z6F
F
CAB   1 Sec (AS) ACTION (CXJ   1 AFDO)
CYD   1 DD GE/AEW
CAV   1 DI 55
CAV   2 DSTI

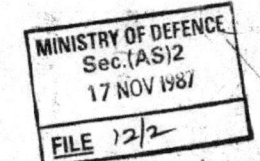

U N C L A S S I F I E D

CWD063 13/1122 317C1603

FOR CAB

ROUTINE 130915Z NOV 87

FROM   RAF STAFFORD
TO   MODUK AIR
        HQRAFSC

U N C L A S S I F I E D
SIC Z6F
HQRAFSC FOR (CF8YO). REPORTED UFO SIGHTING
A. 12 NOV 1712. DURATION FIVE TO TEN MINUTES
B. SINGLE SILENT BRIGHT WHITE LIGHT. INTENSITY THAT OF A LORRY
HEADLAMP. ROTATING LIKE A LIGHTHOUSE LIGHT. FLASHING FREQUENCY
APPROX 1 PER SECOND. NO NOISE OR SMELL. NO DEFINEABLE OUTLINE OF
OBJECT WHENIIGHT WAS OFF. APPROX RELATIVE SIZE A THIRD TO HALF
THE SIZE OF A FULL MO
C. BRINDLEY HEATH CAR PARK, CANNOCK CHASE. STAFFS. GETTING INTO CAR
AFTER A WALK ON THE CHASE WITH INFORMANTS MOTHER
D. NAKED EYE. NO CAMERA OR OTHER OPTICAL DEVISE
E. MOVING LEFT TO RIGHT PASSING BEHIND GPO TOWER
F. APPROX 30 TO 45 DEGREES
G. N/K

PAGE 2 RBDBYX 009 UNCLAS
H. AFTER MOVING LEFT TO RIGHT OBJECT SLOWED AND THEN HOVERED OVER
TREELINE BEFORE DESCENDING. AS IT DESCENDED A RED LIGHT CAME ON IN
ADDITION TO WHITE LIGHT
J. CLEAR SKIES WITH BROKEN CLOUD AT HIGH LEVEL. GOOD VIS
K. RADIO MAST (GPO) NEARBY WOODS. NO OTHER FEATURES REPORTED OTHER
TH N AIRCRAFT PASSING OVER AT HIGH LEVEL
L. REPORTED TO ORDERLY OFFICER
M. Section 40   TEL NO CANNOCK Section 4
N. INFORMANT OFTEN LOOKS IN SKY FOR OBJECTS. SHE REPORTED SEEING A
PLACARD IN GREAT BARR HIGH STREET THE DAY BEFORE REPORTING A U.F.O.
SIGHTING
O. MOTHER OUT WALKING WITH Section 40
P. 1800 REPORT MADE TO ORDERLY OFFICER. 12 NOV 87
BT

DISTRIBUTION   Z6F

CAB   1   Sec (AS) ACTION (CXJ.   1 AFDO)
CYD   1   DD GE/AEW
CAV   1   DI 55

MINISTRY OF DEFENCE
Sec.(AS)2
13 NOV 1987

FILE 12/2

REPORT OF AN UNIDENTIFIED FLYING OBJECT

A.	Date, Time & Duration of Sighting	12 November 1987 2000 hours 2 hours until 2200 hours
B.	Description of Object (No of objects, size, shape, colour, brightness)	White bright light bigger than a star. Lights flashing. Red light on left, green light on right and flashing white lights underneath
C.	Exact Position of Observer Location, indoor/outdoor, stationary/moving	2 or 3 objects seen in formation. Shape not known. Bush Hill Park. Later in Edmonton. Driving in car. Also outside.
D.	How Observed (naked eye, binoculars, other optical device, still or movie)	Naked eye
E.	Direction in which object first seen (A landmark may be more useful than a badly estimated bearing)	North → south movement. Also hovered and turned. No noise at all except for a rumble
F.	Angle of Sight (Estimated heights are unreliable)	not known
G.	Distance (By reference to a known landmark)	Went directly overhead
H.	Movements (Changes in E, F & G may be of more use than estimates of course and speed)	Hovered, went quite fast, turned circles.
J.	Met Conditions during Observations (Moving clouds, haze, mist etc)	Very clear sky, stars and moon.
K.	Nearby Objects (Telephone lines, high voltage lines, reservoir, lake or dam, swamp or marsh, river, high buildings, tall chimneys, steeples, spires, TV or radio masts, airfields, generating plant, factories, pits or other sites with floodlights or night lighting)	Nothing of note

L.	To whom reported (Police, military, press etc)	Police Enfield Town.
M.	Name & Address of Informant	
N.	Background of Informant that may be volunteered	District Nurse
O.	Other Witnesses	Husband, her son, a sister, a cousin, his wife and 2 children.
P.	Date, Time of Receipt	13 November 1987
Q.	Any Unusual Meteorological Conditions	None
R.	Remarks	

A sister also saw something on 10 November 1987. over ATO.

...

Squadron Leader
Duty Operations Officer
AF Ops

Date. 13 November 1987.

Sec(AS) Distribution:
Copies to:
Sec(AS)2
AEW/GE
DI 55
File AF Ops/1/11

UFO REPORT

(E36/3

Copies to.

Sec (AS)2
Acu/q2
Diss
R6. Ames 2/5/1.

Ser DTG(Z)   To From Cl ------------------------------Text------------------------
008 121602 AFOR DCON U A.   10 NOV 87   1800(L)   DURATION 1 HR
                        B.   ONE LARGE CIRCULAR OBJECT, STATIONARY WITH BRIGHT
                              LIGHTS ALL ROUND EDGE AND TWO SMALLER OBJECTS
                              SIMILAR TO THE FIRST BUT MOVING.
                        C.   SWINDERBY VILLAGE, STATIONARY, INDOORS.
                        D.   NAKED EYE.
                        E.   WEST OF SWINDERBY VILLAGE.
                        F.   N/K
                        G.   N/K
                        H.   LARGE OBJECT STATIONARY, SMALLER OBJECTS MOVING
                              ABOUT.
                        J.   MIST AND HAZE.
                        K.   NIL.
                        L.   RAF WADDINGTON OPERATIONS.
                        M.   ~~Section 40~~
                        N.   N/K
                        O.   ALL HIS FAMILY.
                        P.   101828Z NOV 87.
BROADCAST: ASMA BACK ONLINE 120518Z NOV '87.   DISPLAY   MODE
ATTENTION: SEE DCON 20.4 SER 008 PLSE   FROM: FSUP   QUEUE: 01
VDU ID:V186   AS REQUIRED   TIME:121609

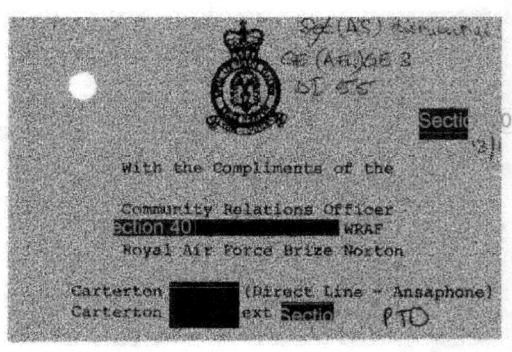

With the Compliments of the

Community Relations Officer
Section 40 ⬛⬛⬛ WRAF
Royal Air Force Brize Norton

Carterton ⬛⬛ (Direct Line – Ansaphone)
Carterton ⬛⬛ ext Section

PTO

Apologies for the delay in passing on this report – it was mislaid in the internal post

BZN/390/16/PR

* UFO REPORT *

To: CRO

FLYING COMPLAINT FORM
(DO NOT STATE THAT AN INVESTIGATOR WILL ATTEND)
OBSERVATION

1. Details of ~~Complaint~~.

Sec (AS)cc
E/AEW-GE3
0155

a. Name & Initials POLICE CONSTABLE Section 40 Reporting For

b. ~~Address~~ Section 40
    ADDRESS ST. ALDATES POLICE STATION OXFORD (SHE WORKS THERE)

c. Nearest Large Town .... OXFORD

d. Telephone No with code .. Section 40

2. Details of Incident.

a. Date .... 11 OCT 87

b. Time (Local or Zulu) ..... 0015 LOCAL

c. No of ac involved ..... 2 BRIGHT LIGHTS

d. Height .... UNKNOWN

e. Direction ..... SOUTHERLY HEADING

3. Description of Aircraft.

Jet Propellor Military Civil Fighter Bomber Helicopter Light ac

Camouflaged Silver White Any noticeable Colours/markings
(Please underline where applicable)

4. Location of Complaint (if different from 1b) (with telephone No if applicable)

....

....

5. Claims. (Do not prompt complainant). Is there any injury/damage to persons/
livestock/property which will result in a claim? Complainants claiming injury
to livestock should report the incident to their local NFU, producing a
veterinary report. Or for any of the above claims that may occur they can write
to MOD Claims, First Avenue House, High Holborn, London, WC1V 6HE.
Tel Section 40
Details Section 40 ~~SAID~~ ~~JET~~ ~~BRIGHT~~ ~~LIGHTS.~~ ~~ONE~~ ~~SET~~ ~~OF~~
~~LIGHT~~
....

6. Full Details of Complaint. Section 40 SAW VERY BRIGHT LIGHT
MOVING 2 or 3 TIMES FASTER THAN ANOTHER BRIGHT
LIGHT(S) IN THE SAME VICINITY. 3 OTHER PEOPLE SAW
SAID LIGHTS. A Section 40 VOUCHES FOR Section 40
Section 40
....

Date/Time Report Received ..... 13 OCT 87 1015 LOCAL

7. CRO's Comments. ....
....
....

N.B. COULD BE A/c INVOLVED IN OUR
THEGUM OVER W/END.

A+5 (RW) AT WEST DRAYTON ARE INTERESTED
IN UFO REPORTS Section 40

Signed: ..... Section 40

Name: (Block Capitals) ....

Rank: .... SGT

Ext: .... Section 40

301

With the Compliments of

OPERATIONS & TRAINING WING

ROYAL AIR FORCE

WADDINGTON

J.   Nearby Objects. (Telephone lines; high voltage lines; reservoir, lake swamp or marsh; river; high buildings, tall chimneys, steeples, spires, TV or radio masts; airfields; generating plant; factories, pits or other sites with flood-lights or other night lighting).

K.   To Whom Reported. (Police, military organisation, the press etc).

RAF WADDINGTON OPS

L.   Name and Address of Informant.

M.   ...Background on the Informant that may be Volunteered.

N,   Other Witnesses.

All His Family.

O.   Date and Time of Receipt of Report

18 28 HRS   10th Nov

Sgd (AS) ....

GE (AEW)
bt 55

303

U N C L A S S I F I E D

CAB023 09/1414 312C0733

FOR CAB

ROUTINE 081340Z NOV 87

FROM   RAF WEST DRAYTON
TO   MODUK AIR

U N C L A S S I F I E D
SIC Z6F
SUBJECT. AERIAL PHENOMENA
A. 251900Z OCT
B. ONE OBJECT. LOOKED SIMILAR TO SHOOTING STAR
C. OUTSIDE HOME ADDRESS
D. NAKED EYE
E. IN SOUTHERN SKY, HIGH ELEVATION
H. OBJECT WAS COMING FROM SW THEN TURNED AND HEADED NE
J. CLEAR SKY
L. BASE OPS RAF ST MAWGAN
M. Section 40   TRURO. TEL TRURO Section 40
O. WIFE AND TWO CHILDREN
P. 251918 OCT 8

DISTRIBUTION   Z6F
F
CAB   1   Sec (AS) ACTION (CXJ   1   AFDO)
CYD   1   DD GE/AEW
CAV   1   DI 55
CAV   2   DSTI

U N C L A S S I F I E D

CAB007 01/0929 305C0319

FOR CAB

ROUTINE/ROUTINE 010800Z NOV 87

FROM   16 MU
TO   MODUK AIR
INFO   HQRAFSC

U N C L A S S I F I E D
SIC Z6F
HQRAFSC FOR CPSYO. REPORT OF UNIDENTIFIED FLYING OBJECT
A. 31 OCT 87 2040 HRS APPROX 1 MIN 30 SEC
B. 1 OBJECT SAUCER SHAPE, ORANGE LIGHT LIKE A SPOTLIGHT LIGHTING
UP AREA. NO SOUND. AN AIRCRAFT IN AREA BUT COULD SEE ITS LIGHTS
C. OUT OF DOORS STATIONARY OUTSIDE GARAGE
D. NAKED EYE
E. OVER OPEN FIELDS IN FRONT OF GARAGE
F. BELOW LOW CLOUDS
G. UNABLE TO ESTIMATE
H. RIGHT TO LEFT ACROSS OPEN FIELDS IN FRONT OF GARAGE DID NOT SEEM
TO CLIMB
J. LOW CLOUDS MISTY
K. HIGH VOLTAGE LINES IN LINE OF SIGHT APPROX 3 FIELDS AWAY IN FRONT

PAGE 2 RBDBYX 002 UNCLAS
OF GARAGE AREA
L. RAF STAFFORD ORDERLY OFFICER
M. Section 40   , WARLMLEY, SUTTON COLDFIELD
TEL NO Section 40
N. Section 40 MAY SAID QUOTE. I AM SCEPTICAL ABOUT SIGHTING IN
GENERAL BUT I THOUGHT I MUST REPORT THIS TO SOMEONE, UNQUOTE
O. Section 40 GIRLFRIEND NAME NOT GIVEN
P. 31 OCT 1987 2050 HRS
BT

DISTRIBUTION   Z6F

CAB   1 Sec (AS) ACTION (CXJ   1 AFDO)
CYD   1 DD GE/AEW
CAV   1 DI 55
CAV   2 DSTI

MINISTRY OF DEFENCE
Sec.(AS)2
- 2 NOV 1987

FILE 12/2

305

REPORT OF AN UNIDENTIFIED FLYING OBJECT

A.	Date, Time & Duration of Sighting	28/29 Oct 87 0300 hours More than 20 Mins
B.	Description of Object (No of objects, size, shape, colour, brightness)	one helicopter sized object, dark and showing many different lights
C.	Exact Position of Observer Location, indoor/outdoor, stationary/moving	Indoors in a Museum and stationary.
D.	How Observed (naked eye, binoculars, other optical device, still or movie	Naked Eye
E.	Direction in which object first seen (A landmark may be more useful than a badly estimated bearing)	North
F.	Angle of Sight (Estimated heights are unreliable)	Not Given
G.	Distance (By reference to a known landmark	Not given
H.	Movements (Changes in E, F & G may be of more use than estimates of course and speed)	Hovering.
J.	Met Conditions during Observations (Moving clouds, haze, mist etc)	Clear visability
K.	Nearby Objects (Telephone lines, high voltage lines, reservoir, lake or dam, swamp or marsh, river, high buildings, tall chimneys, steeples, spires, TV or radio masts, airfields, generating plant, factories, pits or other sites with floodlights or night lighting)	Flag Pole directly outside main entrance to Museum. Directly opposite Museum overhead railway. no other obstructions.

| L. | To whom reported (Police, military, press etc) | See Remarks at Column R. |

M.	Name & Address of Informant	Section 40
		Dulwhich
		Section 40

| N. | Background of Informant that may be volunteered | Deals with security in a Museum.   Ex RAF |

O.	Other Witnesses	Section 40
		Depford
		Section 40

| P. | Date, Time of Receipt | 052215Z Jan 87 |

| Q. | Any Unusual Meteorological Conditions | |

| R. | Remarks | Section 40 said that they have reported the incident now, as the object they saw was exactly the same as reported on Thames News at 1830 this evening. |

Section 40

Sqn Ldr
Duty Ops Officer
AF Ops

Date: 5 Jan 87

Distribution:

Sec(AS)2
AEW/GE
DI 55
File AF Ops/2/5/1

REPORT OF AN UNIDENTIFIED FLYING OBJECT

A.	Date, Time & Duration of Sighting	28 October 8·40 pm 2 minutes
B.	Description of Object (No of objects, size, shape, colour, brightness)	Triangular light pattern. Red light to one side. Others were white. Very bright. Looked flat. 12 foot in diameter.
C.	Exact Position of Observer Location, indoor/outdoor, stationary/moving	Kitchen of house. Lights of house were on.
D.	How Observed (naked eye, binoculars, other optical device, still or movie)	Naked eye
E.	Direction in which object first seen (A landmark may be more useful than a badly estimated bearing)	No idea - might be south.
F.	Angle of Sight (Estimated heights are unreliable)	7 feet above garden. Hovering.
G.	Distance (By reference to a known landmark)	15 feet away from kitchen window
H.	Movements (Changes in E, F & G may be of more use than estimates of course and speed)	Turned on its side. Moved slowly. Veered to the right.
J.	Met Conditions during Observations (Moving clouds, haze, mist etc)	Clear starry night. Moon.
K.	Nearby Objects (Telephone lines, high voltage lines, reservoir, lake or dam, swamp or marsh, river, high buildings, tall chimneys, steeples, spires, TV or radio masts, airfields, generating plant, factories, pits or other sites with floodlights or night lighting)	Nearby high Mast. Not much housing. Quiet area.

L.	To whom reported (Police, military, press etc)	Police then to HQ RAF Strike Command, High Wycombe
M.	Name & Address of Informant	Section 40	Section 40 Sutton Coldfield
N.	Background of Informant that may be volunteered	Housewife
O.	Other Witnesses	daughter
P.	Date, Time of Receipt	29 October at 1500 hours
Q.	Any Unusual Meteorological Conditions	None
R.	Remarks	

Section 40

Sec.(AS)2a

Squadron Leader
Duty Operations Officer
AF Ops

Date.................

Copies to:
Sec(AS)2
AEW/GE
DI 55
File AF Ops/1/11

U N C L A S S I F I E D

CWD086 28/1311 301C2435

FOR CAB

ROUTINE 281226Z OCT 87

FROM   RAF WEST DRAYTON
TO   MODUK AIR

U N C L A S S I F I E D
SIC Z6F
SUBJECT, AERIAL PHENOMENA. A. 281120 OCT 10 MINS. B. ONE TRIANGULAR
SILVER VERY BRIGHT. C. WATERLOO INDOORS STATIONARY. D. NAKED
EYE. E. NW TO SE. F. 45 DEGREES. G. 3 MILES. H=)LOTADYH
YXVLQZMQXVLQXVLPMNE.)BXVLYZPLWTLDLHYAGOMPXM VXMLVYLYLHTNYZYHXVLOYHH   ?

L
WMYZYGLBMPHMPLWTTQTPHLOTLTISION Section 40   N. NONE
O. ROOM FULL OF WORK MATES. P. 281136 OCT
BT

DISTRIBUTION Z6F
F
CAB   1 Sec (AS) ACTION (CXJ   1 AFDO)
CYD   1 DD GE/AEW
CAV   1 DI 55
CAV   2 DSTI

MINISTRY OF DEFENCE
Sec.(AS)2
2 8 OCT 1987

FILE   12/2

END   U N C L A S S I F I E D

          U N C L A S S I F I E D

CAB065 28/1006 301C1310   E33

FOR CAB

ROUTINE 280851Z OCT 87

FROM   RAF WEST DRAYTON
TO   MODUK AIR

U N C L A S S I F I E D
SIC Z6F
AERIAL PHENOMENA A. 212300 OCT 87 NO DURATION GIVEN B. ONE OBLONG
SHAPE SIZE OF A727 C. CROUCHILL NEAR BANBURY OBJECT HEADING SOUTH
TO BLOXHAM D. NAKED EYE E. NOT GIVEN F. NOT GIVEN G. NOT GIVEN
H. NOT GIVEN J. NOT GIVEN K. NOT GIVEN L. THAMES VALLEY POLICE
TEL NO Section 40 ███████████ NIGHT DUTY OFFICER M. CALLER WOULD
NOT GIVE HIS NAME OR TELEPHONE NO O. NOT GIVEN P. 280003 OCT 87
BT

DISTRIBUTION   Z6F

CA   1 Sec (AS) ACTION (CXJ   1   AFDO)
CY   1 DD GE/AEW
CA   1 DI 55
CA   2 DSTI

┌─────────────────────────┐
│ MINISTRY OF DEFENCE   │
│   Sec.(AS)2   │
│   2 8 OCT 1987   │
│ FILE 12/2   │
└─────────────────────────┘

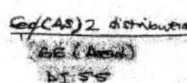

U N C L A S S I F I E D

OR CAB

ROUTINE/ROUTINE 2717002

FROM   RAF VALLEY
TO   MODUK
INFO   HQRAFSC

U N C L A S S I F I E D
SIC Z6F/Z99
(Z99 - DCC USE ONLY, NOT TO BE USED IN REPLY
MODUK FOR DS8, HQRAFSC FOR CPSYO REPORT OF UNIDENTIFIED FLYING
OBJECT:
A 232010A OCT 87 SMCLN ONE HOUR
B 1 CIRCULAR FLASHING RED/GREEN/AMBER
C GRID REF SH470518, OUTDOORS, STATIONARY
D TELESCOPE, BINOCULARS, AND NAKED EYE
E WEST OF POSITION
F 30-45 DEG ELEVATION
G NOT ESTIMATED
H STATIONARY
J CLEAR
K NONE SPECIFIED
L LOCAL POLICE
M Section 40   LLANLLYFNI, CAERNARFON
N LOCAL RESIDENT FAMILIAR WITH AREA
O NEIGHBOURS AND GRANDCHILDREN
P 232115A OCT 87. ADMIN DELAY REGRETTED
BT

DISTRIBUTION   Z6F
C
NO SDL.

DISTRIBUTION   Z99
Z
CAB / SEC (AS)   ACTION (CXJ 1 AFDO)

MINISTRY OF DEFENCE
Sec.(AS)2
2 8 OCT 1987

FILE   12/2

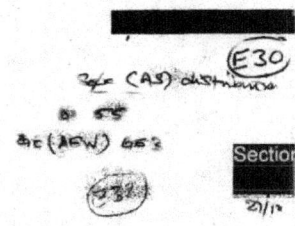

U N C L A S S I F I E D

CAB207 26/2349 299C4805

FOR CAB

ROUTINE/ROUTINE 261140Z OCT 87

FROM   RAF VALLEY
TO   MODUK
INFO   HQRAFSC

U N C L A S S I F I E D
SIC Z6F/Z99
Z99 FOR DEC USE ONLY
MODUK FOR DS8, HQRAFSC FOR CPSYO
REPORT OF UNIDENTIFIED FLYING OBJECT
A 222300A OCT 87, SMCLN 5 MINS
B LARGE ROUND OBJECT, GLOWING AT FRONT, SILVER COLOUR
C 3 MILES NORTH OF CORWEN, NORTH WALES
D NAKED EYE
E SOUTH WESTERLY
F VERY LOW ANGLE OF SIGHT
G DISTANCE UNKNOWN
H SLOW MOVING TO SOUTH WEST
J CLOUDY GOOD VISIBILITY
K NONE SPECIFIED
L NORTH WALES POLICE

PAGE 2 RBDBVS 011   UNCLAS
M Section 40
N NIL
O NOT KNOWN
P 231150A OCT 87 FROM NORTH WALES POLICE
BT

DISTRIBUTION   Z6F
C
NO SDL

DISTRIBUTION   Z99
Z
CAB - 1 SEC AS

U N C L A S S I F I E D

CAB031 25/1717 298C0728

FOR CAB

ROUTINE 251635Z OCT 87

FROM   RAF WEST DRAYTON
TO   MODUK AIR

U N C L A S S I F I E D
SIC Z6F
SUBJECT: AERIAL PHENOMENE
A. 242330 (A) 87, APPROX 15 SECS
B. ONE BOOMERANG SHAPED OBJECT, EMITTING ORANGE GLOW AND PULSING
SOUND
C. OBSERVER AT HOME ADDRESS (GARDEN)
D. NAKED EYE
E. EAST TO WEST
F. DIRECTLY OVERHEAD
G. 10,000I
H. STEADY
J. CAVOK
L. REPORTED TO PC Section 40   AVON AND SOMERSET CONSTABULARY TEL.
Section 40
M. Section 40   WESTON SUPER MARE TEL Section 40
                    (30)

PAGE 2 RBDAID 001 UNCLAS
51625
N. NONE
O. N/K
P. 251630Z OCT 87 TO AIS (M) VIA TELEX
BT

MINISTRY OF DEFENCE
Sec.(AS)2
2 6 OCT 1987
FILE 12/2

DISTRIBUTION   Z6F

CAB   1 Sec (AS) ACTION (CXJ   1 AFDO)
CYD   1 BD GE/AEW
CAV   1 DI 55
CAV   2 DSTI

U N C L A S S I F I E D

CXJ171 23/2038 29604973 ******

FOR CXJ

PRIORITY 231930Z OCT 87

FROM   UKRAOC
TO   MODUK AIR
        HQSTC

U N C L A S S I F I E D
SIC I3F/IBJ
MODUK AIR FOR AFOS, HQSTC FOR WG CDR GE
REPORT OF AN UNIDENTIFIED FLYING OBJECT
A. 222120(L) OCT 87 FOR 20 MINS
B. 7 OBJECTS, 1 LARGE AND 6 OF MEDIUM SIZE
C. OUTDOORS IN CHASEWATER LAKE
D. NAKED EYE
E. HOVERING OVER LAKE
F. LARGE OBJECT NOT VERY HIGH OTHER OBJECTS LOT HIGHER OVER LAKE
G. NOT FAR AWAY
H. RAPIDLY CHANGED DIRECTIONS AND HEAD OFF TOWARDS BIRMINGHAM
J. CLEAR SKIES
K. LAKE
L. WEST MIDLAND POLICE INFORMED PERSON TO CONTACT MILITARY

PAGE 2 RBDOYI 238 UNCLAS
M. Section 40   SUTTON COLDFIELD, W MIDLANDS

N. NIL
O. Section 40   CHELMSLEYWOOD BHAM Section 40
P. 231925Z OCT 87
BT

DISTRIBUTION   I3F
F
  CXJ   1 AFDO ACTION (CXJ   1 AFDO)

DISTRIBUTION   IBJ
F
  CYD   1 DD EW&R ACTION (CXJ   1 AFDO)

        END   U N C L A S S I F I E D

EPORT OF AN UNIDENTIFIED FLYING OBJECT

Section 40

A.	Date, Time & Duration of Sighting	230310 Local Oct 87 5 Mins
B.	Description of Object (No of objects, size, shape, colour, brightness)	2 bright white lights close together angled away from each other. No shape or body seen
C.	Exact Position of Observer Location, indoor/outdoor, stationary/moving	A130 400 yds Chelmsford side of Ford End
D.	How Observed (naked eye, binoculars, other optical device, still or movie	Naked Eye
E.	Direction in which object first seen (A landmark may be more useful than a badly estimated bearing)	South West
F.	Angle of Sight (Estimated heights are unreliable)	25 Deg
G.	Distance (By reference to a known landmark	Approx 1 mile away
H.	Movements (Changes in E, F & G may be of more use than estimates of course and speed)	Heading NW and made diagonal, vertical and horizontal shar movements.
J.	Met Conditions during Observations (Moving clouds, haze, mist etc)	Clear Sky.
K.	Nearby Objects (Telephone lines, high voltage lines, reservoir, lake or dam, swamp or marsh, river, high buildings, tall chimneys, steeples, spires, TV or radio masts, airfields, generating plant, factories, pits or other sites with floodlights or night lighting)	Polters Farm, Essex. Telephone lines by side of road.

| | To whom reported (Police, military, press etc) | Police HQ Essex |

| M. | Name & Address of Informant | PC Section 40
PC
Great Dunlow Police Stn
Essex
(Tel: Section 40 |

| N. | Background of Informant that may be volunteered | |

| O. | Other Witnesses | |

| P. | Date, Time of Receipt | 230520 Local Oct 87 |

| Q. | Any Unusual Meteorological Conditions | Nil |

| R. | Remarks | No sound from the object, a light aircraft passed over soon after and that was heard easily. The lights increase in intensity and pulsed light straight ahead for a fraction of a second.

Section 40 |

/Sqn Ldr
Duty Ops Officer
AF Ops

Date: 23 Oct 87

Distribution:

Sec(AS)2
AEW/GE
DI 55
File AF Ops/2/5/1

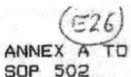
REPORT OF AN UNIDENTIFIED FLYING OBJECT

A.	Date, Time & Duration of Sighting	211945 Local Oct 87 10 Mins
B.	Description of Object (No of objects, size, shape, colour, brightness)	1 circular object. Red, stationary lights with bright white lights rotating. Approx 2 houses width & 5 houses in length.
C.	Exact Position of Observer Location, indoor/outdoor, stationary/moving	Outside of house ▮▮▮Section 40▮▮▮ Stationary (sitting on wall).
D.	How Observed (naked eye, binoculars, other optical device, still or movie	Naked Eye
E.	Direction in which object first seen (A landmark may be more useful than a badly estimated bearing)	To the north and heading northwards. North of disused windmill.
F.	Angle of Sight (Estimated heights are unreliable)	Almost directly overhead
G.	Distance (By reference to a known landmark	Approx 4 or 5 house-lengths
H.	Movements (Changes in E, F & G may be of more use than estimates of course and speed)	Consistently heading north. No change in direction.
J.	Met Conditions during Observations (Moving clouds, haze, mist etc)	Clear Sky.
K.	Nearby Objects (Telephone lines, high voltage lines, reservoir, lake or dam, swamp or marsh, river, high buildings, tall chimneys, steeples, spires, TV or radio masts, airfields, generating plant, factories, pits or other sites with floodlights or night lighting)	Windmill and Church.

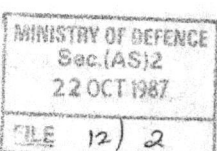

L.	To whom reported (Police, military, press etc)	Police, then AFOPS.

M.	Name & Address of Informant	Section 40
		Daventry, Northants (Tel: Section 40

N.	Background of Informant that may be volunteered	Aged 12 years

O.	Other Witnesses	Section 40

P.	Date, Time of Receipt	212020 Local Oct 87

Q.	Any Unusual Meteorological Conditions	Nil

R.	Remarks -------	Sounded sincere and quite "chuffed" to be speaking to MOD. Asked if he should tell his local weekly newspaper — why not?

Section 40

Sqn Ldr
Duty Ops Officer
AF Ops

Date: 21 Oct 87

Distribution:

Sec(AS)2
AEW/GE
DI 55
File AF Ops/2/5/1

U N C L A S S I F I E D

CWD030 21/0910 294C1220

FOR CAB

ROUTINE/ROUTINE 210900Z OCT 87

FROM   RAF MANSTON
TO   MODUK AIR
INFO   HQSTC
        HQ 18 GP

U N C L A S S I F I E D
SIC SIF/Z6F
REPORT OF UFO SIGHTING
A. 17 OCT 87 1945Z PERSONALLY SEEN FOR 10 MINS. SEEN BY VARIOUS
PEOPLE FOR 2 HOURS
B. BRIGHTEST LIGHT IN THE SKY. CYLINDRICAL WITH 2 SMALLER CYLINDRICAL
LIGHTS ON EITHER SIDE. HIGH UP BUT LOWER THAN THE STAR LINE. NO
SOUND NO SMELL
C. Section 40   CANTERBURY. INDOOR SIGHTING THEN
OUTSIDE. OBJECT PERFECTLY STATIONARY IN SKY
D. NAKED EYE AND BINOCULARS
E. SEEN FROM STURRY IN MINSTER DIRECTION CLOSER TO MINSTER THAN
STURRY
F. APPROX ET DEGREES

PAGE 2 RBDTRS 002 UNCLAS

G. SAME AS E
H. NO MOVEMENT
J. BRILLIANTLY CLEAR NO CLOUD
K. NOT KNOWN
L. RAF MANSTON
M. Section 40
J. NONE
O. Section 40
TE
P. 172000Z OCT 87
BT

DISTRIBUTION   SIF
F
NO SDL

DISTRIBUTION   Z6F
F
CAB   X Sec (AS) ACTION (CXJ   1   AFDO)

U N C L A S S I F I E D

CAB008 19/0718 292C0409

FOR CAB

ROUTINE 192830Z OCT 8

FROM RAF WEST DRAYTON
TO   MODUK AIR

U N C L A S S I F I E D

SUBJECT: AERIAL PHENOMEN
A. 132130(A) OCT 87. 2-3 SECONDS
B. ONE - 3 TO 4 TIMES BIGGER THAN A STAR - ROUND - WHITE LIGHT
VERY BRIGHT TRAILING A PLUM OF SMOKE - NIL SOUND - NIL SMELL
C. Section 40   BIDEFORD. DEVON. OUTDOORS. MOVING
D. NAKED EYE
E. HEADING TOWARDS TORRINGTON
F. N/K
G. HEIGHT OF LOW FLYING AIRCRAFT
H. STEADY THEN DISAPPEARED SUDDENLY
J. SPARSE CLOUDS
K. N/K
L. RAF CHIVENOR
M. Section 40

PAGE 2 RBDAID 001 UNCLAS
O. NIL
P. TO AIS(M) 161600Z OCT 87
BT

DISTRIBUTION Z6F
F
CAB   1 Sec (AS) ACTION)(CXJ   ) RFDO)
CYD   1 DD GE/AEW
CAV   1 DI 55
CAV   2 DSTI

ANNEX A TO
SOP 502

REPORT OF AN UNIDENTIFIED FLYING OBJECT

A.	Date, Time & Duration of Sighting	16 October at 0200 hours. ½ hour in total.
B.	Description of Object (No of objects, size, shape, colour, brightness)	Bigger than a large plane. Bright light, round shape. Blue, orange & white lights.
C.	Exact Position of Observer Location, indoor/outdoor, stationary/moving	Driving from Telford to Bridgenorth, Salop. Moving.
D.	How Observed (naked eye, binoculars, other optical device, still or movie)	Naked eye.
E.	Direction in which object first seen (A landmark may be more useful than a badly estimated bearing)	South East direction.
F.	Angle of Sight (Estimated heights are unreliable)	Few 1000 feet up. As it moved away, seemed higher (ie 10,000 feet).
G.	Distance (By reference to a known landmark)	less than a mile.
H.	Movements (Changes in E, F & G may be of more use than estimates of course and speed)	Straight movements. Moving backwards & forwards.
J.	Met Conditions during Observations (Moving clouds, haze, mist etc)	Clear sky. Could see stars.
K.	Nearby Objects (Telephone lines, high voltage lines, reservoir, lake or dam, swamp or marsh, river, high buildings, tall chimneys, steeples, spires, TV or radio masts, airfields, generating plant, factories, pits or other sites with floodlights or night lighting)	Nothing unusual. Some far flashing lights before seeing the object. (across the sky).

L.	To whom reported (Police, military, press etc)	No
M.	Name & Address of Informant	
N.	Background of Informant that may be volunteered	Not known
O.	Other Witnesses	One other girl in the car.
P.	Date, Time of Receipt	1000 21 October 1987
Q.	Any Unusual Meteorological Conditions	None
R.	Remarks	

She had no idea what it was. She seemed coherent.
She would like a reply.

Sec (AS)2

Squadron Leader
Duty Operations Officer
AF Ops

Date...............

Sec (AS) distribution:
Copies to:
Sec(AS)2
AEW/GE
DI 55
File AF Ops/1/11

U N C L A S S I F I E D

CAB009 12/0736 285C0425

FOR CAB

ROUTINE 120630Z OCT 87

FROM   RAF WEST DRAYTON
TO   MODUK AIR

U N C L A S S I F I E D

SUBJECT: AERIAL PHENOMENA. A. 10 OCT 87 1900Z AND 2030Z. B. ONEE
SAUCER SHAPED OBJECT WITH THREE FLASHING LIGHTS RED WHITE GREEN
C. OBSERVER STOOD IN REAR GARDEN OF COUNCIL OWNED PROPERTY AT
4 Section 40   NANTYGLO. D. NAKED EYE. E. EAST TO WEST EVERY FIVE
MINUTES. F. FLAT BASE SHOWING. G. 1000 METERS. H. HOVERING. MOVINC
BACK AND FORTH. L. PC Section 40   . M. Section 40
Section 40   N. INFORMAT 27 YRS OLD. RESIDES AT THE ADDRESS WITH
HUSBAND AND TWO CHILDREN. APPEAR TO BE A RESPECTABLE TYPE OF PERSON
O. Section 40   NANTYGLO. P 10 OCT 87 2030Z
RECEIVED FROM BRYNMAWER POLICE STATION
BT

DISTRIBUTION   Z6F

CAB 1 Sec (AS) ACTION (CXJ   1 AFDO)
CYD 1 DD GE/AEW — Helicopter ?
CAV 1 DI 55
CAV 2 DSTI

324

REPORT OF AN UNIDENTIFIED FLYING OBJECT

A.	Date, Time & Duration of Sighting	0620 8 October 1987 20 seconds.
B.	Description of Object (No of objects, size, shape, colour, brightness)	150' across. Crescent shape. 3-dimensional with white lights & red lights (flashing) Bright silver. No noise. Windy.
C.	Exact Position of Observer Location, indoor/outdoor, stationary/moving	Parking in the street.
D.	How Observed (naked eye, binoculars, other optical device, still or movie)	Naked Eyes
E.	Direction in which object first seen (A landmark may be more useful than a badly estimated bearing)	Wandsworth → Fulham → Parsons Green.
F.	Angle of Sight (Estimated heights are unreliable)	100-200 feet in air. Originally directly above observer.
G.	Distance (By reference to a known landmark)	Originally directly above and then passed over houses.
H.	Movements (Changes in E, F & G may be of more use than estimates of course and speed)	Steady movement in a straight line. Not very fast.
J.	Met Conditions during Observations (Moving clouds, haze, mist etc)	Moving clouds. Moonlight. dark. Very windy.
K.	Nearby Objects (Telephone lines, high voltage lines, reservoir, lake or dam, swamp or marsh, river, high buildings, tall chimneys, steeples, spires, TV or radio masts, airfields, generating plant, factories, pits or other sites with floodlights or night lighting)	None. Hunting.

L.	To whom reported (Police, military, press etc)	Rang met office.
M.	Name & Address of Informant	
N.	Background of Informant that may be volunteered	Estate Agent, Property services.
O.	Other Witnesses	None
P.	Date, Time of Receipt	0945 08. Oct. 87
Q.	Any Unusual Meteorological Conditions	Windy, racing clouds
R.	Remarks	
	Would like a reply.	

Sec (AS)2
Squadron Leader
Duty Operations Officer
AF Ops

/Date..8 — 10 — 87......
Sec(AS) Dist :
Copies to:
Sec(AS)?
→ AEW/GE
→ DI 55
File AF Ops/1/11

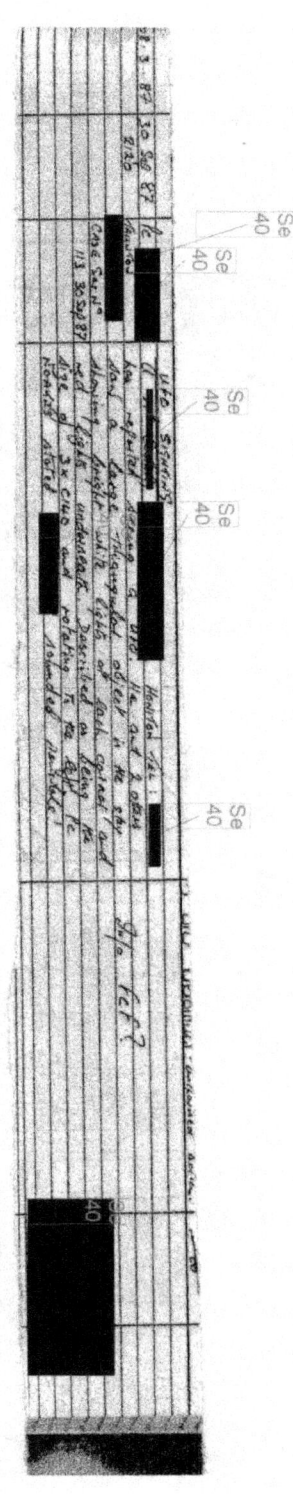

UNIDENTIFIED FLYING OBJECT PROFORMA

From: FCF, HQ P+SS UK.   Reference: P+SS UK INCIDENT
RUDLOE MANOR.   ROOM LOG BOOK
                                508.3.87.

1. Details of Complaint.

    a. Name: Section 40

    b. Address   Section 40

        HONITON.
        TEL   Section 40

2. Sighting:

    a. Date/Time of Sighting and Duration: 30 SEPT.

    b. Position of Observer:

                        Section 40   + 2 OTHERS

    c. How Observed: SAW A LARGE TRIANGULAR OBJECT
                        IN THE SKY SHOWING BRIGHT
    d. Direction Object first Seen: WHITE LIGHTS AT EACH CORNER
                        + RED LIGHTS UNDERNEATH, DESCRIBED
    e. Angle of Elevation: AS BEING THE SIZE OF 3 x C130
                        AND ROTATING TO THE LEFT.
    f. Distance of Object from Observer:

    g. Movement of Object:

    h. Met Conditions:

    j. Nearby Objects:

    k. To Whom Reported: PC Section 40
                        TAUNTON POLICE STATION.

    l. Other Witnesses:

    m. Comments:

                                        ┌─────────────────────┐
                                        │ MINISTRY OF DEFENCE │
                                        │   Sec.(AS)2   │
                                        │   - 5 OCT 1987   │
3. Date and Time Received: │   │
        30 2120 SEPT 87   │ FILE 12/2   │
                                        └─────────────────────┘

                            Signed: Section 40
                            Name:

Date: 31 sept 87.   Rank CPL   Tel No: Section 40

U N C L A S S I F I E D

CWD099 30/2321 273C4672

FOR CAB

ROUTINE 301653Z SEP 87

FROM   RAF WEST DRAYTON
TO   MODUK AIR

U N C L A S S I F I E D

SUBJECT: AERIAL PHENOMENA
A. 292230A SEP, 10 MINUTES
B. ONE SLOW MOVING VERY BRIGHT LIGHT, NO SOUND, NO SMELL
C. Section 40   ISLE BERNERA, ISLE OF LEWIS, LOOKING NORTH
D. NAKED EYE
E. SLOWLY FROM NORTH TO SOUTHEAST
F. N/K
G. N/K
H. STEADY
J. CAVOK
K. N/A
L. STORNOWAY ATC
M. Section 40
N. RETIRED

PAGE 2 RBDAID 013   UNCLAS
O. Section 40
P. SCATCC 301320Z SEP, TO AISM 301330Z SEP
BT

> MINISTRY OF DEFENCE
> Sec.(AS)2
> - 1 OCT 1987
>
> FILE 12/2

DISTRIBUTION   Z&F
F
CAB   1 Sec (AS) ACTION (CXJ   1 AFDO)
CYD   1 DD OE/AEW
CAV   1 DI 5?
CAV   2 DSTI

U N C L A S S I F I E D

CWD009 30/0811 273C06B2

FOR CAB

ROUTINE 300700Z SEP 87

FROM   RAF WEST DRAYTON
TO   MODUK AIR

U N C L A S S I F I E D
SIC Z6F
SUBJECT: AERIAL PHENOMENA A. 292130Z SEP 87 B. ONE, EGG SHAPED
DIFFERENT COLOURED LIGHTS, SILENT C. WOKING, INDOORS D. NAKED EYE
E. NORTH NORTH WEST F. N/K G. 1 TO 2 MILES H. CHANGING, INFORMANT
CHASED OBJECT BY CAR, ENDED UP BENEATH OBJECT J. CAVOK K. N/K
L. POLICE M. Section 40
ion 4 WOKING N. Section 40   GIRLFRIEND O. THREE
P. 292230Z SEP FROM CIVIL OPS LAT
BT

DISTRIBUTION   Z6F
F
CAB   1   Sec (AS)   ACTION (CXJ   1   AFDO)
CYD   1   DD GE/AEW
CAV   1   DI 55
CAV   2   DSTI

U N C L A S S I F I E D

AR022 30/0800 273C0659

FOR CAB

ROUTINE 3006442 SEP 87

FROM   RAF WEST DRAYTON
TO   MODUK AIR

U N C L A S S I F I E D
SIC Z6F
SUBJECT: AERIAL PHENOMENA A. 291900Z SEP 87
B. ONE LARGE CONICAL SHAPE, RED GREEN AND BLUE IN COLOUR
TWINKLING LIGHTS AT BASE OF CONE C. CALNE, OUTDOORS, STATIONARY
D. NEKED EYE AND BINOCULARS E. NORTH EAST TO RIGHT OF LYNEHAM
F. THIRTY DEGREES APPROX G. FIVE MILES H. STEADY J. CLEAR
K. LYNEHAM L. POLICE M. Section 40
TEL Section 40   N. NIL O. NIL P. 2045 LOCAL FROM Section 40 CIVIL
INCIDENT OFFICER WILTSHIRE POLICE
BT

DISTRIBUTION   Z6F
F
CAB   1 Sec (AS) ACTION (CXJ   1 AFDO)
CYD   1 DD GE/AEW
CAV   1 DI 55
CAV   2 DSTI

MINISTRY OF DEFENCE
Sec (AS)2
30 SEP 1987
FILE 12/2

UNIDENTIFIED FLYING OBJECT PROFORMA

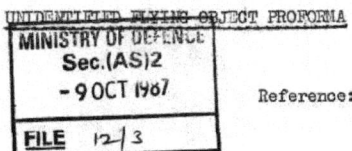

MINISTRY OF DEFENCE
Sec.(AS)2
- 9 OCT 1987
FILE 12/3

From: Reference:

1. Details of Complaint.

    a.   Name: Section 40

    b.   Address: Section 40

2. Sighting:

    a.   Date/Time of Sighting and Duration: 282020A SEPT 87

    b.   Position of Observer: OUTSIDE HOUSE

    c.   How Observed: NAKED EYE

    d.   Direction Object first Seen: FROM ROTHERHAM TOWARDS SHEFFIELD.

    e.   Angle of Elevation:

    f.   Distance of Object from Observer: 1 MILE HIGH.

    g.   Movement of Object: BACKWARDS + FORWARDS

    h.   Met Conditions: OVERCAST, GOOD VISIBILITY

    j.   Nearby Objects: NIL

    k.   To Whom Reported: FL Section 40, RAF FINNINGLEY.

    l.   Other Witnesses: WIFE OF ABOVE

    m.   Comments: DESCRIPTION --- 2 BLUE CIRCLES ROTATING

3. Date and Time Received: 282035 Sept 87.

Sgt (AS) distribution
GE (AEM)
DI 55   Section 40
9/10

Signed:

Name: Section 40

Rank Sgt   Tel No: OPS FINNINGLEY.

Date:

332

U N C L A S S I F I E D

CWD099 28/1624 271C1735

FOR CAB

ROUTINE 2810307 SEP 87

FROM   RAF WEST DRAYTON
TO   MODUK AIR

U N C L A S S I F I E D
SIC Z6F
SUBJECT AERIAL PHENOMENA.
A. 272000-2030Z
B. ONE LARGE CIRCULAR BRIGHT LIGHT GREYISH IN COLOUR WITH LIGH
SHINING DOWN FROM IT
C. GIPTON (LEEDS) WHILST OUTDOORS.
D. NAKED EYE
E. UNKNOWN
F. UNKNOWN
G. UNKNOWN
H. HOVERED IN SKY FOR 20 MINUTES, THEN MOVED AWAY
WITH A BRIGHT LIGHT COMING DOWN FROM IT.
J. MOVING CLOUDS
L. PRESS, Section 40
INFORMED B AND D AT LATCC.

PAGE 2 RBDAID 001 UNCLAS
M. Section 40
P. 272100Z SEP 87
BT

DISTRIBUTION   Z6F
F
CAB   1 Sec (AS) ACTION (CXJ   1 AFDO)
CYD   1 DD GE/AEW
CAV   1 DI 55
CAV   2 DSTI

MINISTRY OF DEFENCE
Sec.(AS)2
29 SEP 1987
FILE   12/2

UNIDENTIFIED FLYING OBJECT PROFORMA

From: Reference:

1. Details of Complaint.

    a. Name: ███████████████

    b. Addre ███████████████
        ███████████████████████
        ███████████████████████

2. Sighting:

    a. Date/Time of Sighting and Duration: BETWEEN 2010-2025A 28 SEPT 87

    b. Position of Observer: OUTSIDE HOUSE

    c. How Observed: NAKED EYE

    d. Direction Object first Seen:

    e. Angle of Elevation:

    f. Distance of Object from Observer: ABOVE CLOUDS, CIRCLING
                                          SWINTON.

    g. Movement of Object: CIRCLED SWINTON, LARGE RADIUS TORN
                             NO NOISE, VERY FAST

    h. Met Conditions:

    j. Nearby Objects: NIL.

    k. To Whom Reported: S. YORKSHIRE POLICE → F/L ███Section 40███
                          RAF FINNINGLEY.

    l. Other Witnesses:

    m. Comments:

                                         Sec (AP) distribution: GE (Aew)
3. Date and Time Received: DI 55
                                                                 Section 40 a/10

        ┌─────────────────────┐
        │ MINISTRY OF DEFENCE │   Signed:
        │   Sec.(AS)2   │   Name: ████Section 40████
        │   - 9 OCT 1987   │
        └─────────────────────┘
Date: FILE 12/3   Rank Sgt   Tel No:

ANNEX A TO
~~SOP 502~~

REPORT OF AN UNIDENTIFIED FLYING OBJECT

A.	Date, Time & Duration of Sighting	Tues 22 Sep 87 2300 to 2400 Wed 22 Sep 87 0200 to 0215 Also Thursday 24 & Friday 25 Sep.
B.	Description of Object (No of objects, size, shape, colour, brightness)	Stationary hovering 3 white lights in a triangle. Very bright & star like.
C.	Exact Position of Observer Location, indoor/outdoor, stationary/moving	At home windows & in garden. Standing still.
D.	How Observed (naked eye, binoculars, other optical device, still or movie)	Naked Eye & Video camera. * * phoned Section 40 on 6/10. Re-recording does not show anything. Section 40
E.	Direction in which object first seen (A landmark may be more useful than a badly estimated bearing)	West North West
F.	Angle of Sight (Estimated heights are unreliable)	500' to 600' above ground level.
G.	Distance (By reference to a known landmark)	1 to 1½ miles away
H.	Movements (Changes in E, F & G may be of more use than estimates of course and speed)	No movement initially. Moving away at a speed faster than helicopter.
J.	Met Conditions during Observations (Moving clouds, haze, mist etc)	22/23 : clear nights 24/25 : } not known 21 : }
K.	Nearby Objects (Telephone lines, high voltage lines, reservoir, lake or dam, swamp or marsh, river, high buildings, tall chimneys, steeples, spires, TV or radio masts, airfields, generating plant, factories, pits or other sites with floodlights or night lighting)	Large TV mast River Medway Milk Quarries Electricity Pylon West Malling Airfield Also close to Rochester Airport & M2 motorway + M20 motorway

335

L.	To whom reported (Police, military, press etc)	Reported to Army & Air Force (RAF Manston)
M.	Name & Address of Informant	Rochester, Kent (medium)
N.	Background of Informant that may be volunteered	Very persistent, convinced not aircraft. Housewife
O.	Other Witnesses	None
P.	Date, Time of Receipt	25 Sept 2230 26 Sept 2400 / 0030
Q.	Any Unusual Meteorological Conditions	None
R.	Remarks	

Rang Air Force. 1st time observer of UFOs. Also rang Kent Maling police.

Pilot officer Air Traffic RAF Manston.

Sec (A5)2a

Squadron Leader
Duty Operations Officer
AF Ops

/ Date. 28—09—87

Sec (A5) distribution :
 Copies to:
 Sec (A5)2
✓ AEW/GE
✓ DI 55
 File AF Ops/1/11

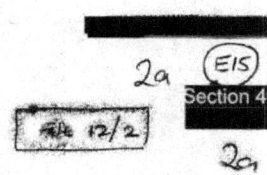

U N C L A S S I F I E D

CAB010 24/0846 267C0995   Section

FOR CAB

ROUTINE 240340Z SEP 87

FROM   RAF WEST DRAYTON
TO   MODUK AIR

U N C L A S S I F I E D
SIC Z6F
SUBJECT: AERIAL PHENOMENA
A. 232055 - 2130Z SEP 87, OBJECT WAS STILL IN VIEW WHEN PHONED
THROUGH
B. ONE - SMALL - STAR SHAPE - WHITE LIGHT - VERY BRIGHT - NIL - NIL
C. Section 40   HESTON, MIDDLESEX Section 4 - INDOORS -
STATIONARY
D. NAKED EYE - PHOTOGRAPH TAKEN
E. EAST OF HOUSE
F. 75 DEGREES
G. ABOVE CLOUDS (HEATHROW CLOUD 1/1800FT)
H. STEADY
J. MOVING CLOUDS
K. N/K
L. NIL

PAGE 2 RBDAID 001 UNCLAS
M. Section 40   ADDRESS AS ABOVE
N. NIL
O. BROTHER
P. REPORT RECIEVED BY AIS(M), RAF WEST DRAYTON 232130Z SEP 87
BT

DISTRIBUTION Z6F   FILE 7/1

CAB   1 Sec (AS) ACTION (CXJ / 1 AFDO
CYO   1 DD GE/AEW
CAV   1 DI 55
CAV   2 DSTI

337

U N C L A S S I F I E D

CAB117 23/1249 266C2608

FOR CAB

ROUTINE 231225Z SEP 87

FROM   RAF WEST DRAYTON
TO   MODUK AIR

U N C L A S S I F I E D
SIC Z6F
SUBJECT: AERIAL PHENOMENA. A. 222030A-222115A SEP 87. B. 3 REP ORBS
IN LINE THEN 2 ORBS STARTED CIRCLING DISPLAYING WHAT LOOKED LIKE
A/C LANDING LIGHTS WHILST THE THIRD APPEARED STATIONARY. C. 18.
Section 40   WHETSTONE N20. INDOORS. STATIONARY. D. VIEWED THROUGH
BINOCULARS SOME PHOTOS ALSO TAKEN. E. EASTERLY DIRECTION. F. N/K
G. N/K. H. CHANGING. J. CAVOK. K. N/K. L. POLICE-SCOTLAND YARD
REF NO CAD6324. M. Section 40
Section 40   N. NIL. O. WIFE PLUS FRIEND Section 40   P. REPORT
RECEIVED BY AIS(M) RAF WEST DRAYTON 221950Z SEP 87
BT

DISTRIBUTION   Z6F   (E15)
F

CAB   1   Sec (AS) ACTION (CXJ (1) AFDO)
CYD   1   DD GE/AEW

CAV   1   DI 55
CAV   2   DSTI

REPORT OF AN UNIDENTIFIED FLYING OBJECT

A.	Date, Time & Duration of Sighting	2000 on Tuesday 22 sep 87. Duration 10 minutes. (initially) Then later up until 2300 hours.
B.	Description of Object (No of objects, size, shape, colour, brightness)	Similar to planet but much brighter. modulating light. Yellow in colour. Large but not sure of size. Totally silent craft. Crescent shape *
C.	Exact Position of Observer Location, indoor/outdoor, stationary/moving	In car driving from Gt Rollright to Hook Norton. Moving. Then few minutes later, object passed over Hook Norton.
D.	How Observed (naked eye, binoculars, other optical device, still or movie)	Naked eye.
E.	Direction in which object first seen (A landmark may be more useful than a badly estimated bearing)	Due East.
F.	Angle of Sight (Estimated heights are unreliable)	30° (approx)
G.	Distance (By reference to a known landmark)	Hard to assess (10 miles) Passed over directly overhead. (later). (300')
H.	Movements (Changes in E, F & G may be of more use than estimates of course and speed)	object stationary. Craft. Slow steady movement. No noise. on curved course towards South.
J.	Met Conditions during Observations (Moving clouds, haze, mist etc)	Clear, stars, dark twilight.
K.	Nearby Objects (Telephone lines, high voltage lines, reservoir, lake or dam, swamp or marsh, river, high buildings, tall chimneys, steeples, spires, TV or radio masts, airfields, generating plant, factories, pits or other sites with floodlights or night lighting)	None.

* Full of lights (white). Spar at the back (Red light).

L.	To whom reported (Police, military, press etc)	To Sec (AS) 2a, after obtaining phone number from CAA.
M.	Name & Address of Informant	Oxfordshire.
N.	Background of Informant that may be volunteered	Quantity Surveyor.
O.	Other witnesses	Wife and daughter.
P.	Date, Time of Receipt	1200 hours on 29 Sep 87.
Q.	Any Unusual Meteorological Conditions	None.
R.	Remarks	

Friend saw it from near Shipston on Stour.

Wants a reply.

Sec (AS) 2a
Squadron Leader
Duty Operations Officer
AF Ops

Date.. 29 - 09 - 87 ....

Copies to:
Sec(AS)2
AEW/CE — Any aircraft ops at Heyford on 22/09? or large aircraft from surrounding areas
DI 55
File AF Ops/1/11

28/9

U N C L A S S I F I E D

CWD059 18/1206 261C2224

FOR CAB

ROUTINE 180920Z SEP 87

FROM   RAF WEST DRAYTON
TO   MODUK AIR

U N C L A S S I F I E D
SIC Z6F
SUBJECT: AERIAL PHENOMENA. A. 132120 TO 2130 SEPT 87 B. ONE ONLY.
ORANGE/RED FLICKERING BRIGHT LIGHTS OVAL IN SHAPE WITH DARK BAND
ACROSS THE MIDDLE. INFORMANT STATED IT WAS THE SIZE OF A FOOTBALL
PITCH. C. Section 40 BATLEY, WEST YORKSHIRE. OUTDOORS AT BACK
OF HOME ADDRESS, STATIONARY. D. SEEN WITH NAKED EYE ONLY. E. SEEN TO
MOVE FROM EAST TO WEST. F. ALMOST ON A LEVEL WITH OBSERVER (FROM ONE
HILLSIDE TO ANOTHER). G. BETWEEN ONE HALF AND THREE QUARTERS OF A
MILE. H. SEEN TO HOVER, MOVE ACROSS BATLEY, HOVER AGAIN THEN MOVE OFF
NORTH WEST. J. CLEAR NO CLOUD K. GROSVENOR ROAD CHURCH, BATLEY
WITH SPIRE AND TOWER ON, BLAKERIDGE MILLS AND M62 MOTORWAY. L.
PC Section 40 AND PC Section 40 STATIONED A BATLEY SUBDIVISION,
WEST YORKSHIRE POLICE, TEL Section 40 M. Section 40 AND
Section 40 N. NIL O. NONE P. REPORT
RECEIVED BY AISM, RAF WEST DRAYTON 180900Z SEP 87, BY POST

PAGE 2 RBDAID 003 UNCLAS
BT

DISTRIBUTION   Z6F
F
CAB   1   Sec (AS) ACTION (CXJ   1   AFDO)
CYD   1   DD/GE/AEW
CAV   1   DI 55
CAV   2   DSTI

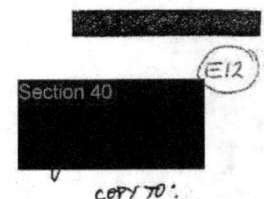

E12

U N C L A S S I F I E D

CXJ045 16/1413 259C3177

FOR CXJ

ROUTINE 161250Z SEP 87

FROM   RAF LYNEHAM
TO   MODUK AIR

U N C L A S S I F I E D
SIC I3F
ATTN AF OPS. REPORT OF AN UNIDENTIFIED FLYING OBJECT
A 13 SEP 1650 LOCAL FOR APPROX 10 MINS
B ONE OBJECT AIRLINER SIZE, LONG THIN ROCKET SHAPE-LIKE CONCORDE
WITHOUT WINGS, WHITE OR SILVER COLOURED WITH VERY BRIGHT ALTERNATING
GREEN/WHITE LIGHTS FLASHING. NO SOUND APPARENT, NO SMELL
C INFORMANTS IN GARDEN AT ADRESS PARA M
D NAKED EYE FIRST THEN BINOCULARS
E APPEARED TO BE SLOW MOVING IN WEST TO SOUTH EAST WIDE TURN
F ABOVE AND TURNING
G APPROX 38000FT (COMPARING WITH AIRLINERS ON AIRWAY)
H AS E/F/G
J HIGH CLOUD, BRIGHT, SUNNY, BLUE SKY, CLEAR, NO HAZE
K ELECTRIC PYLONS NEARBY-NO SPARKS ETC. RESERVOIR 2 MILES WEST
L BRISTOL/LULSGATE AIRPORT (THEY TOLD HIM TO PHONE US AS THEY WERE

PAGE 2 RBDOYF 033 UNCLAS
BUSY) THEN CPL Section 40 LYNEHAM OPS
Section 40   BATHFORD, Section 40 TEL BATH

M AMATUER PLANE OBSERVER (VERY AMATUER RECKONED A TOMCAT HAS A
SPY PLANE). NEVER SEEN ANYTHING LIKE THIS, ETC, ETC
O HIS WIFE
P 13 SEP, 1620Z
BT

DISTRIBUTION. I3F
F
  CXJ   1 AFDO ACTION (CXJ   1 AFDO)

END   U N C L A S S I F I E D

U N C L A S S I F I E D

CWD099 15/1251 258C2360

FOR CAB

ROUTINE 141030Z SEP 87

FROM   RAF WEST DRAYTON
TO   MODUK AIR

U N C L A S S I F I E D
SIC Z6F
SUBJECT: AERIAL PHENOMENA
A. 142030 LOCAL SEP 87, 5 TO 7 MINS
B. APPEARED LIKE AN ELONGATED DIAMOND, SIZE OF LARGE AIRCRAFT,
BRIGHT LIGHT LOOKED LIKE COCKPIT LIGHT WITH ANOTHER BRIGHT LIGHT
FURTHER BACK
C. MAPLE CROSS RICKMANSWORTH, HERTFORDSHIRE, IN CAR
D. NAKED EYE
E. NORTH EAST
F. TREE HEIGHT
G. PASSED NEARLY OVERHEAD
H. STEADY
J. CLOUDLESS
K. TWO BUILDINGS
2. RAF WEST DRAYTON

PAGE 2 RBDAID 005 UNCLAS   F
M. Section 40
MK.
O. NONE
P. 142230Z SEP 87
BT

DISTRIBUTION   Z6F
F
CAB   1 Sec (AS) ACTION (CXJ   1 AFDO)
CYD   1 DD GE/AEW
CAV   1 DI 55
CAV   2 DSTI

MINISTRY OF DEFENCE
Sec.(AS)2
15 SEP 1987
FILE 12/2

BRISTOL AIRPORT PLC

BRISTOL Section 40 **TEL. LULSGATE** Section 40

Sec (AS) 2a distribution:
    GE (AEW)
    DI 55

Section 40

27/9

WITH COMPLIMENTS
Section 40 – *MANAGING DIRECTOR*

REPORT OF UNIDENTIFIED FLYING OBJECT

A. Date, Time and Duration of Sighting Local times to be quoted	1650 . 13-9-87 APPROXIMATELY 15 MINS
B. Discription of Object Number of objects, size, shape, colours, brightness, sound, smell, etc.	ROCKET SHAPE BRIGHT WHITE/GREEN LIGHT NO SOUND. BRIGHTER THAN AIRCRAFT STROBE LIGHTS
C. Exact position of observer Geographical location, indoors our out, stationery or moving.	BATHFORD OUTDOORS STATIONERY.
D. How Observed Naked eye, binoculars, other optical device, still or movie camera.	NAKED EYE AND BINOCULARS
E. Direction in which Object was First Seen A landmark more useful than badly estimated. bearing.	TO THE SE OF BATHFORD 80° - 90 DEGREES.
F. Angular Elevation of Object Estimated heights are unreliable.	80 DEGREES. NO VAPOUR TRAIL.
G. Distance of Object from Observer Ref. to known landmark when possible.	HIGHER THAN JET TRAFFIC ON GREEN ONE WITH VAPOUR TRAIL
H. Movements of Object Changes in E, F & G more use than est. course and speed.	SLOW MOVING. TRACKING TOWARDS MELKSHAM.
J. Met. Condition During Observation Moving clouds, haze, mist, etc.	SOME HIGH CIRRUS BUT MAINLY CLEAR BLUE SKY
K. Nearby Objects Telephone or high-voltage lines; dam, lake or reservoir; swamp or marsh; river; high building, tall chimney, steeples, spires or masts; airfields, generating plants; pits, factories or other lighted sites, or lighting.	NOTHING SPECIAL.
L. To Whom Reported Police, Military org. the press, etc.	A.T.C BRISTOL AIRPORT
M. Name and Address of Informant	Section 40
N. Any Background Information on Informant that may be Volunteered	VERY KEEN AIRCRAFT OBSERVER
O. Other Witness	Section 40
P. Date and Time of Receipt of Report	1700A 13-9-87

Section 40

Signature Section 40

please see draft reply. GE/AEW WOULD LIKE A REPLY.
have no comments & D/SS have
received no other reports.
16/9

UNIDENTIFIED FLYING OBJECT PROFORMA

E10/1

FCE

From: RYDROE MANOR.

Reference:

MINISTRY OF DEFENCE
Sec.(AS)2
- 8 SEP 1987
FILE 12/2

1. **Details of Complaint.**

   a. Name:

   b. Address:

   CASE WINFIELD.
   Telephone

2. **Sighting:**

   a. Date/Time of Sighting and Duration: 4 Sep 87 at 21:17 hrs
   for 2 minutes

   b. Position of Observer: In the Back garden on
   the patio dogs started barking.

   c. How Observed: Through the naked eye

   d. Direction Object first Seen: In a SW direction
   travelling to NW direction

   e. Angle of Elevation: overhead at an angle
   of 50°.

   f. Distance of Object from Observer: Difficult to assess
   but lower than any average they
   have seen

   g. Movement of Object: Diagonally across the sky

   h. Met Conditions: Clear moonlit night.

   j. Nearby Objects: None.

   k. To Whom Reported: Chesterfield Civilian Police

   l. Other Witnesses: Two children aged 14 and
   12 yrs.

   m. Comments: Egg shaped with red/white
   lights at front. Green light at back.

3. **Date and Time Received:** At 2138 hrs a shooting star
   was seen in the sky.

Signed:

Name:

Date: 7 September 87. **Rank** SGT **Tel No:**

copies to D/SS / AEW/AEW 10/9

Section 4

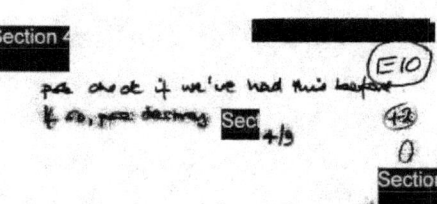

E 10

pls chk ot if we've had this before
If so, pse destroy Sec 4/3   +2
                                   0
                              Section

41

U N C L A S S I F I E D

CWD055 04/0959 247C1167 SUSPECTED DUPLICATE

FOR CAB

ROUTINE 040800Z SEP 87

FROM   RAF WEST DRAYTON
TO   MODUK AIR

U N C L A S S I F I E D
SIC Z6F
SUBJECT AERIAL PHENOMENA
A. 28 AUGUST 1987 2330 HRS LOCAL TIME
B. LARGE FAST CIRCLE, BLUE LIGHTS, CENTRE OF WHITE, YELLOW, ORANGE.
HOVERED MAKING A NOISE, LOUD HUM TO TOTAL SILENCE
C. TREHARRIS
D. NAKED EYE
E TO K. N/I
L. MERTHYR TYDFIL POLICE TO ST ATHAN GUARDROOM
M. Section 40
N. APPEARD TO BE SOBER. 03 SEP 2144Z
BT

MINISTRY OF DEFENCE
Sec.(AS)2
- 4 SEP 1987

E 11   FILE 12/2

DISTRIBUTION   Z6F
F
CAB   1   Sec (AS) ACTION (CXJ   1   AFDQ)
CYD   1   DD GE/AEW
CAV   1   DI 55
CAV   2   DSTI

REPORT OF AN UNIDENTIFIED FLYING OBJECT

A.	Date, Time & Duration of Sighting	01 September 1987 2115 hours 10 - 15 seconds
B.	Description of Object (No of objects, size, shape, colour, brightness)	Elliptical — Airship. Slightly larger than an aircraft. Lights along the side. Longer mass (shaped)
C.	Exact Position of Observer location, indoor/outdoor, stationary/moving	outside in garden. Sitting down.
D.	How Observed (naked eye, binoculars, other optical device, still or movie)	Naked Eye
E.	Direction in which object first seen (A landmark may be more useful than a badly estimated bearing)	North. Travelled south. Aircraft travel diagonally across garden.
F.	Angle of Sight (Estimated heights are unreliable)	Below cloud level. Aircraft are usually above.
G.	Distance (By reference to a known landmark)	overhead
H.	Movements (Changes in E, F & G may be of more use than estimates of course and speed)	Straight line. Aircraft speed.
J.	Met Conditions during Observations (Moving clouds, haze, mist etc)	Cloud cover. Dark
K.	Nearby Objects (Telephone lines, high voltage lines, reservoir, lake or dam, swamp or marsh, river, high buildings, tall chimneys, steeples, spires, TV or radio masts, airfields, generating plant, factories, pits or other sites with floodlights or night lighting)	Open area.

L.	To whom reported (Police, military, press etc)	First reported to us.
M.	Name & Address of Informant	Section 40 Winchmore Hill London
N.	Background of Informant that may be volunteered	-
O.	Other Witnesses	Wife.
P.	Date, Time of Receipt	1100 02 September 1987
Q.	Any Unusual Meteorological Conditions	None observed.
R.	Remarks	No sound. Didn't travel in the same usual direction as airliner traffic.

Section 40

Sec (AS)2a

Squadron Leader
Duty Operations Officer
AF Ops

Date.. 02 September 1987.

Copies to:
✓Sec(AS)2
AEW/GE
PRESS
File AF Ops/1/11

REPORT OF AN UNIDENTIFIED FLYING OBJECT

A.	Date, Time & Duration of Sighting	012205 Local Sep 87 1_2 Mins
B.	Description of Object (No of objects, size, shape, colour, brightness)	1 Cigar shaped object Gold/Orange Bright/lights out on descent
C.	Exact Position of Observer Location, indoor/outdoor, stationary/moving	On corner of, Section 40 Newcastle Stationary
D.	How Observed (naked eye, binoculars, other optical device, still or movie	Naked Eye
E.	Direction in which object first seen (A landmark may be more useful than a badly estimated bearing)	To the North
F.	Angle of Sight (Estimated heights are unreliable)	Approx 50 Deg upwards
G.	Distance (By reference to a known landmark	Unknown
H.	Movements (Changes in E, F & G may be of more use than estimates of course and speed)	Initially stationary then descended rapidly and disappeared
J.	Met Conditions during Observations (Moving clouds, haze, mist etc)	Clear Sky, little cloud dark.
K.	Nearby Objects (Telephone lines, high voltage lines, reservoir, lake or dam, swamp or marsh, river, high buildings, tall chimneys, steeples, spires, TV or radio masts, airfields, generating plant, factories, pits or other sites with floodlights or night lighting)	Houses and Newcastle Airport. Aircraft clearly identified in sky.

L.	To whom reported (Police, military, press etc)	Newcastle Airport, then AFOPS

M.	Name & Address of Informant	

N.	Background of Informant that may be volunteered	Customs Officer
O.	Other Witnesses	NIL
P.	Date, Time of Receipt	012215 Local Sep 87
Q.	Any Unusual Meteorological Conditions	Nil
R.	Remarks -------	Chap sounded rational and intelligent tho' a little breathless! Sees lots of aircraft and was adamant not an aircraft.

Sqn Ldr
Duty Ops Officer
AF Ops

Date. 01 Sep 87.

Distribution:

→Sec(AS)2
AEW/GE
DI 55
File AF Ops/2/5/1

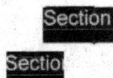

CYD037 01/0909 244C0776

FOR CAB

ROUTINE 010830Z ~~AUG~~ SEP 87

FROM   RAF WEST DRAYTON
TO   MODUK AIR

U N C L A S S I F I E D
SIC Z6F
SUBJECT: AERIAL PHENOMENA
A. 312030Z AUG 87
B. ONE, NON FLASHING
C. ARLESFORD, HANTS - OUTDOORS
D. NAKED EYE
E. FROM THE WEST
F. 35 DEGREES FROM HORIZONTAL
G. N/K
H. GOING ROUND AND ROUND
J. SKY CLEAR
K. TELEPHONE LINES
L. ATC BRISTOL
M. Section 40
P. 312110Z AUG 87

PAGE 2 RBDAID 001 UNCLAS
BT

DISTRIBUTION   Z6F

CAB   1   Sec (AS) ACTION (CXJ   1   AFDO
CYD   1   DD GE/AEW
CAV   1   DI 5F
CAV   2   DSTI

MINISTRY OF DEFENCE
Sec.(AS)2
7 SEP 1987

FILE 12/2

REPORT OF UNIDENTIFIED FLYING OBJECT

07/09

A. Date, Time and Duration of Sighting Local times to be quoted	30·8·87 2230(Local)
B. Discription of Object Number of objects,size,shape,colours, brightness,sound,smell,etc.	ONE. STARLIKE IN BRIGHTNESS & APPEARANCE
C. Exact position of observer Geographical location,indoors our out, stationery or moving.	STATIONARY, OUTDOORS LOOKING WEST.
D. How Observed Naked eye,binoculars,other optical device,still or movie camera.	NAKED EYE.
E. Direction in which Object was First Seen A landmark more useful than badly bearing.	IN VICINITY OF "THE PLOUGH" (URSA MINOR ?)
F. Angular Elevation of Object Estimated heights are unreliable.	45°
G. Distance of Object from Observer Ref. to known landmark when possible.	
H. Movements of Object Changes in E,F & G more use than est. course and speed.	SMALL CIRCULAR ORBITS STOPPING FROM TIME TO TIME.
J. Met. Condition During Observation Moving clouds, haze, mist, etc.	MISTY. CLEAR SKY.
K. Nearby Objects Telephone or high-voltage lines; dam, lake or reservoir; swamp or marsh; river; high building, tall chimney, steeples,spires or masts; airfields, generating plants;pits, factories or other lighted sites, or lighting.	NONE KNOWN.
L. To Whom Reported Police, Military org. the press, etc.	A.T.C. BRISTOL ONLY.
M. Name and Address of Informant	Section 40 ITCHENSTOKE, Nr ARLESFORD, HANTS
N. Any Background Information on Informant that may be Volunteered	TEL Section 40 NONE (CASUAL OBSERVER
O. Other Witness	NONE
P. Date and Time of Receipt of Report	30·8·87 2323 (L)

Signature ..... Section 40 .....

✓ ATCO (WATCH SUP.)

REPORT OF AN UNIDENTIFIED FLYING OBJECT

A.	Date, Time & Duration of Sighting	30 AUG 87, 2145 HOURS LOCAL. APPROX 3 TO 4 MINUTES DURATION OF SIGHTING.
B.	Description of Object (No of objects, size, shape, colour, brightness)	ONE OBJECT, OVAL SHAPED, APPROX SIZE OF A HOUSE ROOF. TWO RED LIGHTS AT FRONT WITH TWO WHITE LIGHTS ON UNDERSIDE. BRIGHTNESS "LIKE SPOTLIGHTS".
C.	Exact Position of Observer Location, indoor/outdoor, stationary/moving	THREE OBSERVERS, ALL INDOORS, ALL STATIONARY.
D.	How Observed (naked eye, binoculars, other optical device, still or movie	NAKED EYE.
E.	Direction in which object first seen (A landmark may be more useful than a badly estimated bearing)	HOVERING OVER TURN HIGH ROAD IN WHITBURN, WEST LOTHIAN.
F.	Angle of Sight (Estimated heights are unreliable)	DIRECTLY OVERHEAD (APPROX 40 FEET ABOVE).
G.	Distance (By reference to a known landmark	APPROX 100 - 200 YARDS (NO LANDMARKS).
H.	Movements (Changes in E, F & G may be of more use than estimates of course and speed)	HOVERED FOR APPROX TWO MINUTES, THEN DESCENDED APPARENTLY TO BELOW HOUSE LEVEL.
J.	Met Conditions during Observations (Moving clouds, haze, mist etc)	CLOUDS IN SKY BUT NO MIST OR HAZE
K.	Nearby Objects (Telephone lines, high voltage lines, reservoir, lake or dam, swamp or marsh, river, high buildings, tall chimneys, steeples, spires, TV or radio masts, airfields, generating plant, factories, pits or other sites with floodlights or night lighting)	NOTHING.

L. To whom reported (Police, military, press etc)

CONSTABLE ██Section 40██
WEST LOTHIAN POLICE
·TEL No :
DIV HQ : ██Section 40██

M. Name & Address of Informant

██Section 40██ (BOTH AGED 16 YEARS)

██Section 40██

WHITBURN
WEST LOTHIAN

WHITBURN
WEST LOTHIAN
SCOTLAND.

N. Background of Informant that may be volunteered

AGES SUPPLIED - SEE 'M' ABOVE.

O. Other Witnesses

SEE 'M' ABOVE

P. Date, Time of Receipt

TO WEST LOTHIAN POLICE - 2215 LOCAL, 30 AUG 87.
TO AF OPS - 2310 LOCAL, 30 AUG 87.

Q. Any Unusual Meteorological Conditions

NONE

R. Remarks

CONSTABLE ██Section 40██ REPORTED THAT ALL THREE INFORMANTS SEEMED TO BE SINCERE AND SENSIBLE.

██Section 40██

Sqn Ldr
Duty Ops Officer
AF Ops

Date. 28 Aug 87.

Distribution:

Sec(AS)2
AEW/GE
DI 55
File AF Ops/2/5/1

To: MOD Sec(AS)2b
Room Section 40
Main Building
Whitehall
London

From: HQ P&SS (UK)
FCF
RAF RUDLOE MANOR
Hawthorn
Wilts SN 13 OPQ

Date   9 OCT 87

FLYING COMPLAINT

1. The attached complaint was recieved at this Headquarters as per date stamp from a first time complaint.

2. The complaint location is/is not listed as an avoidance area and is situated as follows:

   a. OS Sheet Number . . . . *128* . . . .

   b. Grid Reference . . *SK 3536* . . . .

   c. LFA . . . . *8* . . . .

3. This Headquarters will take no further action unless directed by you.

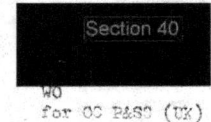

WO
for OC P&SS (UK)

356

FLYING COMPLAINT FORM

(DO NOT STATE THAT AN INVESTIGATION WILL ATTEND)

From: HQ P&SS (UK)   TO: MOD Sec (AS) 2b

1. Details of Complaint.

    a. Name & Initials   [Section 40] ....

    b. Address .... [Section 40] ....
        ....

    c. Nearest Large Town .... *Derby* ....

    d. Telephone No with code [Section 40] ....

2. Details of Incident.

    a. Date .... 29 Aug 87 ....

    b. Time (Local or Zulu) 2300 hrs ....

    c. No of ac involved .... 1 ....

    d. Height .... High ....

    e. Direction .... Going West ....

3. Description of Aircraft.
    Jet Propellor Military Civil Fighter Bomber Helicopter Light ac (UFO)
    Camouflaged Silver White Any noticeable Colours/markings

4. Location of Complaint (if Different from 1b)(with telephone No if applicable.)
    ....
    ....

5. Claims. (Do not prompt complainant). Is there any injury/damage to persons/
    livestock/property which will result in a claim? Complainants claiming injury to
    livestock should report the incident to their local NFU, producing a veterinary
    report. Or for any of the above claims that may occur they can write to MOD Claims,
    First Avenue House, High Holborn, London, WC1V 6HE. Tel [Section 40]
    Details ....
    ....
    ....

6. Full Details of Complaint. [Section 40] saw a small
    ...... Solid white light sighting lasted 3 seconds
    Info passed by: Sgt [Section 40] - Derbshire Civ Pol HQ
    ...... [Section 40] No other sightings reported.
    Date/Time Report Received ... 30 Aug 87 0830 ...

                                          Signed [Section 40] ....
                                          Name .. [Section 40]
                                          Rank .... Sgt Tel No. [Section 40]

                                                            DDCO

REPORT OF AN UNIDENTIFIED FLYING OBJECT

A.	Date, Time & Duration of Sighting	292300 Local Aug 87 2-3 Mins
B.	Description of Object (No of objects, size, shape, colour, brightness)	1 Spherical Object Blue/Orange Bright
C.	Exact Position of Observer Location, indoor/outdoor, stationary/moving	Smallheath, Birmingham Outdoors and Stationary
D.	How Observed (naked eye, binoculars, other optical device, still or movie	Naked Eye
E.	Direction in which object first seen (A landmark may be more useful than a badly estimated bearing)	Unknown
F.	Angle of Sight (Estimated heights are unreliable)	Unknown
G.	Distance (By reference to a known landmark	Unknown
H.	Movements (Changes in E, F & G may be of more use than estimates of course and speed)	Initialy Stationary then moved of at a speed estimated at 2-3000 MPH
J.	Met Conditions during Observations (Moving clouds, haze, mist etc)	Clear Sky
K.	Nearby Objects (Telephone lines, high voltage lines, reservoir, lake or dam, swamp or marsh, river, high buildings, tall chimneys, steeples, spires, TV or radio masts, airfields, generating plant, factories, pits or other sites with floodlights or night lighting)	Unknown

L.	To whom reported (Police, military, press etc)	Civil Police Birmingham

M.	Name & Address of Informant	

N.	Background of Informant that may be volunteered	Nil

O.	Other Witnesses	

P.	Date, Time of Receipt	292350 Local Aug 87

Q.	Any Unusual Meteorological Conditions	Nil

R.	Remarks	Nil

Sqn Ldr
Duty Ops Officer
AF Ops

Date. 30 Aug 87.

Distribution:

Sec(AS)2 ✓
AEW/GE
DI 55
File AF Ops/2/5/1

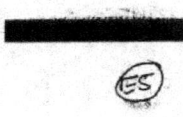

Secti

U N C L A S S I F I E D

CYO259 28/1953 240C4091

FOR CAB

ROUTINE 280916Z AUG 87

FROM   RAF WEST DRAYTON
TO   MODUK AIR

U N C L A S S I F I E D
SIC Z6F
SUBJECT: AERIAL PHENOMENA
A. 272130(L) AUG
B. THREE REVOLVING OBJECTS IN THE SKY
C. REAR GARDEN OF INFORMANTS HOME, OUTSIDE, STATIONARY
D. BINOCULARS
E. N/K
F. N/K
G. SEVERAL MILES
H. TWO STATIONARY ONE MAKING ZIG ZAG MOVEMENTS AROUND THEM
J. DRY, VISIBILITY GOOD
K. N/K
L. POLICE STATION EBBW VALE, PC Section 40
M. Section 40   RASSAU, EBBW VALE
N. RELIABLE PERSON KNOWN TO LOCAL OFFICERS

DISTRIBUTION   Z6F)
F
CAB   1 Sec (AS) ACTION (CXJ , 1 AFDO)
CYD   1 DD GE/AEW
CAV   1 DI 55
CAV   2 DSTI

UNCLASSIFIED

CAF033 28/0404 240C0580

FOR CAB

ROUTINE 272215Z AUG 87

FROM   RAF MARHAM
TO   MODUK AIR

UNCLASSIFIED
SIC LGZ/Z6F
(SIC Z6F INSERTED BY DCC)
FROM MARHAM OPS
A 272130(A) AUG 87. DURN 1 HR 25 MIN
B ONE OBJECT SIZE AND BRIGHTNESS OF SMALL STAR. VARIED IN BRIGHTNESS.
FINALLY EXTINGUISHED AT 2255A
C OBSERVED OUTDORRS DUE EAST OF ASHWICKEN KINGS LYNN NORFOLK. SOME
MOVEMENT OBSERVED
D NAKED EYE
E AS IN PARA C
F ELEVATION OF TWENTY DEGREES FM HORIZON
G NOT ABLE TO ESTIMATE
H AS IN PARA C
J CLEAR SKY
K NONE
L LOCAL
M Section 40
TEL Section 40
N NONE
O OPS STAFF AT MARHAM OBSERVED POSSIBLE SAME OBJECT WHEN INFORMED.
DISAPPEARED AT SAME TIME
P 272230 (A) AUG 87
BT

DISTRIBUTION   LGZ

NO SDL

DISTRIBUTION   Z6F
F
CAB   1 Sec (AS) ACTION (CXJ   1 AFDO)
CYD   1 DD GE/AEW
CAV   1 DI 55
CAV   2 DSTI

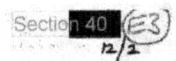

REPORT OF AN UNIDENTIFIED FLYING OBJECT

A.	Date, Time & Duration of Sighting	272115 Local Aug 87 2 Mins
B.	Description of Object (No of objects, size, shape, colour, brightness)	One
C.	Exact Position of Observer Location, indoor/outdoor, stationary/moving	Outdoors
D.	How Observed (naked eye, binoculars, other optical device, still or movie	Naked eye.
E.	Direction in which object first seen (A landmark may be more useful than a badly estimated bearing)	Near Collegate (Haelsowen)
F.	Angle of Sight (Estimated heights are unreliable)	Very High
G.	Distance (By reference to a known landmark	Difficult to say
H.	Movements (Changes in E, F & G may be of more use than estimates of course and speed)	Veered off at very high speed
J.	Met Conditions during Observations (Moving clouds, haze, mist etc)	Very Clear
K.	Nearby Objects (Telephone lines, high voltage lines, reservoir, lake or dam, swamp or marsh, river, high buildings, tall chimneys, steeples, spires, TV or radio masts, airfields, generating plant, factories, pits or other sites with floodlights or night lighting)	No significant objects

L.	To whom reported (Police, military, press etc)	West Midlands Police Force Control Room

M.	Name & Address of Informant	

N.	Background of Informant that may be volunteered	Nil

O.	Other Witnesses	Boyfriend

P.	Date, Time of Receipt	272345 Local Aug 87

Q.	Any Unusual Meteorological Conditions	Nil

R. Remarks

Sqn Ldr
Duty Ops Officer
AF Ops

Date. 28 Aug 87.

Distribution:

Sec(AS)2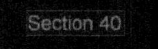
AEW/GE
DI 55
File AF Ops/2/5/1

UNCLASSIFIED

CWY029 24/0917 236C0694

FOR CAB

ROUTINE 2480467 AUG 87

FROM : RAF LEUCHARS
TO   MODUK AIR
        UKRADC
        HQSTC

UNCLASSIFIED
SIC Z6F
FOR ATTN OF MOD AFOR(RAF)
A 2120Z 21ST AUG 87
B STAR LIKE BUT MOVING, 2 BY LIGHTS WHICH WERE CHANGING COLOUR
FROM GREEN AND WHITE TO RED
C 4 MILES SOUTH OF PITLOCHRY   OUTSIDE AT TIME
D NAKED EYE
E NORTH EAST INVERNESS WAY
F 11 OCLOCK
G SAME AS STARS
H ERRATIC LIKE A DOG FIGHT
J VERY CLEAR
K NIL

PAGE 2 RSDDXJ 011 UNCLAS
L SAR Section 40 WING OPS, RAF LEUCHARS
M Section 40   PERTHSIHIRE. TELEPHONE
BALLINLUIG Section 40
N NIL
O 7 OTHERS
P 2137Z 21ST AUG 87
Q YES
BT

DISTRIBUTION   Z6F

CAB   1 Sec (AS) ACTION (CXJ   1 AFBO)
CYD   1 DD GE/AE4
CAV   1 DI 55
CAV   2 DGYI   Section 4

                                         File : 12/2
                                         Date : 24/08

U N C L A S S I F I E D

CY0010 23/0819 235C0242

FOR CAB

ROUTINE 230702Z AUG 87

FROM   RAF WEST DRAYTON
TO   MODUK AIR

U N C L A S S I F I E D
SIC Z6F
SUBJECT: AERIAL PHENOMENA
A. 22235X(L) AUG
B. ONE ROUND OBJECT WITH BRIGHT LIGHT
C. GRANGE ROAD, OUT DOORS, STATIONARY
D. NAKED EYE
E. N/K
F. N/K
G. LOWER IN SKY THAN AIRCRAFT
H. STEADY
J. STORMY
K. N/K
L. GUILDFORD POLICE POSection 40
M. Section 40   GUILDFORD Section 40
N. NIL

PAGE 2 RBDAID 001 UNCLAS
O. MEMBERS OF THE FAMILY
P. 230020(L) AUG
BT

Section

DISTRIBUTION Z6F
P
CAB   1 Sec (AS) ACTION (CXJ/ /± AFDQ|)
CYD   1 DD GE/AEI
CAV   1 DI 5!
CAV   2 DSTI

Section

File 12/2

24 Aug 87

Index

UFO REPORTS DECLASSIFIED MINISTRY OF DEFENCE

FIELD OFFICE AERIAL INVESTIGATION
AND ADMINISTRAIVE FILES

With special thanks to
Brian, Annette and Amy

www.ingramcontent.com/pod-product-compliance
Lightning Source LLC
Chambersburg PA
CBHW061956280526
45787CB00005B/1886